Spital~~~
a battle for land~~~

Charlie Forman

Hilary Shipman
London

First published 1989 by
Hilary Shipman Limited
19 Framfield Road
Highbury
London N5 1UU

British Library Cataloguing in Publication Data
Forman, Charlie
  Spitalfields: a battle for land
  1. London, Tower Hamlets (London Borough).
  Spitalfields. Proposed redevelopment. Attitudes of community
  action groups
  I. Title
  711′.4′094215

ISBN 0-948096-17-9

Cover design by David Bennett

Typeset by Florencetype Ltd, Kewstoke, Avon
Printed and bound by Biddles Limited
Guildford & King's Lynn

Contents

List of maps

Acknowledgements

Somewhere, while climbing yet another spongey staircase, where each tread sags as you put your weight on it, where your shoes soak up rain blown in through the broken window panes, this book began.

I started as a housing rights worker in Spitalfields in 1979. I thought I'd seen bad housing conditions. But what I was shown as I went in and out of the rented rooms around Brick Lane left me stunned. I couldn't believe anyone in Britain was still living in housing conditions which I'd only read about in history books of the Victorian slums. Yet here it was – street after street of just such appalling housing. This was no natural disaster. Recovering from the shock, I was angry. What authority was responsible for letting such housing stand? Why had nothing been done about it? The people of Spitalfields already knew the answers – and they knew what to do about it. Ten years have gone by since then, and much has been achieved. I hope I learnt enough to make this book a reasonable record of what happened.

Over those years I have had hundreds of conversations with people about their housing, and how they wanted it improved. Eating creamy rasmalai at a kitchen table, or sitting at the end of a bed, when there's no space in the room for other furniture, and sipping hot sweet tea, I've listened to many families' histories. Their determination to stay in Spitalfields and get somewhere decent to live is at the heart of this book. I hope they think it was worthwhile, and that by now most have got the housing they wanted. I'm grateful to them all for what I learnt. Certainly, if they hadn't been prepared to talk through their housing problems, there would have been no book. But even when they did talk, most only spoke Bengali. I would have understood very little of what they had to say if it hadn't been for the interpreters who have worked with me. Lots of people have interpreted for me, but I'd especially like to thank Saima Akbar, Abdul Asad, Razia Sadeq, Komla Rahman, Abdul Bari and Konor Ali for all their help.

There would still have been no book without all the people who worked with me, and after me, at the Housing and Planning Rights Service in Spitalfields: Mark Adams, Philippa Fawcett, Osman Gani, Ala Uddin, Maria Mercedes Clarkson, Richard Backes, Sarah Lerner, Shishu Choudhury, Brian Williams, Rumi Altaf and Mujib Osmani. Although obviously I take sole responsibility for what is written down here, an enormous amount of what appears in this book we compiled together, we discussed together, we campaigned on together. A lot of the book is their work. Their support continued as I tried to pull all this material together – giving advice, finding information, suggesting ways of redrafting. The debt is immeasurable.

It's just not possible to give full recognition to all the people who've been important influences on what I've written. But I must mention some. I'll always be indebted to the people who introduced me to Spitalfields, and who continued to be so supportive – especially Michael Myers, the late Ahmed Fakhruddin, Pat and Alan Heuman, the late Jafur Khan, Phyllis Barber and Cathy Peters. Two 'veterans' of community work in Spitalfields, Bill Blair and Clare Murphy, have not only been great supports, but gave invaluable comments on the text. Barbara Brooks, Abdus Shukur and many other local people gave their time to manage the Housing Rights Service and keep it going for the nine years it did survive.

Other people have been a special help in particular areas of this work. What I've learnt of Bangladesh owes much to Abdul Karim, Soyful Alom and Shoaib Chowdhury. In many things, but especially for the work on housing allocation, Kumar Murshid and Sue Davis have been inspirational. Shofor Ali and Gulam Mustafa taught me much through their work in the Homeless Families Campaign. I also learnt a lot that went into this book by working with everyone at the Spitalfields Housing Co-op – and I have a particular debt of gratitude to Abbas Uddin and Brendan O'Sullivan. Though I was a lazy pupil, what Bengali I ever learnt was due to the efforts of Nurul Hoque. I must also thank Andy Coupland, Rick Middleton, Anjum Rahmatulla, Terry Fitzpatrick, Kay Jordan, Maggie Jones, Jane Deighton and Heather Williams for their information and advice and David Cross for drawing the maps.

I should add here that I've used the term Bangladeshi and Bengali to mean much the same thing in this book. Although one emphasizes national identity, the other is more commonly used when they speak about themselves.

I wrote the book at home, with great support from Alison Lowton, and help too from Linda Buckley who gave me the child-free time to write. I did a lot of research at the Tower Hamlets Local History Library. The people working there deserve a medal – I ran them ragged some days. Nothing I asked them was ever too much trouble. Then the book would never have shaped up without the editing of Hilary Macaskill and Michael Shipman.

Finally – thanks to the late Romesh Thapar who first suggested I should write the book.

Foreword

Things are moving with alarming speed in Spitalfields. As this book was being written, it needed constant updating. I have tried to ensure that all the information here is correct as at the beginning of November 1988. Some very important later events have been acknowledged, while some of the most difficult statistics about future house-building plans have not been updated since the summer of 1988. With such a large spread of material, it has not been possible to update any further. You need to bear this in mind when you read the book – the story will continue.

Charlie Forman
May 1989

1 | Threadneedle streets of Spitalfields

Take a walk down Brick Lane in London's East End. It is like nowhere else. It's a narrow street, crowded with shops opening straight onto the pavement. It's blocked with traffic. Somewhere a wide van is parked, half-keeled over, two wheels on the pavement, two on the road. A man, almost submerged under a pile of thick women's coats, is loading it from the back. He pops in and out of an open doorway, up the steep stairs to the workshop above. A car could get by. But a lorry is stuck – piled high with empty beer kegs going back to Truman's brewery just beyond.

It's Friday. There's a queue in the take-away cafes for the meat pancake ketlama, cooked only once a week. Someone pushes his way out with an armful of polystyrene cups of steaming tea and vegetable samosas, carried in a cut-down cardboard box, which he uses as a tray. He heads back to the other machinists in his workshop. They're on piece rates, there's no time for anyone else to stop and have a break.

The doors of the mosque fly open. Men burst out into the frosty street and the flow of those leaving prayer is traced in the crowds by the bobbing of their white skull caps, called *tokis*. Some of the men filter past the wicker baskets of vegetables into the New Taj Stores for the weekend shopping. As ever, the shop is packed. Someone is explaining with intricate gestures how he wants his fish cut up. Others from the mosque pass the shops by and gather round the knots of people at the talking corners of Princelet Street and Hanbury Street. As conversations build, the traffic jam of the street is repeated on the pavement.

A woman wearing a cardigan over her sari reaches the

bottom of her tenement staircase and turns out from Hanbury Street against the flow from the mosque. She's heading for her doctor's appointment. Her daughter holds her hand, walking slowly, wearing her knee-length skirt over long trousers. They cross the road, past old Weinberg the printers, where until recently metal letters were still laid out waiting for a compositor. Next door, the black-hatted orthodox Jews sort their bales of cloth.

The mosque has emptied as they cross Fournier Street with its town houses, gleaming shutters, polished knockers and locked front doors. The girl is embarrassed. As they reach the Church of England school, her mates are coming out in a long ragged crocodile. 'Why aren't you in school?' they shout. But they push on past the Seven Stars, its topless dancers advertised, as the traffic jams up again. Someone hoots half-heartedly. Through the round porthole windows of the new health centre other women can be seen, children beside them – some silent and still, others squirming with impatience. The girl holds the door for a pensioner who shuffles out unsteadily. Into the warm they go.

This is Spitalfields, the capital of Britain's Bangladeshi community. Like most capitals, it is a busy, dynamic, energetic place. But it is also poor. Here are the worst-paid jobs and the most overcrowded homes in London. Half a mile away from Brick Lane is the ancient boundary of the City of London, heart of Europe's financial institutions. For 400 years the two have faced each other, first across the real walls of the city, and now across an imaginary line on a map which is no less formidable. The silk weavers avoided the restrictions of the City Guilds by living outside its gates – Aldgate, Bishopsgate, Folgate are still the boundaries today. Spitalfields has been described as London's first industrial suburb. But now the City is moving outwards. It wants the land of the outcasts for itself.

This is land which London's poorest community depends on for its survival – it has nowhere else to go. But the capital's richest institutions also want it – and their desire turns land values to gold. Democratic planning is often seen as a means of mitigating the raw power of such institutions. Yet the policies of elected authorities have assisted the rich in trying to expropriate the people of Spitalfields.

In Margaret Thatcher's third term in office, expropriation is a real threat to all working-class communities who are using land which could be put to more profitable use. Forcing up rents, taking away security of tenure and breaking up council estates are all part of this. The London borough of Wandsworth has provided a foretaste: council tower blocks become luxury housing; Labour estates become Conservative. Battersea, Labour for a hundred years, now votes Tory. Tenants who wouldn't move out of Battersea tower blocks found themselves living on a building site with asbestos being stripped out all around them. They soon moved. Where profits can be made, working-class communities must now be expendable and the law that has protected their security needs to be stripped away. Forcing tenants out through clouds of asbestos dust was too crude. The law has already been changed so that bailiffs, rather than asbestos dust, carry out the evictions. William Waldegrave, Housing Minister at the time, said in a speech at Bristol in August 1987 that the idea of working-class people having the right to choose where they live 'must be nonsense'. There are echoes here of what has happened with Soweto and the townships.

Breaking up a working-class community to make profits from the land it lives on isn't a new idea – it just hasn't been made so easy before. For 15 years the policies of successive Tower Hamlets councils have smoothed the way for the take-over of Spitalfields. To get the land, it has had to break the back of the Bangladeshi community. This it has failed to do. Like Wandsworth, it too had its eye on its electoral base and wanted to get rid of a growing opposition. But it has not been so adept. The way the Bangladeshi community has fought for its land is important in its own right. Ten years ago, they were clinging to Spitalfields by their fingertips. Now the community is certain of a future in the area for a generation to come. But sadly, that fight for land is only

3

a harbinger of more struggles. There are lessons to be learnt – perhaps the Tories have already learnt them, because they are tilting the odds immeasurably further in favour of the profiteers.

History

Without luggage, it takes less than half an hour to walk from the London Docks to Brick Lane. And many have walked it. Not just the Irish migrants fleeing from famine, and the Jews from the Pale fleeing persecution. Sailors from many countries came too – Maltese, Cypriots, Keralans, Punjabis, Somalis. Even closer is the great railway terminus at Liverpool Street. From there came the landless labourers of East Anglia. Great Eastern Buildings, hanging over the railway tracks, housed many of them.

The fruit and vegetable market, now exclusively whole-sale, has been on the same site for over 300 years, as has Truman's Brewery. It's a measure of the changes hanging over Spitalfields that both may have closed by the time you read this. Many of the galleries which housed 18th century silk weaving looms can still be seen in the town houses at the side of Nicholas Hawksmoor's Christ Church. There was silk in Spitalfields before the Huguenot refugees arrived in the late 17th century. Clothing is still a mainstay today – with leatherwear being the latest addition.

For 300 years people have come to Spitalfields. Some stayed, some passed through. Despite that flux, the market, the brewery and, above all, the textile industry survived those same 300 years. It is an extraordinary paradox – an area in constant change and yet unchanging. Spitalfields has been the haven for each new migration. It has been a place to settle, a place to rebuild broken lives. But it has also been a place of poverty. Migrants haven't chosen Spitalfields, but were forced into its bad housing and its sweated labour in the clothing trade. There was nowhere else to go. And because there was nowhere else, they have defended it,

4

cherished it, changed it as best they could to make it meet the needs of their different cultures and civilizations. Without money they make do. Bengali machinists turn out jackets in old synagogues, pray in council flats built for large Irish families 50 years ago and live in tenements built for the refugee Jews.

At different times, Huguenots, Jews and now Bangladeshis have made up the majority of the population. Today only a third of Spitalfields residents are British in origin. The clothing trade, paying badly and with enormous variations in its labour needs, has always drawn on migrant labour. But it has also relied on low overheads – buy a sewing machine and you're in production. For centuries people have lived and worked, sewing and weaving, in the same houses. Even today, 12 per cent of the population has economic activity going on at home.

With each migration Spitalfields has been charged by the struggle of village people in the vast metropolis – coming from small communities to one of the largest masses of humanity on earth. The village was self-sufficient. Spitalfields has been expected to provide the same self-sufficiency. Home, work, food, clothing, friends, relatives, doctors, schools, places of worship, markets must all be within that walking distance which was the pattern back in the village. The demands of the village being stitched into the complex design of metropolitan life make Spitalfields a place of unique richness and variety. But its tight-knit self-reliance has also been forced upon it by the legacy of racism of the East End. The people of Spitalfields have had to take the violence and intimidation which are the practical effects of this.

Despite the repeated pattern of successive migrations of peoples from rural areas to the same bad housing and the same jobs, the different groups of migrants share little else. They have found themselves in Spitalfields for many reasons, and have expected a multitude of different things from their stay. The Jews were fleeing pogroms, their previous existence was unstable, they had nowhere to return to. They came in desperation. Bangladeshis came from settled rural communities whose basic patterns were unbroken even by the British Empire. They came in hope; they never expected to settle here.

Whatever their aspirations, they have had to fight for them against a back-drop of abject poverty. Few new arrivals brought any money with them, and few have made their fortune from the work that Spitalfields offered them. When the Greater London Council (GLC) used the information from the 1981 Census to pinpoint the most 'deprived' wards in London, Spitalfields didn't just come out worst of all the wards in the metropolitan area, it was in a different league. On four of the seven indicators used, it was amongst the worst three. Only one ward (in Newham) had a higher level of unemployment, only one ward (in Ealing) had worse overcrowding, only one ward (again in Ealing) had a higher percentage of unskilled and semi-skilled workers. Despite these enormous pressures, the traditional family structure is very strong. Nowhere in Tower Hamlets had a lower proportion of single parents bringing up families on their own.

Spitalfields is no island. Its problems are not contained only within its boundaries. Surrounding wards, especially St Mary's and St Katharine's to the south, face many of the same issues. There too the Bangaldeshi community has established itself. Conditions there, on the western edge of Tower Hamlets, stand out as being worse than elsewhere in the borough. That is saying something. Tower Hamlets as a whole had become a generally desolate place before the old Docklands were sequestered.

The docks of Tower Hamlets were once as important to trade as Heathrow Airport now is to travel, each a fulcrum of international movement. An enormous workforce had to service those docks. Communities developed over 150 years which were left with their hearts cut out when the docks closed. Rebuilding the docklands for those communities was going to be a slow and difficult process. It had hardly started when the Tories took power. They took the docklands away from its people, imposed the dictatorship of the London Docklands Development Corporation and it is now a land of the wealthy. For the old dockers' families the unemployment and poverty is still there, but there is no land left which could offer a new start.

The north of the borough has not fared well either. The furniture trade in Bethnal Green has dwindled, while many of the functions of the big breweries of Stepney have been moved elsewhere. The Lea Valley has the best of what is left of local industry. But it is not enough to prevent Tower Hamlets having the highest rate of unemployment in London. People with skills have moved out. What is left is an unskilled workforce and the many elderly people forced to fend for themselves now their relatives have gone.

As well as the decline in the industrial base, there was a staggering decline in the population of Tower Hamlets, from 600,000 people in 1901 to just 140,000 recorded in the 1981 Census. Enormous numbers of people moved out before and during the war, and never came back. The drain continued until recently. Now the presence of both the Docklands bonanza and the Bengali community means that the population is growing again. It is one of the few areas of London where increased populations are predicted in the 1991 Census.

Today, over 80 per cent of Tower Hamlets residents still live in council housing despite all the Tories' schemes to sell off such housing. Most of this housing, built in the grand manner of municipal socialism, is badly designed, badly maintained and lacking essentials like decent playspace and launderettes. Yet, when housing association and co-operative housing is added in, virtually 90 per cent of the housing stock is in 'social ownership' – possibly the highest proportion anywhere in the western world.

In a London context, bad housing and unemployment in Tower Hamlets stand out. But even in a Tower Hamlets context, conditions in Spitalfields are still shocking. Tower Hamlets people know this, but sometimes their anger is diverted by racism. There are people who, because they are badly off, don't recognize that Spitalfields has had it worse. To them, Spitalfields gets the money, housing, new community centres, jobs and training. Why don't they? 'Because we're white.' In reality, what Spitalfields has achieved has been through concerted work by Bengali and white people alike. Sometimes they've operated separately but often enough they've worked together too.

Geography

Spitalfields, which is 250 acres – the size of a small farm – divides into four distinct parts. Its western edge shares a boundary with the City of London – known as Middlesex Street during the week, it is Petticoat Lane on Sundays with the market bursting out to fill every nook and cranny of surrounding streets. From there Wentworth Street leads east, stuffed with clothes shops and fast food restaurants, it is now only fully alive in the two hours every day when the City takes its lunch and pours eastwards to buy beigels and winter boots. Above the shops are the skeletons of the last tenement blocks, while off to each side is the council housing of the Holland Estate, the old part to the north and west built in the 1920s, the new part to the south finished 50 years later. Still hugging the City border, but moving north, a few passages and lanes of 18th century Spitalfields remain. They disgorge onto the old Artillery ground, now the parking space for lorries loading and unloading at the market, where life starts at midnight, reaches its peak at 6am and at midday leaves streets empty of people but stacked high with broken packing cases and piles of rotting fruit and veg which even the scavengers couldn't make a meal of. North again, and more remnants of the 18th century streets meet up with the boundaries of Hackney.

Mixed in amongst these activities are the growing numbers of office blocks, smart cars, and wine bars to match. At the City boundary, the Victorian shapes of Liverpool Street station have disappeared. The new outlines

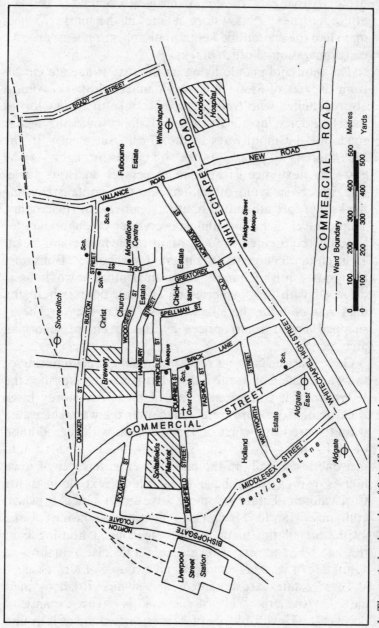

1. The main landmarks of Spitalfields ward.

of the Broadgate development now dominate. By late afternoon, new shadows are falling on the market, which may, like the station, be about to disappear under a massive conglomeration of office blocks.

The thousand people living on the City fringe are cut off from the rest of Spitalfields by Commercial Street. Almost always choked with traffic, it used to take the heavy lorries that thundered up the A13 from Tilbury onto the feeder roads for the motorways to the north. But even with the M25 there is no peace – traffic still crawls through. Moving east, the next slice of Spitalfields centres on Brick Lane. The streets splaying off either side still contain clothing workshops, private rented housing, leatherwear storerooms, shops, travel agents and almost everything else necessary for the daily requirements of life. Many of the houses are mean, 19th century tenements or converted warehouses. But some, alongside Christ Church, are 18th century town houses, designed with long galleries on the top floors where the light was best for the silk weavers. Today they are being snapped up at smart prices by the lovers of Georgian architecture.

Going east again, you reach the main council housing of the ward. The Chicksand Estate has kept growing since the 1930s when it comprised a few of those five-storey brick walk-up blocks. More were added after the war. The estate wasn't spared the worst of 1960s design, with the addition of a 19-storey tower and six-storey blocks divided into maisonettes. Finally in the last few years, terraces of town houses with gardens have been built. Next door is the Christchurch Estate – more five-storey blocks which epitomize Harold Macmillan's utilitarian housing of the 1950s. So all the main fashions in council housing over the last 60 years are in evidence. Little else remains – a sprinkling of workers' cottages and a couple of terraces.

These estates are bounded by Vallance Road to their east. On the other side of the road is a vast expanse of derelict land, with blocks of houses tucked uneasily round the edges. In this land are railway cuttings, old goodsyards, car auction rooms, scrap dealers and the like. Underneath is Whitechapel tube station, with trains rumbling below on the Metropolitan Line's East London Branch. Beyond the dereliction is Brady Street and the Collingwood Estate – someone else's patch. On its southern edge Spitalfields is bounded by Whitechapel High Street, which becomes Whitechapel Road further east. Surrounding Whitechapel tube station is a shopping parade, overlooked from across the road by the London Hospital in St Mary's ward.

St Mary's has more of the mean 19th century housing, and at Fieldgate Mansions one of the last complete tenement estates. The multiplicity of activities flows on down from Brick Lane. The City end of St Mary's is as strongly part of the Bangladeshi community as anything in Spitalfields. Going down further towards the river and Wapping is St Katharine's ward. Even here, on estates like the Berner, Bangladeshis are well-established.

To the north of Spitalfields, it is different. The railway lines from Liverpool Street Station divide the ward off from Bethnal Green as they have for 100 years. The other side of the tracks really is a different world. The migrants of Stepney and Spitalfields have never moved far beyond the tracks. Even in 19th century London, with its enormous inflow of peoples from all over the British Isles, nearly everyone in Shoreditch and Bethnal Green was London born and bred.

The peoples of Spitalfields

Spitalfields is not an exclusively Bengali area inherited from the Jews. It contains instead a wealth of different peoples, though since 1980 Bangladeshis have made up at least half of Spitalfield's population. Until recently, their housing cut them off from the rest of the ward. They lived in the remaining Victorian streets of private rented rooms and flats and filled the oldest of the council blocks. The remaining population was mostly in the newer council housing – but although it was newer, its condition was often run down.

Pensioners make up a third of all households. Many of them are what remains of a Jewish community whose grandchildren are spread far and wide across south-east England. A very few still hold distant memories of eastern Europe, a few more still speak Yiddish. A tower block like Denning Point, with many Jewish pensioners, rarely has empty flats. People who have shared a life time together are still under the same roof, and that's the way they want to stay.

A few of the next generation stayed on too. Still of working age, theirs may be the last generation of Spitalfields Jews. The days of the Jewish Free School with its 1,000 students are over, and most of the synagogues have closed. But there are still Jewish traders on Brick Lane, Jewish clothing firms, at least one synagogue alive – and many reminders of how Spitalfields used to be – beigel shops open on Sunday mornings, Bloom's the restaurant, Marks' the delicatessen and many more.

Irish people have come in numbers to the East End, from the navvies who dug the docks. Others claim Huguenot roots – families who have moved only inside the small circle of Stepney for as long as anyone can remember, with children still expecting a future in Spitalfields. Since the war, Maltese and Cypriot families have arrived. There's a population of West Pakistanis and Punjabis which has waxed and waned over the last 20 years. Afro-Caribbeans have settled in small numbers. Spitalfields has been a resting place for the single homeless from all over Britain and Ireland who live in the big Salvation Army and Providence Row hostels. None of these people is wealthy. Most work in clothing or service jobs, if they work at all. They all share Spitalfields as a home. Bound together by circumstance, divided by history, both the differences and the things held in common have shaped the way Spitalfields has developed.

Those 250 acres of Spitalfields are wanted badly. They are

wanted by the people who live there now, and by the hundreds of homeless families scattered across the seedy hotels and private lettings of London at the council's expense. They are wanted just as badly by the kind of property developers who can make Liverpool Street Station disappear beneath the steel and glass of monolithic offices.

This book is about the fight for that land.

2 | Point of departure: point of arrival

The population of Tower Hamlets is now a quarter of what it was at the beginning of the century. The people who have left would fill a city the size of Bristol. This hasn't all happened 'naturally'. From the 1920s onwards, planners have deliberately tried to reduce the number of people in the East End, because they could see no other solution to its problems. After 50 years' work they left an ageing population dependent on dying industries. Most people of working age have gone. The process went into a spiral, with the population getting smaller and smaller, older and older. Between the end of the war and the rebuilding of Docklands, the Bengalis have been the only large group to come in and fill the gap, providing new families of working age with children looking to the East End for their future.

The County Plan

Central to this process was the County of London Plan. Published in 1944, it was a vision for post-war London. It was full of unchecked enthusiasm for all the planning ideas which we now recognize to have been disasters for the inner city. But the ideas were important. Sir Patrick Abercrombie, the chief author of the plan, singled out the East End for detailed study. An attempt was made to put his ideas into practice, and the East End is still living with the consequences.

Throughout the war, planners keenly anticipated post-war reconstruction. It was seen as the once-in-a-lifetime opportunity to reorganize cities on a 'rational' basis. They saw themselves as public-spirited – fighting the forces of development for profit in order to build cities to meet peoples' needs. The mood of the time is well expressed by the architect Ralph Tubbs in his book *Living in Cities*, published during the war:

> Profit-seekers will try to break any attempt at control, and if we fail to make the necessary preparations now, the demand for speed will tempt those without conviction to shelve any large-scale planning schemes. We must not fail. Often we may have to pull down more. 'Re-destruction' may have to precede reconstruction. In that day, our faith in our own civilisation will be tried.

The idea of controlling the rebuilding of post-war Britain had enormous popular appeal. Penguin sold a quarter of a million copies of Thomas Sharp's book *Town Planning*, published in 1940. The people of the bomb-damaged cities were expecting more than speeches about 'homes for heroes'. To head off disaffection, the government deliberately encouraged the feeling that post-war Britain would be *planned* to meet the needs of the British people. This mood was still alive in the post-war Labour government's Town and Country Planning Act of 1947, which attempted to end land speculation and to get public control of all development.

Planning on this scale had never been attempted before outside Russia – the way the Russians were rebuilding their war-torn cities was often admired. In Britain as in Russia, enormous power was vested in the architects and planners. Here the ideas of planning were new and little understood outside professional circles. This meant the class assumptions about reconstruction were devastating. Almost all working-class housing was seen as slums that had to be 'swept away'. The mock Tudor of the petty bourgeoisie was sneered at too. Instead of the slums, Tubbs had this vision:

The solution is surely terraces around open quadrangles of lawns and trees, punctuated with high blocks of flats. How pleasant to walk from one quadrangle to another, to enjoy the sense of seclusion and the peace of the inner courts, with a skyline ever changing with the silhouettes of towering flats. For centuries men enjoyed some of these pleasures in the mediaeval cloisters, in the university 'quads', and in the courts of the Temple and Lincoln's Inn in London.

These were the sort of ideas which formed the County of London plan. Working-class areas were to be rebuilt with a mixture of houses and widely spaced high-rise flats with large open spaces in between. Industry and shopping were to be separated off. Each area would be divided from the next by motorway standard roads, which could take people quickly to the 'country'. The East End was to be developed into 'neighbourhoods' of about 100 acres each, within which all community facilities would be provided. In all 1,900 acres of the East End were to be razed to the ground. This wasn't some massive bombsite, like Dresden or Tokyo. In Abercrombie's special study of Shoreditch, only 6 per cent of the housing was irreparably bomb-damaged. For Abercrombie, all working-class housing was unfit to live in and had to wiped off the face of London.

The new city was planned with scarcely a mumble of consultation with the East End itself. The planners admitted that their new city with its open spaces wouldn't fit all the East Enders into it – even if they built it all of ten-storey tower blocks. So as the people didn't fit into the plan, they planned to get rid of the people. They decided to rebuild the East End at a density of 136 people to an acre. This would mean moving out over 40 per cent of the population, leaving two thirds of the rest in high-rise flats. The idea of moving working-class people to satellite towns far beyond the city boundary was much in vogue, and strongly supported by Abercrombie. On the one hand this was inspired by the Garden City movement earlier in the century. On the other, it could be seen as a means of social control. These two strands were entwined in the Town and Country Planning

Association's journal in January 1945. One article cites the benefits of new satellites 'where large overspill populations must inevitably be accommodated at some distance from the parent town'. The next, written by a Colonel Bowling of the South African branch of the Institute, latches onto these arguments eagerly:

> The advantages of living in a large city are merely illusory. There are admittedly more opportunities for the rich to get richer, but the poor usually get poorer and lead a more unhealthy and artificial existence.

His solution was to build separate new townships for the blacks.

In fact the grand plan for the East End never happened. The only neighbourhood development completed was the Lansbury Estate in Limehouse. This was given priority treatment as it was an exhibit in the 1951 Festival of Britain. It was also in the heart of Poplar, where the people had dared to boo the King and Queen on their war-time visit to inspect the bomb-damage. It was the only neighbourhood which incorporated the community facilities, shops open spaces and schools that Abercrombie envisaged.

Otherwise development was piecemeal. Bomb sites were rebuilt first – and because of the pressure for new housing, were almost all developed at the highest possible densities with high-rise flats. Comprehensive Development, as it was called, became too expensive, especially with the restrictions put on borrowing by the Tories in the 1950s. Estates were built one at a time and usually the community facilities just got left out. A mix of one third houses and two thirds flats had been promised. In fact, 96 per cent of everything built was flats. But many estates bear the hallmarks of the plan. On Mile End Road, the blocks from Ocean Estate stand up almost straight out of the pages of the plan.

Spitalfields and St Mary's wards were at the heart of the East End's bad housing. The triangle made up of White-chapel Road, Commercial Road and Sidney Street in

St Mary's was one of Abercrombie's special study areas. He recognized it needed immediate attention. The County Plan had exact diagrams showing the new ten-storey blocks, the simplified road layout, the annihilation of 'non-conforming' industries, and the collecting together of other industrial activity at the apex of the triangle near the City. No brick would remain standing.

In fact, scarcely a single brick has ever been disturbed. Forty years later, the area is a unique example of what the pre-war streets of East London looked like. It is also an example of why the County Plan was so wrong to try and demolish the East End. As will be detailed later, much of this 19th century housing, through internal conversion, will provide good quality accommodation well into the 21st century.

Spitalfields did not receive much more attention than St Mary's. In the 20 years after the war only two small estates were built. Stepney Council put about 170 units of housing on their Christchurch Estate, while the London County Council added 230 more units to the Chicksand Estate. At the heart of the Jewish community, these two wards were no priority for early rehousing.

But although the County Plan did not alter the fabric of these wards very much, it left a deadly legacy. It established the legitimacy of simply moving people out of an area when they didn't fit into the plan that has been drawn up. In fact the County Plan was based on false assumptions. Although it was full of radical ideas, it was planning for the pre-war East End which had disappeared before the plan was even published. For example, it assumed the population had not changed since the 1931 Census. In fact, Tower Hamlets lost nearly half its population between then and the end of the war. Many evacuees had seen how the other half lived, and liked it. The Plan set its heart on moving out 40 per cent of the population, when that 40 per cent had already gone. And yet emigration to the estates of Dagenham, Harold Hill and the new towns of Harlow and Basildon continued to be encouraged. Tower Hamlets' population went down from

230,000 to 140,000 between 1951 and 1981. By then planners were talking about *underpopulation* being a problem. By 1981 Tower Hamlets had just half the population envisaged in the Plan, 80 per cent of whom were living in council housing. Yet it still had a major housing shortage and some of the worst housing conditions in Britain. Reducing the population had not been the solution.

Even so, when Spitalfields did come up for redevelopment, the old arguments of the County Plan resurfaced. There were too many people living in impossible conditions at desperate densities. And the only solution, these people were told, was for them to move out of the area, because there wasn't any room for them. It's remarkable how this argument persisted, even as bigger and bigger tracts of Tower Hamlets land became empty and derelict. And although, throughout the post-war period, there have been plenty of people happy to move out when offered suitable out-of-London housing, this has never been true for everyone, least of all for members of the Bengali community who have been told to move out before many of their families have even had the chance to move in.

The 'disappearance' of the Jewish population of Stepney has to be seen in this context. It's true that those who could afford it went north and west – through Stamford Hill and Tottenham to Finchley, Hendon and beyond. But many Jewish people could only afford council housing. A few found it locally on estates like Sidney Street. Many more moved on to the London County Council estates of east London – the Jewish population in Becontree was so great by 1965 that the Ilford United Synagogue had to split in two. How much was such a move a real choice, and how much was it simply the only option available, because the LCC had been able to buy 1,000 acres of Ilford before the war? There isn't much evidence. *Family and Kinship in East London*, a study published in 1957 of what happened to the younger generation of families from Bethnal Green who were moved to outlying estates, suggested that they, at least, were very unhappy about being moved out. Yes, they wanted better housing, but, no, they didn't want the severing of links with their families and the break-up of established communities that this entailed. It would be surprising if Jewish Stepney felt very different.

The journey from Sylhet

The arrival of the Bengalis of Sylhet in East London has deeper roots than the Jewish and Huguenot migrations from persecution, As far back as the 17th century the British East India Company was already heavily involved in trade with Bengal, which was still part of the Mughal empire and had a highly developed mixed industrial and agricultural economy. Britain needed her manufactured goods – particularly the high-quality cottons and silks – as well as saltpetre, the vital ingredient in the gunpowder for Britain's European wars. In exchange, Bengal needed little of what Britain could export – raw materials like tin, lead and quicksilver being the most important. The East India Company was running a trade deficit, with the balance paid for in silver.

In the middle decades of the 18th century, the Mughal empire was collapsing. The East India Company's agents and merchants seized this opportunity to ruin the Bengali economy. Robert Clive's forces effectively gained military control of Bengal. Under his shield, the Company's agents got their hands on the land revenue which the Mughals had collected. But the checks and balances which had prevented the peasants from being overtaxed were jettisoned. The country was squeezed for far more than it was worth. There were desperate famines, but the Company would not lighten the tax burden. Company merchants were also exempted from local taxation, thus undercutting all local trade. Much of the enormous wealth leached out of Bengal didn't go to the Company, but to the individuals working for it. Some of these privateers settled down with country estates back in Britain, but a lot of their money was re-invested in the British Industrial Revolution. Roles were reversed. Bengal became the producer of raw materials – jute (made into sacking and rope in Dundee), tea (consumed in London) – while Britain exported its inferior cloth and other manufactured goods. Dhaka's silk industry was ruined. It is hard to see how Britain could have gained such pre-eminence as an industrial power, if it had not used the wealth of Bengal to finance it.

The British Raj never let Bengal recover. The last famine, during the Second World War and just three years before Independence, killed 2 million people. Small wonder so many people see the Bengali Subash Bose and his Indian National Army, who attempted to liberate India through armed struggle in collaboration with the Japanese, as heroes. Bengal was always one of the most militant areas to oppose British rule. Curzon's attempt to divide it in two at the beginning of this century failed. In the process Calcutta became too hot to handle as the capital of British India, and the administration moved to Delhi. When Partition came with Independence, Sylhet, which has an unbroken Islamic tradition going back to the 14th century, voted to go into Pakistan.

Sylhet district, with its head in the Assam hills and its feet in the flood-plains is a startlingly beautiful, emerald land. Of course it did not escape the Raj. But unlike most of India, a great deal of its land remained the property of the people who worked it, even if they were excessively taxed for what they were able to grow on it. In bad years, moneylenders paid the taxes – and some families never got out of their clutches. Through debt and land-subdivision, there were growing numbers who needed to look for work elsewhere. From the early 19th century Sylhetti men were travelling to the Calcutta waterfront to get work crewing British ships. Through a complex system of pay-offs, there were men in the docks who could arrange to get the Sylhettis jobs in the boiler-rooms of merchant ships and who could give them board and lodging till something came up. These Sylhetti men, paid very little, working in execrably hot conditions, played their part in the system that turned the wealth of Bengal into the fortunes of the British ruling class.

Most of their ships passed through London – the largest port of the most powerful Empire on earth. Still at the heart of that port were the docks of Millwall, Limehouse, Shadwell and Wapping, now all part of the London borough of Tower Hamlets. Seamen from many British colonies passed through. Some – from Africa, Somalia, China, and India – stayed. Their descendants are an integral part of the Tower Hamlets of today. Sometimes seamen were marooned on the London quaysides, their shipping companies having no further need of them. They had to wait to work another passage home. Until the first seamen's hostels opened in the 1850s, many of these men slept rough or in dockside sheds. This fate also befell young women employed in Calcutta as ayahs to accompany the children of the Raj on return journeys to London. Many of these women were also left on the quaysides, with no money, nowhere to live, and no way of getting home.

But in living memory, most of the seamen who came to stay in East London jumped ship and, penniless, made their way to Aldgate to seek their fortune. They were citizens of the British Empire and had every right to live in London. But they were breaking their contracts with the shipping companies. For this they could have been apprehended – although they rarely were. From the 1930s just a couple of men had safe houses in Spitalfields – addresses which were already known or soon discovered by those jumping ship. They lived from there until they could establish themselves and get a job. In the early days, most worked in hotels and restaurants.

During the war, many of those still working on ships serving the British Merchant Navy were killed by German torpedoes. Stoking the boilers below sea-level put them in the firing line. Although they had a reputation for reliable hard work, the shipping companies which employed them held them in such low esteem that there is no absolute record of the numbers, let alone the names, of those who died. In all it is estimated 6,600 Indian seamen were killed crewing British ships.

The end of the war saw the first mass arrival of people from the colonies to make good the labour shortage in Britain. The *Windrush* brought the first boat-load of Jamaicans in 1948. Sylhettis did not join them. With the formation of Pakistan, systematic discrimination soon developed against those from the East, while power and government remained in the West. The East Pakistanis, who would have been welcomed in Britain, couldn't get permission from the government in the West to let them leave. This wasn't resolved until 1956. Then for just six years friends, relatives and neighbours of the original Sylhetti seafarers came across. Britain then shut its doors to its own black Commonwealth citizens through the 1962 Immigration Act. For a further nine years, until 1971, decreasing numbers were allowed in on rationed work permits. Sylhettis still came over, mostly to fill jobs created by the small community which had established itself before 1962. After the 1971 Immigration Act only the dependants of those here already were allowed in, while with the 1988 Act many husbands, wives and children will be divided forever. As immigration was being stopped in 1971, the People's Militias were fighting for the independence of East Bengal, and many millions of the new Bangladeshis were sitting it out in refugee camps on the Indian border, sheltering from the atrocities of the Pakistani army. Out of that bloody war, they won citizenship of their new country of Bangladesh, and at the same time they lost the right to be settlers and citizens of Great Britain. British citizenship had been the only compensation Bengalis had been offered for the plunder of their country. When they claimed it, it was taken away.

Bangladesh is largely made up of the delta of the Brahmaputra and Ganges rivers. The silt brought down makes it one of the most fertile places on earth – three rice crops a year can be grown. It is a country the size of England and Wales, although in the wet season much of its land is under water. This tiny area supports a population of nearly 100 million people, 93 per cent of whom live in the countryside, and 85 per cent of whom rely on subsistence agriculture. The pressure on the land is increasing. A rising population needs more land for housing at the same time as requiring ever greater crop production. Deforestation in the Himalayas means more rainwater and silt running off the mountains into the rivers. Floodings in Bangladesh get worse year by year.

Bangladesh is a village society split apart by water. Communication is often enormously difficult. In the wet season, when the low-lying land is ten feet under water, journey times are much the same as in 18th century England. This isn't surprising, as from the 18th century until the time they left, the British did little to improve on the natural transport infrastructure provided by the waterways, building only the main roads to each district. In many places bridges are only replacing ferries now. Water is still often the only means of transport. And as the big rivers break up into many channels, there are numerous major river crossings just as disruptive and sometimes almost as long as the English Channel. As a result the villages remain self-contained and self-sufficient. It is said that regional variation in speech is still so pronounced that people's places of origin can be guessed to within a few miles by the way they talk.

This self-sufficiency is reinforced by the poverty of central government which can offer each village very little. Electricity is still not widespread. Road maintenance, bridge building and the like are the responsibility of the villagers. Although the government pays the salaries of teachers, schools have to be built through the efforts of villagers themselves. Local planning issues like these, and internal disputes, are still resolved as far as possible by the 'panchayat', or committee of elders, in each village.

At the heart of each villager's life is the extended family. This bears no relation to the term as it is used in Britain. An extended family can often include 100 or even 200 people. It will live in houses built round a compound, or

24

down a street, making a small village in its own right. A great-grandfather might have one house, while three or four sons each have another for their wives and children. And these children, as they marry, will also be setting up new households in further houses. On this scale the family is a mini 'welfare state' providing for those who cannot provide for themselves. To preserve this security, the family has great collective discipline and loyalty.

The family and the village were both enormously influential when men from these Sylhetti villages began arriving in Britain. Village loyalties ensured that once someone had got a foothold here, he would do what he could to help others from the same place. The seamen who arrived first drew in others from their own villages. When the British state did not provide for their needs, this was nothing new. There was already a village tradition of self-organization to make good the shortcomings of the state. This tradition was important in the East End as organizations developed to confront the state's failure to meet their needs. Meetings and discussions to resolve dificulties were already part of the way of life.

Only one Bangladeshi in four can read, while around 40 per cent are unemployed; but it was not the landless illiterates who came to Britain. They had no money to get here. It was the families who could use their land as security against the cost of the fare who could afford to send someone over. So, by and large, the people who came were the sons of landed families where the land was reaching the limits of the numbers it could support. Originally most families hoped that the breadwinner in Britain would be able to save enough money to return and buy more land to improve the family's long-term position.

This meant that the young men who arrived saw their stay as temporary. They were here for their families, were sending money back to them regularly, and were still taking directions from the head of the family back in Bangladesh. While this continued, they needed to minimize their living costs in Britain to maximize the amount they could send the family at home. Unlike the earlier seamen, many of whom

25

settled here marrying English women, the new arrivals were either married before they left, or had marriages arranged for them back home while they were working here. Being separated from their most immediate family when family ties were so vitally important meant that most men were living double lives. They would work for one or two years here, returning to spend as long as possible with their families. Time at home could almost equal the amount of time spent in England working.

Settling in Spitalfields

It's hard to be precise about how many people came over. Until the 1981 Census, Bangladeshis were classified as Pakistanis. Census returns are anyway notoriously inaccurate in enumerating houses in multiple occupation, where there are people who don't read or speak English or are frequently abroad visiting their families. In 1951 there were just 300 Pakistanis recorded in the Tower Hamlets area. This figure has more than tripled with each succeeding Census to reach the total of 9,800 Bangladeshi-born people living in the borough in 1981. This was probably a serious underestimate, but any estimate is difficult as the population has continued to grow fast. Health visitors, in the autumn of 1984, did a head count of their Bangladeshi caseload. On the basis of this alone, they were confident that the Bangladeshi population by then was well over 15,000. The council's own 'Count of the Bangladeshi Population' of May 1987 established that numbers around Spitalfields had increased by 81 per cent between the 1981 Census and 1987.

Between 1951 and 1961 the Census figure had increased to 800. Many of these people followed in the footsteps of the earlier seafarers. They would stay awhile at one of the tiny number of addresses with Bengali landlords, while they looked for a room. Nawab Ali of the Welfare Association, once had 95 people signing on for work at the Settles Street Labour Exchange from his address! They moved where they

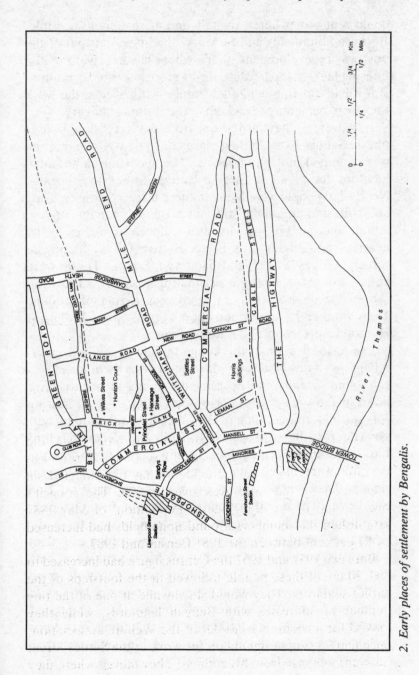

2. *Early places of settlement by Bengalis.*

could rent somewhere privately and as cheaply as possible. Because Spitalfields and St Mary's had been left out of the post-war redevelopment, that's where cheap private rented housing lay – cheap because it was in such terrible condition. But it had one immediate advantage – it was near the work they were beginning to pick up in the clothing industry.

However, as they moved out from the 'reception' houses like 13 Sandys Row, finding places wasn't easy. The housing was crammed into tiny pockets. The agent for an absentee landlord let seven houses in Settles Street to Bengalis. Nearly 100 people were living in these terraced houses. They are still standing, and still have Bengali tenants today. About another 120 men lived at a dozen addresses in the heart of Spitalfields – at Princelet Street, Old Montague Street, Wilkes Street and Heneage Street. These were largely houses in multiple occupation – some had Bengali owners, some had resident landladies letting off rooms. Then another 75 men found rooms in six of the 12 flats at Hunton Court just off Hanbury Street.

The concentration of this community in so few addresses, reliant on so few landlords who would offer them tenancies, gives some idea of the hostility the young men must have faced in those early years. However, their style of sharing flats was not unique. One of the other flats at Hunton Court was occupied by Irish workers – with the electoral roll of 1961 recording 37 men living there. To that extent the Bengalis were fitting into a previous tradition of migrant labour. They were living in the very worst the East End could offer. The houses were in a shocking state of disrepair. The rooms usually had space for little more than the beds. Lavatories, shared by many, were in the back yards. Hot water was virtually unknown – washing facilities of any sort were very basic. The housing was indivisible from the clothing trade. Workshops and rooms to let would frequently be in the same terraced house. If not, a ground floor kitchen might be a 'right of way' to clothing workshops in the backyard. And sooner or later machines were set up in many of the rented rooms.

Several factors tied the Bangladeshi workforce into the clothing trade. It is seasonal work, peaking for the spring and autumn fashions when many extra hands are needed. Arriving at a time of full employment, the Bengali workers were readily absorbed at these seasonal peaks, especially as much of the work was semi-skilled and could be picked up quickly, The slack season gave some the chance to rejoin their families in Bangladesh. It's labour-intensive work. A tiny amount of capital will hire a few sewing machines and a cheap workshop. Like the Jews before them, Bengalis found they could become their own sub-contractors, winning orders to knock out the 'shells' of garments for bigger manufacturers. As sub-contractors they could employ relatives and people from their village, ensuring a high level of loyalty and commitment. When work became slack, it could still be shared out equally, rather than having people laid off. So everyone in that workshop 'unit' could survive at some level. Achieving this was only possible by working on the margins of health and safety, for some of the lowest hourly rates of pay.

Taking this process one step further produces the home-worker. These people are officially 'self-employed'. They turn their own bedrooms into workshops, using old industrial machines. Cut cloth is delivered to their homes and taken away again when it has been made up. The firms using home-workers have an entire workforce at their disposal without having to pay any overheads, and without carrying any employment responsibilities. The firms have almost complete power to dictate the piece-rate for each garment. It is an unholy system, dating back in the East End to the 19th century homeworkers sticking together matchboxes. It can only thrive where other avenues to work are blocked – as they were for the Bangladeshi migrants. Even after the migrants settled the system has continued. When the women started arriving, they faced a battery of extra difficulties in getting work outside the home. Many became homeworkers, each trying to keep one eye on the seams she was stitching and the other on her children.

On these foundations – the worst of the private rented housing and employment in the clothing industry – the Bangladeshi community developed. The Census records that the number of 'Pakistanis' in Tower Hamlets quadrupled from 800 to 3,500 between 1961 and 1971. If the figures are wrong, the proportionate increase is probably right. These new arrivals had to be accommodated. Yet some of the first havens for the migrants of the 1950s had gone. Hunton Court had been pulled down, as had the houses in Old Montague Street and Wilkes Street. Just because the area had a history of immigration didn't make access to housing easy. In 1966 a third of all adverts in the local press for privately rented rooms actually specified 'no coloureds'. But the Bangladeshis found two new sources of housing.

The first came from local Asian business people. Some of them invested money in run-down properties which they then rented out room by room to the Bangladeshi workers. Being in poor condition the houses were cheap to buy. But it needed someone with the cash – building societies weren't going to advance mortgages on such derelict places. In 1961 only one house in Brick Lane had Bangladeshi residents. By 1971 there were over 20, housing more than 200 people. Another 200 were living in 16 addresses in Princelet Street. The new landlords didn't change traditional management practice – overcrowding continued, and the minimum was spent on repair and improvement. The most notorious of these was a man known locally as 'Musa' who owned dozens of properties. He spent some time in prison for illicit business practices while his property portfolio rotted.

The other source of housing was the old privately owned Victorian tenement estates. In Spitalfields, St Mary's and St Katharine's, many of these estates were still untouched by redevelopment. Landlords had their own systems for selecting tenants and collecting rent. But most of them put these jobs in the hands of agents. Unofficial networks developed: outgoing tenants would select someone new for the tenancy. The new tenant would be charged money for taking over the rent book. This money was split between the outgoing tenant who had set up the deal, and the landlord's agent, who had to co-operate by issuing a rent book in the new tenant's name. This followed on from a long tradition in the East End, where many of the superintendents of the Model Dwelling Companies in the 19th century were known to be corrupt.

Because Bengalis were excluded from so much of the private sector, the 'key money' they were charged to get into these tenements was exorbitant. Thus, 'buying' a rent book became the second big investment that a family had to make when sending someone over to London. Key money was apparently not money down the drain – it could always be charged to the next person to move into the flat when you moved out. But sums of money were very large relative to weekly incomes – equivalent to perhaps half a year's wages. Paying key money either involved raising cash from inside the family, or borrowing it from travel agents and other money lenders at very disadvantageous rates of interest. One way of paying this money back was by sub-letting parts of the tenements to relatives and friends who would pay rent to the person holding the rent book. It wasn't difficult to find these people – they had nowhere else to live.

This was an insidious system. It meant the tenements weren't economically viable unless they were overcrowded. It involved very poor people having to find very large sums of money for very dilapidated housing. None of the money went into improving the housing conditions. As the laws against charging these premiums tightened, it meant the money borrowed could only be recouped unlawfully.

But it had more deep-seated effects. Someone who had invested money in a tenement rent-book would lose it if the tenement was redeveloped and he was rehoused. He therefore held a vested interest in the maintenance of slum housing. The sub-tenants had family and village loyalties to the tenant who had done them a favour by giving them somewhere to live at all. So they didn't want to do anything to jeopardize the tenant's position. If the tenant told them to go, they went, regardless of their rights in law. In rare cases where there were disputes, Spitalfields had its own 'panchayat' where elders in the community would arbitrate. Nothing went to court. So complaining above the tenant's head about overcrowding or repairs was a very serious step to take. This loyalty extended into the terraced housing too. Conditions could be tolerated so long as the rent was cheap enough to save money out of their low wages to support their families back home. This all militated against organized resistance to the appalling conditions.

In this way, men moved first into the Hanbury Street tenements and Harris Buildings in St Katharine's, and then into places like Wentworth Dwellings. At Wentworth there were no Bengali tenants in 1960, just 19 in 1971 and around 200 by 1979, which was nearly the whole estate. There had been a lot of Sikh families there – as they moved on, Bengalis moved in. But other tenement owners weren't so accommodating. The Industrial Dwellings Society, which owned Brady Street Dwellings, did nothing to house Bengalis till the day they were demolished. The Society still owns property in the East End and continues to maintain the same housing management traditions.

A typical household would have been a group of between three and eight men sharing a tenement or a couple of rooms in a terraced house. Most likely they would all be relatives or from the same village. At any one time, a couple of them might be home with their families in Bangladesh. Sometimes this group would include younger brothers of school age who were sent over into the care of their elders. They shared cooking between them and would pay a small weekly rent to the person among them who held the rent book. Apart from beds, cooking utensils and a table to eat from, there was little furniture. If they'd wanted more furniture, there would have been nowhere to put it anyway. There was no space.

This pattern was to be broken. In the mid-1960s a survey by Mariyan Harris suggested that over 80 per cent of the Bengalis in the East End had no intention of settling here. Fifteen years later the Spitalfields Survey, carried out by the Spitalfields Housing and Planning Rights Service and the

Catholic Housing Aid Society, suggested that 89 per cent of Bangladeshis in Spitalfields had decided to stay. Over that period an enormous shift in perception had taken place.

A few people made enough money to return to Bangladesh and set up their own businesses there successfully. But for most, this was not an option. Wage levels in the clothing industry have always been notoriously low. As late as 1980, average male wages were below £80 a week, when the equivalent figure for Greater London as a whole was £144. It was not easy to earn enough to survive in the East End *and* support a family at home *and* pay the fares for regular visits *and* save enough to buy more land in Bangladesh. What compounded this was the very village network which had helped get people across to Britain. Villages with a lot of wage-earners in Britain will have several families with extra cash offering money for land. The result is inflation in land prices. This has got worse since contract workers started going to the Middle East in the 1970s. Altogether Bangladesh is now earning $600 million a year in foreign exchange from its workers abroad. The families with London connections became known as the 'Londhoni' – 'dhoni' being the Bengali word for rich. But money saved in London simply doesn't have the purchasing power that had been envisaged.

This has left three choices: returning, remaining separated from the family, or bringing the family over. Returning means facing the difficulties that had first prompted people to leave. How will the families be supported when the men get home? Few have chosen this course except for those retiring with a British pension. But staying in Britain and visiting the family from time to time becomes a terrible strain if it goes on indefinitely. So most men have chosen to bring their families here. At the start, some were worried about how Western culture would affect them, while all were anxious about the racist violence which intensifed when families began arriving, and the terrible housing that the women and children would have to move into. Families started coming at the beginning of the 1970s. They're not all here yet, and some may never make it. Once families have decided to join up, immigration controls have been manipulated by the British government to slow this down as far as possible. Now, the 1988 Immigration Act will stop families coming at all unless they've already got somewhere to live. The Tories want to use the housing shortage as a tool of immigration control.

Families weren't going to fit easily into the terraces and tenements that their menfolk had been living in. It was out of the question for a woman with her children to come and share a room already occupied by several men, even if there had been the space. The conditions which had been tolerated as a temporary expedient by single men, were unthinkable when considering a permanent home for a whole family. So from the mid-1970s, when the arrival of families began in earnest, housing quickly became a central issue for the emerging Bangladeshi organizations.

The decision to bring the immediate families over to Britain changed the men's relationship with their extended families, whether they liked it or not. Once a man's family arrived, he was effectively setting himself up as the head of the household. The extended family could no longer be the day-to-day support. Many of the benefits which this family had provided could only continue in Britain within a very different framework. As heads of their families, the men in Britain could not wield the same authority as they would have had at home. This wasn't just because most of the family was no longer there. In the village enormous respect is paid to its elders – the head of a family being in its oldest extant generation. In the stable social structure of village life, the wisdom gathered through a lifetime's experience is extremely valuable. In Britain this no longer applied. The men had had little contact with the institutions of the British state. Of working age, they had rarely used the health service. There had been no children at school. Few had been given council housing. Few even claimed unemployment benefit when work was slack. With Bengali employers, shopkeepers and landlords, there was

34

scarcely a need to learn to speak English (and many never did learn).

When the children arrived they were thrown straight into English-speaking schools and had to deal in their own way with the racism of English institutions which they had not been warned about. Although their fathers may have decided to centre their lives in Britain, they had the habits of a lifetime to change. Many youths at 16, with just three or four years of British schooling behind them, were far more focused on Britain as their home, had a greater understanding of British institutions and had the English language as an immediate tool with which to deal with their life here.

The arrival of the Bangladeshi women provided the greatest challenge to the existing set-up. In Bangladesh middle-class women take an active part in public life. The leaders of the two main opposition parties are women – Hasina Wasil, daughter of Bangladesh's first leader, Sheikh Mujib, heads the Awami League, while General Zia's widow leads the Bangladesh National Party. But in the rural areas purdah still prevails. Women are rarely seen in public – even the buying and selling in the markets is done by men. However, with the size of the family unit, women are far from being isolated. They are in constant contact with each other and with the many other members of an extended family, while they often share cooking and childcare. There was no way of translating this to the East End. When the women arrived, they had to come to terms with many of the problems their menfolk had experienced a decade or two before. They were moving from ordered village life to one of the biggest cities in the world; they spoke no English; they had nowhere to live. But they had many more things to contend with. They had an immediate responsibility for children, which involved contact with schools and health visitors, that their husbands had never had. They were coming to settle – their husbands had come as migrants. They were making a much bigger break with their own past. They had to make a family home out of slum housing that their husbands had simply used as a place to eat and sleep. It was housing built for a way of life and climate they knew little about: glazing for example, not essential in Bangladesh, was suddenly a necessity. Their children, used to the freedom of the countryside, were scarcely safe outside the front door, let alone out of sight. Their pattern of contact with other women was broken. Sometimes there would be only one woman in the house. Only in rare cases of extreme overcrowding would there be more than two or three women living in the same flat.

The tenements of Spitalfields could not accommodate these women and their aspirations. Their arrival demanded change on the most massive scale. They needed somewhere permanent to live which gave the space for their families to grow and develop. This settlement was going to bring a new, young heart to the East End's ageing population. With young families, which were often large, setting up and with relatively few pensioners, the Bangladeshi population was set to grow rapidly. By 1984, 46 per cent of all live births in the borough were to Bangladeshi mothers, while it is calculated that Bangladeshi children will form a majority of all primary school pupils in the borough by the early 1990s.

All these people expected to be provided for, as other British citizens had been. The rest of Spitalfields had been housed by the council. Now it was their turn. The divide was almost total. The council estates were white. The Bangladeshis were still in the slums. Now, for the first time, the British state was being asked to pay back some of what it had taken from these people – through 20 years of taxation and before that through 200 years of the imperial presence in Bengal. It did not do so willingly.

3 | The battlelines

For decades Spitalfields had been ignored by the local authorities. But when Bangladeshi families started settling permanently, it became a battleground, with the Bangladeshis desperately trying to hold on and the councils unleashing a barrage of weapons aimed at getting them out.

In local government terms, Tower Hamlets has been unusual. Until recently, over half its housing stock was run through the London-wide authority of the Greater London Council. This gave the GLC as much power over people's lives as the borough council had. But whereas there were 50 borough councillors, the GLC had only two representing the area. This meant that officers employed by the GLC, particularly in its housing department, had much greater freedom of movement than their borough counterparts. Indeed, the way that policies were delivered on the ground was a complex mixture of priorities, set by politicians, and practice, which depended on the way their paid officers chose to interpret these priorities. This is important, as in extreme cases officers controlled and carried out their own policies. What's more, the two councils themselves sometimes worked in harness, sometimes in opposition. To keep things clear, there follows a table of the different GLC and borough council administrations.

For 41 years, from 1945 to 1986, local councils in Tower Hamlets were controlled by the Labour Party. For 20 years this was through three separate borough councils in Poplar, Bethnal Green and Stepney, and then from 1965 as one united body. For most of that time, Labour had little opposition. Not a single opposition candidate ever won

The battlelines

a seat on Bethnal Green Council from 1945 till the council's amalgamation in 1964. In Stepney the only dissent came from the Communists, with a tradition there of industrial and housing organization going back to the 1930s. The Liberal Party, now in control, didn't win a single seat until 1978, while the Conservative Party has always been a non-runner.

Administrations in GLC and Tower Hamlets

Year of election	GLC Administration/Leader	Tower Hamlets Administration/Leader
1968		Labour – John Orwell
1970	Tory – Desmond Plummer	
1971		Labour – John Orwell
1973	Labour – Reg Goodwin	
1974		Labour – Paul Beasley
1977	Tory – Horace Cutler	
1978		Labour – Paul Beasley
1981	Labour – Ken Livingstone	
1982		Labour – Paul Beasley John Riley
1986	ABOLITION	Liberal – Eric Flounders Brenda Collins

With 40 years in power and little opposition the Labour Party ossified. In the 1968 elections, a third of the wards were uncontested, and only 11,000 of the borough's 126,000 electors voted. Many councillors served continuously for decades. As the 1982 elections approached, 19 of Labour's 43 councillors had been there for 20 years or more. Joe O'Connor headed the list with an unbroken stint from 1928. As membership of the Labour Party declined, councillors were able to get re-selected by smaller and smaller cliques of supporters. This continuity was also reflected amongst senior officers who worked their way up through the ranks, staying with the council for as many decades as the councillors themselves. This created a cosy and complacent relationship, with the officers finely tuned to the way their councillors operated. Underneath this solid bond, the standard of services delivered by the council – especially in housing – went from bad to worse.

The council's power base was disappearing. It had been built on organized labour. But the docks had gone and most workers in industries like the breweries moved out to areas where they could afford to buy their own homes. Solid support for the councillors aged with them. The younger generation did not seem to be following in the tradition – with one Labour councillor's son joining the National Front. By the mid-1970s a group largely made up of elderly white men, with a record in organized labour, was representing a borough where one person in four was from an ethnic minority, one in five was unemployed and most of the industry had gone elsewhere or closed down. They only reflected the make-up of the borough in as far as they, like most residents, were council tenants.

These councillors had no experience of dealing with political opposition. Many had started their careers without even standing in contested elections. They had never needed to mobilize people, nor even govern by consent. In fact any political organization at all was seen as a threat. They had only got where they were because political organization, either in support or in opposition, didn't really exist. So when opposition arrived, they didn't know how to handle it. In just eight years the Liberals moved from having no seats to controlling the council. At the same time, the Labour Party itself was changing. In 1978 only three of Labour's 43 councillors had not served before. In 1986, when Labour went into opposition 14 of their remaining 24 councillors were new. Belatedly, the process which had turned the London Labour Party leftwards through the late 1970s and 80s also affected the make-up of the Tower Hamlets party. As the Liberal challenge mounted, the turnout in local elections increased. This led to the irony that the Left Labour slate which lost the 1986 election, actually received more votes than any of the winning Labour administrations of the previous 25 years: in 1968, 57 Labour councillors were returned with just 7,800 votes; in 1986 Labour received 21,300 votes and had just 24 councillors. Thus, in losing power, the Labour Party has probably got a stronger real base than it did 20 years ago. It cannot be written off.

Decline of the Labour Party on Tower Hamlets Council

| | Election Year | | | | | |
Number of councillors	*1968*	*1971*	*1974*	*1978*	*1982*	*1986*
Labour	57	60	60	43	31	24
Liberal				7	18	25
Communist	3					
Other					1	1
Total Number	60	60	60	50	50	50
% share of vote						
Labour	71	89	86	64	47	46
Liberal	6	1	7	11	40	44
Conservative	10	5	2	10	7	5
Other	13	5	5	15	6	5
% turnout	14	26	18	28	31	39
Seats uncontested	23	15	13	0	2	0

Turnout calculated only on seats which were contested

(Source: GLC Intelligence Unit)

In order to hold power without opposition for so long, the Labour Party had to accommodate the traditions of racism in the East End. Pressure for the first Aliens Act had centred on Bethnal Green before the First World War. A generation later, and Oswald Mosley stood for Parliament from Shoreditch. A generation after that, the National Front set up its national headquarters there. The northern boundary of the Jewish East End was the Liverpool Street railway line. Beyond was the 'alien' Bethnal Green. When there were 40,000 Jews in Stepney, only 3.5 per cent of Bethnal Green's population were föreign-born. Sixty years later, when Stepney had its first 2,000 residents from the Indian sub-continent, Bethnal Green had less than 100. Even in Stepney, Jews lived only in certain areas. The East End has never assimilated its new arrivals without a struggle.

When Stepney had a very large Jewish population, they had little say in the Labour Party. The main line of Jewish political activity had been through the Communist Party. In 1949, when there were 60 Labour and nine Communist councillors, there were more Jews in the Communist opposition than in the Labour group. When Bethnal Green and Stepney were joined together, it was not surprising that this tradition hardened. Not until the 1982 elections did the Labour Party in Spitalfields give the Bengali community any recognition, and only in 1985 was the first Labour Bengali councillor elected. Before the Labour Party's swing to the left, Bengalis often found it difficult even to join the party.

The figure who presided over the decline of the Labour council was Paul Beasley. Elected in 1970, he became its leader within four years. He was only in his early thirties, he was dynamic. He worked with and for voluntary organizations in the borough, he had Bengali friends. He even went on a visit to Bangladesh. He appeared to be the person who could pull the council out of the 1950s and into the present. His selection was seen as a sign that the party was shifting back to the left.

These hopes were desperately ill-founded. Beasley was to give the Labour council a new look, but not in the way that had been expected. He shed his approachable image, his contact with community organizations and his support for socialist politics. He quickly won the respect of the developers, and gained sufficient experience in the field to set up his own development company after leaving the council. For a time he worked for Asil Nadir, who was owner of the clothing firm Polly Peck and an office development on Commercial Road. He also joined the board of the London Docklands Development Corporation. Then, a few months after standing down as leader, Beasley became a director for the Taylor Woodrow subsidiary the World Trade Centre in London – as, indeed, so later did Jack Wolkind, two years after his retirement from his job as Chief Executive of Tower Hamlets, though there is no suggestion these associations were used improperly.

Beasley carried his Labour councillors with him in the belief that private investment would regenerate the borough. He believed he could harness the aspirations of East Enders who wanted to buy their own homes, move up into white-collar jobs and better themselves generally. These were the people who were leaving the borough and moving to the outer suburbs and new towns. *Family and Kinship in East London* had shown that people didn't necessarily want to move out of the East End. They did so to get on. But if they could better themselves *and* stay in the East End – that was an ideal for many. The private housing would be unaffordable; the office jobs were simply being exported from the City. But he held out the dream of New Town prosperity in the old East End. On the strength of that, he became an enthusiastic backer of international finance capital, backing schemes from 60-storey office blocks to mega-international banking centres. He looked for electoral support by saying he wanted to bring people new jobs and the choice of buying their homes. He looked for developers' support by saying that the borough's problem was its 'unskilled' and 'unbalanced' working class – and housing for a new middle class was needed.

This thinking was part of main-line planning practice too. Throughout, the planners have seen the need to make Spitalfields a 'balanced' community, creating a middle-class core to the area, pushing out unattractive 'non-conforming' workshops. 'Balancing' communities is always used as a means of breaking up and controlling working-class areas, never the other way round. No-one tries to put clothing workshops and council housing into Belgravia or Virginia Water. This planning orthodoxy has provided a base from which politicians have legitimized the breaking-up of communities.

Socialists saw this policy for what it was – jobs and homes for wealthy outsiders. It was no answer to unemployment, and it would further worsen the housing crisis. The Labour Party on the ground, represented in the council chamber from 1982 onwards by a small 'opposition' group of socialist councillors, began to fight against the policies of the Labour majority on the council. They argued for a strategy to redevelop the borough in the interests of the working-class people already living there. To do this, the party needed to forge a new alliance amongst those who clearly had nothing to gain from the private redevelopment of the East End. The Bengali community was central to this plan, as were the borough's other ethnic minorities, the unemployed, the unwaged, the elderly and all those who were relying on a lifetime of council housing. Of all these overlapping groupings, the Bangladeshis were the most highly organized.

The growth in the Bengali vote posed problems for Beasley's Labour administration. It was a solid Labour vote, which, if unchecked, might well amount to a powerful 30 per cent of the electorate by the year 2000. But it was also concentrated on some of the most valuable land in the borough – this was the prime territory for the vision of the 'new East End'. There would be no development further east if the City was cut off from it by the slum housing and workshops of the Bengali community. The Bengalis were occupying the crucial space. They were in the way. They had to go. Although there were a few Bengali right-wingers who were prepared to collaborate with Beasley, most strands in the Bengali community became increasingly

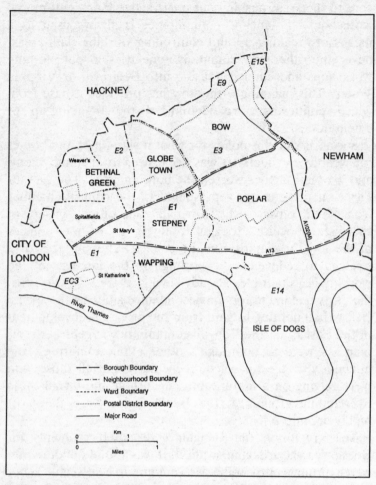

3. Tower Hamlets – neighbourhoods, wards and postal districts.

organized against this attempted break-up. (The colla-
borators ended up joining the Liberals and having to justify
the wilder excesses of the new regime.)

So the Beasley administration was competing with the
Liberals for the votes of those aspiring to white-collar
jobs and home-ownership. The Liberals shared his class
allegiances but they could see his days were numbered. In
their view, socialists were going to take over the Labour
Party, and unless they won the council, there would be a
socialist administration. The Liberals' great asset was the
callousness shown by Labour committees towards the
services delivered by the council. Labour councillors put
absolute faith in the senior officers. Any criticism of services
was treated as personal criticism of these officers and was
therefore offensive and inadmissible. The Liberals worked
doggedly for a decade on the frustrations and alienation of
people who couldn't get answers to their transfer requests,
and who couldn't get anyone round to do the simplest
repairs. They held endless surgeries, sending off letters for
people, and getting councillors to chase up responses.
Beasley preferred talking to developers with big ideas and
big money to the everyday problems of the present. So while
the Labour regime carried out Liberal policies, the Liberals
garnered the votes. The Liberals made headway in the north
of the borough which was largely being left out of the 'new
East End'. But in the riverside wards and along the City
boundary, where development started and Beasley's policies
were turning into reality, left Labour councillors who
opposed Beasley's faction were elected.

With the leftward shift in the Labour Party, Beasley
could not get selected as a Labour candidate for the 1986
election. Along with his brother-in-law and a third deposed
councillor, he stood as an Independent against the Labour
Party in Lansbury ward. They successfully split the Labour
vote – 900 going to the official candidates and 400 to them.
The Liberals were elected with 1,100 votes. Without those
three seats the Liberals would not have controlled the
council. Beasley had given power to the Liberals. On

16th May 1986, just after the election, the *East London Advertiser* quoted him:

> I feel satisfied that our intervention has directly led to the Liberals winning. The effect will be to strengthen the position of moderate members on the council.

We shall see just how moderate the Liberals turned out to be.

The Liberals came into the Town Hall on the populist platform of devolving power to a neighbourhood level. They split the borough into seven such neighbourhoods, apparently giving councillors considerable power over business as it affects their patch. As three of the neighbourhoods were controlled by Labour, this system obviously had safeguards to ensure that decisions made in Labour neighbourhoods could be overturned. Indeed, a fourth neighbourhood went Labour as a result of a by-election in November 1988. Important decisions are taken centrally because they have borough-wide implications. The Labour Stepney neighbourhood, for example, was overruled by the Policy Sub-Committee when it tried to stop office blocks over seven storeys high being built at Aldgate. This suddenly became a 'borough-wide' issue and was taken out of the hands of a Labour-controlled committee.

Two other things are significant for the Bengali community. One is the way the borough was carved up. Spitalfields, St Mary's and St Katharine's wards form a natural group. This isn't just because there is a Bangladeshi majority there. These wards have the same housing problems, the same industries and the same border with the City. This neighbourhood would have given the Bengali community some control over their own area, in theory. But in fact the three wards were put into three different neighbourhoods. Spitalfields is, for the first time in its long history, part of Bethnal Green. Bethnal Green now has a structural means of controlling what happens in Spitalfields. The other issue is one of resources. Instead of being directed towards the areas of greatest need, money is divided equally between the neighbourhoods, based on their relative populations. With no targeting of need, Spitalfields loses out.

The Liberals came to power five weeks after the GLC was abolished. They inherited the entire GLC housing stock, while, with the abolition of the Inner London Education Authority, they will also take on the schools. This gives them greater power than the previous Labour administration ever had.

The importance of Spitalfields

To understand why the fight for the land in Spitalfields has been so intense, it must first be recognized why it is still essential for its existing residents to live there – and especially for its Bangladeshi community. Spitalfields still provides the jobs, and therefore the money to live. The restaurants and the clothing workshops only survive because they are situated where they are – in the heart of London next to the City. There is a complex chain linking the migrant workers to the Spitalfields area. The clothes stores of the West End are very 'fashion sensitive'. Fashion clothing is a volatile business. It is produced in small runs – which are expensive. But a particular style may suddenly take off, needing immediate large re-orders. For the retailers, this requires wholesalers and workshops close by, able to respond to demand at a moment's notice.

This explains why it is possible for there to be so many small employers – all fulfilling different small orders, and why the clothing workshops have traditionally been situated along the eastern edge of the City in Tower Hamlets and Hackney. Bespoke tailoring could afford space in the West End. 'Off the peg' production was forced into the nearest cheap industrial workspace.

Thus the complex inter-relationship of main producers, sub-contractors and wholesalers grew together. Even the famous markets at Wentworth Street and Petticoat Lane are tied into the network. Many of their cheap clothes are bought direct from the workshops on what is known as the 'cabbage'. Workshops are often supplied with the cloth they need to fulfill their orders. If the cutter can find a way of cutting more garments from each piece of cloth than the supplier intended, the extra garments can be kept and sold on the side.

The geographical proximity of wholesalers, manufacturers and smaller contractors makes it easier for small workshop owners to get work. Once they are known as reliable, work will be offered to them. They will not have to market themselves, they can rely on their reputation to keep going.

The whole system depends on a flexible low-paid workforce. The Bengali migrants provided this. Because of the cheap housing, they could survive on the wages. Because it was nearby, they could work anti-social hours and still get meals and get home in relative safety late at night. Sudden fluctuations in the amount of work around mean that most jobs are advertised by word of mouth. Without living in the area, it is hard to know where and when work is coming up. The mixture of housing and workspace made it all the easier for people to set up their own businesses when opportunities arose. People worked at home, and in the worst cases lived at work – when machinists with nowhere to go were left sleeping at night on the cutting room tables. So long as the clothing industry was in Spitalfields, and so long as the Bengali community relied on it for employment, that community also needed to live in Spitalfields.

The other main area of work was in 'Indian' restaurants – almost all of which were run by Sylhettis. Here, anti-social hours and low wages also meant it was important for chefs and waiters to live near the restaurants they were working in. Increasingly, Brick Lane itself has become a centre for such restaurants, and its popularity is pushing up wage rates. But there were also employment opportunities in the West End. Spitalfields was an important base for these workers too, although Fitzrovia and other areas also developed Bengali communities for the same reasons. Until the workforce can break out of its economic dependence on clothing and catering, it will continue to depend on the land of Spitalfields and the surrounding wards for its survival.

But the arrival of the women and children has greatly strengthened the links between the community and the area. The culture shock which the women experienced has already been outlined. Spitalfields was not a totally inhospitable place, however, nor did it demand a total denial of their previous lifestyle. 'Purdah' tends to conjure up stereotypes of women shut away behind veils and closed doors on their own. In the villages, purdah did not exclude the large numbers of both men and women in the extended family. Living in Spitalfields, where some of these people were close by, it was still possible to maintain contact. The daily routine – the working men and schoolchildren coming back for a midday meal, the women friends and family dropping round – was not necessarily broken.

But the city brought new demands too, which led to women being involved more formally with each other – in childcare arrangements; in English classes; in training, first in the skills of the clothing industry and then in better-paid office-based employment. Women's organizations have also begun to provide some of these things for themselves. Gradually women are defining a role for themselves to suit their new situation. This is being accelerated by the increasing numbers of girls leaving school with a British secondary education. Until now it has been crucial for this process that the women live within walking distance of each other – they haven't got cars, and haven't used public transport much on their own.

For these women, freedom from the threat of racist violence is also central. Nothing could have prepared the first women for the level of racism they were to experience on arrival. Although the bleaker side of life in London was usually played down by men on their return visits home, even they cannot have anticipated what was to happen. Spitalfields had never been free from racist attack. But there was an explosion of violence when the women started

49

arriving in the mid-1970s. This coincided with the high-watermark of the National Front, which picked up nearly 10 per cent of the vote in Bethnal Green in the October 1974 election. The climax of fascist activity was at the point when migrants decided to settle.

The Stepney and Bethnal Green Trades Council report on these attacks – *Blood on the Streets* – suggested that they were centred on Spitalfields. Twenty-eight of the 100 incidents they listed happened in the ward. Organized racist violence was focused around the selling of the National Front newspaper on Brick Lane. On 4th May 1978, Altab Ali, a 24-year-old machinist, was knifed to death near Whitechapel Road. Seven thousand people joined the protest funeral march to Downing Street. In June, 150 youths rampaged down Brick Lane in a 'riot' pre-planned by fascist groups. This went unchecked by the large police presence in the area. They smashed windows and seriously injured one storekeeper. There was a protest march against this a week later. On 16th July, by force of numbers, the National Front was unable to sell its paper at the end of Brick Lane for the first time. On 17th July, 8,000 Bangladeshi workers went on strike against the racist violence. On 24th August an attempt by Fascists to march down Brick Lane was thwarted despite the lack of support from the Anti-Nazi League, who were holding a mass rally in south London.

From that point, racist violence in Spitalfields quickly tailed away. The area had been made relatively safe through the Bengali community's proven ability to defend itself. The struggle had strengthened some of the youth groups, and had given birth to others. Spitalfields and St Mary's became havens compared with some places. Safety was not in numbers but in organization. Obviously the value of living in the area was immeasurably enhanced by this victory. It encouraged the growing sense of permanent settlement.

With permanent settlement came a proliferation of institutions, organizations and services provided by the community itself. Until then the mosque and the Bangladesh

Welfare Association had been the pivotal institutions. As the political voice of the Bengali community, these bodies lost their pre-eminence, and they were joined by the youth groups, which took advice from the earlier bodies, but tended to have a more radical perspective. These new groups were increasingly influential on the whole spread of issues relating to community development. They supplemented this with the setting-up of youth centres, sports leagues and out-of-London trips for their membership.

Particularly important was their input to the campaign on Bengali Educational Needs in Tower Hamlets (BENTH) which confronted the ILEA with the need for big changes in what schools taught and how they were run. They were the people who had experienced British schooling – they knew what was wrong with it. This increasing focus on local schooling, the insistence that it met the needs of Bengali children, made it all the more important for families to stay living in the area where these schools were located. This has been underlined by the levels of harassment in secondary schools like Daneford in Bethnal Green, where Bengali pupils have had to organize to confront attacks by white pupils when the teaching staff were not prepared to intervene.

By the same process, many other state and local authority services have had to bend under pressure to meet changing needs. Some health visitors speak Bengali. Bengali social workers have been employed in the Social Services offices. And as we shall see later, even the housing programme changed direction eventually. In parallel, the voluntary organizations also got funding to provide specialist services. The Maternity Support Liaison Service reached nearly every pregnant Bengali mother in the borough; the Asian Unemployment Outreach Project started giving specialist benefit advice; there was also the Housing Rights Service and the Training Forum. All of these were added to the youth and community service provided by Avenues Unlimited which until then had been unique in its work with the Bengali community.

51

The area also has religious importance. The Brick Lane and Fieldgate Street mosques are focuses for the predominantly Muslim community. The Fieldgate Street mosque cost £2 million to build – part of the money was donated personally by King Fahd of Saudi Arabia. It is the largest in Europe, holding 2,000 at a single prayer meeting. On religious festival 'Eid' days, the mosque is filled many times over. For devoted Muslims, who observe the five calls to prayer every day, and who are expected to live within walking distance of their mosque, the proximity of such a place is important. Converted council flats on hostile estates in Poplar are going to be no substitute.

As important as the mosques are the supplementary schools which most Bengali parents want their children to attend after school hours. Here they have the chance to learn to read the Koran and to understand the fundamentals of Islam. Normally added to this are lessons in reading and writing Bengali and, on occasion, supplementary teaching in mainstream school subjects. These schools have sprung up wherever Bengali children are to be found. Often they have to operate from disused basement workshops and other unsuitable premises. But the most longstanding supplementary school – East End Community School – now has its own Portakabin space and serves the children of West Spitalfields. It is indicative of the value placed on this school that one of its teachers, Nurul Hoque, and one of its management committee, Gulam Mortuza, became local councillors.

The Spitalfields Bengali community has now reached a size which makes it viable as a shopping and social centre. Brick Lane is the artery supplying the heart of the ward. It has the clothing workshops and restaurants providing employment. It still has rooms to let. There are over 80 different kinds of retail shops – including the travel agents and money lenders. There are even gambling clubs. Most important are the shops which provide the food Bengali people cannot buy elsewhere – like the freshwater fish flown in from Bangladesh, and the range of fruit and vegetables no-one else would stock. Combine these with the halal meat and spices, sold in the big new supermarkets, and these shops provide a unique resource for those able to live nearby. Ali Brothers and New Taj Stores have become big businesses on the strength of their supermarkets.

Back in Bangladesh, family visits are important. Some of the coherence of family and village life is preserved in London through very regular social visits, functions and family occasions. That way of life makes it all the more valuable for people to live near each other. Spitalfields now has purpose-built premises for big events, and it's often used. The Kobi Nazrul Cultural Centre is a place where such things can be combined with evenings of dance, music, poetry and drama. Other buildings like the Montefiore Centre and – for a time – the Brady Centre which combine sports facilities and function rooms with offices for local groups have become important pivots of community activity.

So many of these benefits have been achieved through the Bengali community's ability to work together for what it wants. It wouldn't have been possible with a community scattered thinly across the borough. Many of the services would not have been viable on that basis anyway. As the community grows, so does its ability to organize over a wider area. For example, there are now youth groups in at least six wards in the borough. But many of the benefits here are still unique to the area in and around Spitalfields. They depend on the present density of population to survive. If the people were to leave, the infrastructure would break down.

So a Bengali family loses a lot when it is forced to live on an outlying estate like Bow Bridge next to the Lea Valley. Women will be cut off from almost all their points of social contact. Training, organized childcare and classes in English will be out of reach. Journeys to pick up children from school won't be safe. Schools are likely to be more violent and less sensitive to need. There will be a greater danger of attack at home. Medical and educational services won't be geared to meet their needs. Community support is at the other end of a telephone, rather than the other end of the street. Shopping will still be done several miles away in Brick Lane. A man employed in clothing or restaurant work will find it very hard to keep in work. But it is women who have to cope with most of these problems, and it has been women who have been most militant about staying in the Spitalfields area. They stand to lose more than their men, and have frequently dissuaded the men from signing for distant flats even when there is apparently no other choice.

Women still do not have a big public presence in Spitalfields, but they have built up their own groups: Mahila Samity, based on the Chicksand Estate, Nari Samity, centred on the Holland, and Jagonari all have active centres in the ward. Even so, women have little control in their community's other organizations. Few attend public forums and committees. Their housing needs are usually mediated through their husbands to the relevant authorities. Despite this, the influence of Bengali women on the development of Spitalfields over the last ten years has probably been greater than that of any other section of the community. They have held onto Spitalfields tenaciously because they have had nothing to gain by being moved out. They have had to pay a most terrible price, enduring housing conditions reminiscent of the 19th century East End. It was expected that this would break their will to stay so they would agree to move out just to get something better. But they did not give in. Instead an electric tension built up between the conditions people were living in and their implacable will to hold on, however bad things got, until they were given the housing they wanted.

Housing conditions

When the Bangladeshi men in Tower Hamlets first sent home for their families, they knew there was nowhere for them to live. It was an act of faith. They hadn't the money to buy anywhere. Without a family in Tower Hamlets, there was no chance of council housing: the council refused to consider it. There was a choice: either the family would be permanently separated, or they would have to move into the slums and fight for decent housing from there.

For people who have not seen these housing conditions, it is hard to convey what they are like. The statistics conjure up little. In the 1981 Census there was only one other ward in London with higher levels of overcrowding (among the Sikh population of Southall). Three households in ten were living with more than one person in every room. One household in seven lacked exclusive use of at least two of the three basic amenities – a bath or shower, hot water and a toilet. The Spitalfields Survey showed that virtually all the people affected by these conditions were Bangladeshis or other Asians. Eighty-three per cent of the people living with more than one person to a room were Asian. Going up above the level of statutory overcrowding – 1.5 to a room – 96 per cent were Asian. In fact 63 per cent of all Asian households were overcrowded – and as these were usually the larger households, this meant the vast majority of all Asian people. With basic amenities it was the same story. Forty-one per cent of Bangladeshi households and 3 per cent of UK households, lacked exclusive use of two or more basic amenities. Missing amenities and overcrowding were worse in the private sector, but they showed up on council estates too.

The human cost of these figures is more difficult to portray. Anyone would be shattered by the the worst of Spitalfields, even today. It seems inconceivable that any local authority could still allow it to exist. The most punishing conditions were in the remaining tenement estates and in the terraces of Victorian housing owned by private companies. The tenements were generally five storeys high, built straight up from the street. Often they were crowded close together, separated by narrow tarmaced yards. This made the lower storeys very dark indeed, and left virtually nowhere for children to play. Social reformers of the 19th century like Octavia Hill, had failed to persuade developers that they could still make a profit by leaving off the top storey, and by spacing the blocks more widely apart. Access to the tenements was usually off a concrete staircase open to the air. At each floor a row of front doors opened straight onto the stairs. What had been considered unfit for the working class of 19th century London was being lived in a century later with a hundred years of disrepair to add to the misery.

For 150 years, Spitalfields has hit the headlines because of its terrible housing. An outbreak of fever, traced back to the housing conditions of the Spitalfields silk-workers in 1837, resulted in the national *Report on Sanitary Conditions of the Labouring Population*, published in 1842, which made many recommendations for change. Jack London inveighed against the slums of Spitalfields in his *Children of the Abyss* published in the first decade of this century. But in the 1970s, many Bengali families were still living in the very rooms that had been described by Charles Booth in his *Life and Labour of the London Poor*, written in the 1890s. His investigators graded the tenements visited and this is a description of a good one:

> The outer door opens into a lobby . . . On the left-hand side is the living room (15ft by 13ft), which is papered and lighted by two windows. The fittings include a . . . sink, the water tap being seen above. Near this is a door leading to a small pantry, fitted with shelves, and having a small window. Another door leads from the lobby into the bedroom, which is about 12ft by 14ft. It has a small fireplace; is papered and painted, and well lighted by two windows. A separate closet, with lock and key, is provided on the landing outside.

No hot water, no inside toilet, no bath. With slight variations, this is how many hundreds of Bangladeshi families were living in the 1970s and even the 1980s. The whole family would sleep in one room and use the other room for cooking, eating and living in. In the larger three-room tenements, the family would still normally sleep in one room, with other male relatives sharing the second bedroom. Even if there had been the money, there was no space for a bathroom.

Reading Charles Booth, Spitalfields present seems to merge into Spitalfields past. There were the same pictures of husband, wife and four children huddled in one room, the same brothers and sisters absent in hospital, the same cracking plasterwork, the same insect infestations. The direct descendants of Booth's silverfish and bedbugs are still at work. But the present brought new problems. Twentieth century rubbish didn't fit down 19th century waste chutes. They got blocked, rubbish rotted, rats multiplied. Soil stacks started leaking, oozing sewage down the sides of the buildings. The flat roofs, originally designed to allow people to hang out washing were completely shot. Top-floor flats were very damp. Windows had rotted; warped front doors opening straight from the living room onto the stone staircases let in draughts.

Yet the front door of a tenement was also a great advantage. However overcrowded the household was inside, once the front door was shut, the space was their own. In the privately owned terraces, this is not the case. For example, take a house in Princelet Street as it was being used in 1985. It was built towards the end of the last century. It is three storeys high, with two rooms on each floor and no back extension. Upstairs the front rooms are about 15ft by 12ft, and the back rooms 12ft by 10ft. One family lives on each floor. The front door opens directly onto the street. A passageway leads past the two ground-floor rooms to the back yard. In that yard there is an outside toilet which serves the three families and 20 men working in the clothing workshops at the back of the yard. These 20 men can only reach their workplace through the front door, walking past the bedroom and kitchen of the family on the ground floor. On the first floor the family of six sleeps in the front room and cooks and eats in the back. Going up to the second floor, there is an old quarter round sink on the turn half way up the stairs. At the top of the stairs a gas cooker is plumbed in. Above it and beside it are cupboards and a tiny workspace to prepare food. The family sleep in the front room, while the back room provides enough space for the husband's brother to put his bed alongside the table they use to eat from.

Overcrowding is one thing. Disrepair is another. Take this house in Sheba Street as it was when surveyed in 1979 and described in a letter to the Chair of the Health and Housing Management Committee. The layout of the house was not dissimilar to the one in Princelet Street, except that it was four storeys high instead of three, and there was no access to the workshops behind the backyard. There was an extra upstairs toilet for the tenants of the top floors:

In the front passageway there is a mass of old meters and wiring. Ahead is the staircase. Several stairs are loose. The plaster on the underside of the stairs is damp and perished – the upstairs toilet leaks. The roof is shot – no-one can survive on the top floor. In storms, water finds its way all the way down to the ground. There's only one door from the passage to the ground-floor rooms, the other has been sealed. So these two rooms have been connected by hacking through the wall dividing them and wedging up a makeshift door frame. A family of seven sleeps in the front room. To fit them in, hardboard has been laid on empty milk crates with mattresses spread across the hardboard. This way the whole family can sleep in one elongated bed. Only the baby has its own cot. There is little room for any other furniture. The windows are broken and boarded up. A draught still comes in, but very little daylight. The electric light doesn't work. Cables loop up from the one power point to provide a light on a hanging lead. The wiring to the power point is old and perished.

The kitchen lighting also depends on a cable from the one power point there. In this room the windows don't shut, whatever the weather. But it's dark here too because the yard is very narrow and light is blocked by the buildings behind. The sash cords are broken and flapping. There is no way out of the kitchen except by going back through the makeshift doorway into the bedroom and from there into the passage. There is a sink in this room, but with no tiling behind it so all the plaster is wet and crumbling away. There is only one cold tap, its washer not working properly so water dribbles out and splashes up continuously. The toilet is in the backyard. The door from the passage to the backyard has no catch and bangs in the wind. The constant movement has pulled the whole door frame away from the brickwork. Four feet above the ground on the outside back wall, the soil stack from the upstairs toilet leaks sewage. The waste pipe from the upstairs sink also leaks down the wall. This makes the wall damp, and sewage seeps through it into the plasterwork inside the kitchen. The pipes don't discharge into the drainhole, so there is a puddle of waste water outside the door to the toilet. The toilet pan is cracked and leaks every time the cistern is flushed. The roof of the lean-to which houses the toilet is made of old doors cobbled together. They are rotting and are supported on a joist which is also just about rotted through. The manhole in the yard overflows regularly, the drains below are almost totally blocked.

This house was worse than average, although many of the things wrong were repeated in house after house and terrace after terrace. But it was spared some of the common problems of infestation. Elsewhere, rats are rampant. They feed on the railway verges, on the rotten vegetables from the wholesale market, on the garbage dumped on derelict sites, on the dustbins at the back of the restaurants. And they come into the houses too. They eat food that had been stored as well as rubbish. They have bitten children in their sleep. Because there are so many places for them to flourish, they have never been eradicated.

Cockroaches are even more prevalent. They are a growing menace across Britain's housing stock – especially where large blocks of flats prone to condensation get central heating installed, creating the consistent damp warmth that cockroaches like. They were also virulent in these slums. Sometimes, taking mirrors and pictures off walls would, for an instant, leave a perfect outline made up of solid cockroaches on the wall beneath, before the pattern exploded and the creatures ran for cover. They could live and breed in the cracks in the plaster, coming out at nigh and feeding off anything left in the kitchens. They can spread diseases in this way. As they travel through the tiniest cracks, spraying a whole house rarely controls them. They are attracted back to the warm damp darkness of the inhabited rooms. It is not unknown for children to wake with them in their ears.

These conditions take a terrible toll on the health of the women and children living in them. They are conditions which kill. For children, coughs and colds are endemic. These can develop into respiratory infections in damp overcrowded conditions. Pulmonary tuberculosis has resurfaced in the Bengali community as a growing threat. Some children also suffer from chronic dysentery. In the most severe cases this causes incontinence and seriously interferes with their schooling. Even rickets, whose ghost was apparently laid to rest after the war, has re-emerged. Housing is perhaps less directly to blame here: in Bangladesh the absorption of vitamins through sunlight prevents rickets. The same children in Spitalfields are often confined indoors in a single room with no safe outdoor playspace. As well as diet, this contributes to the disease.

In the Spitalfields Health Survey of 1984, carried out in conjunction with the Spitalfields Local Committee, Bengali mothers were particularly concerned about children's lack of appetite and their being undersize for their ages. These women considered personal hygiene and diet to be the two most important means of remaining healthy. And yet their housing conditions prevented them from providing either of these things adequately either for themselves or their children. These concerns combine with their daily need to manage a large household of children in a very confined space. This is only possible by severely restricting what the children are allowed to do. No less than 30 per cent of the Bengali women in the Health Survey complained of constant headaches, dizziness or pains all over their bodies. Some experienced all these symptoms. None felt they had been adequately dealt with by the health services; all thought their problems were continuing.

Traditionally Bangladeshi families are large. This tradition has changed little so far with the move to Britain although there are signs that women are beginning to challenge assumptions about family size. In the meantime, many of them can expect to bring up between four and six children. Managing large numbers of children while pregnant is bad enough. But trying to bring up very small babies in the housing conditions described here is extremely stressful. Given the conditions it is not surprising that Tower Hamlets has the highest rate of perinatal mortality in the country.

For many women, the enormous conflict between these conditions and their need to stay in the area contributes to mental breakdown. St Clement's Hospital is treating some Bengali women suffering from mental stress although there are more not being reached. The hospital is unequipped to provide help. Until the end of 1988 there was no Bengali-speaking woman psychiatrist – there is now one. Without more people like this, there is little basis for psychiatric support, and indeed every chance of perpetuating and exacerbating the problems.

Overcrowding brings all sorts of other stresses. Children who need space to study just haven't got it. It certainly doesn't help their chances of passing exams and getting qualifications doing homework in the corridors or surrounded by screaming younger brothers and sisters. Often the families of two brothers or other relatives have to share the same space. If the adults can contain themselves, the children are likely to quarrel. Very unfair and almost unreal demands are put on family structures, which were built to give support but which crack under these new circumstances. Time and again, newly arrived families staying with relatives are forced out by the irreconcilable tensions of overcrowding. These are the extremes – but many have had to experience them. In 1980 there were nearly 100 households living at *over twice* the levels of statutory overcrowding.

In 1980, there were 350 families on the council waiting list in Spitalfields who were either desperately overcrowded or were living without hot water and baths. The Spitalfields Survey suggested there were another 300 in equally bad conditions who hadn't even registered with the council. So the council was badly underestimating how serious things were. What's more, at least 75 council tenants were statutorily overcrowded and the council was breaking the law by not rehousing them. Altogether, more than 700 households needed immediate rehousing.

Things could only get worse. Four hundred and ninety men were still waiting for their families to arrive. They would all need a place of their own. There were already 600 households in the ward wanting to split up and get their own homes. There were also 120 people in the Salvation Army hostels asking for self-contained flats. This was another 720 households.

Added together, these 1,400 households were equivalent to two thirds of the total number of households living in Spitalfields at the time. That is some measure of the housing need. But it didn't account for everyone. There were also council tenants with baths in their kitchens who wanted flats with bathrooms. Homeless families in hotels wanted to come back to Spitalfields. So did people who'd been moved out by slum clearance. So did victims of racist attack living elsewhere. So did many others in bad housing who wanted to remain in Spitalfields for what it had to offer. The total demand was immense and not easily quantifiable.

It wasn't just that the council hadn't got enough houses to meet this demand. Equally significant was the mismatch between the size of council flats, and the size of the families waiting to move into them. Council flats were built for the two-baby families of post-war Britain. In all Spitalfields there were fewer than 50 four-bedroom council flats.

The organization of the Spitalfields community

It was one thing for each of these many households to recognize the importance of living in Spitalfields for themselves. It was quite another to establish a united front of all those in bad housing, which would be capable of fighting for the new housing that was needed.

Spitalfields was not a homogenous community. There was little contact between the 'white' and Asian population before the mid-1970s. As we've seen, the white population itself had many strands – Jewish, Irish, Maltese as well as British – all with their own different roots. By and large, these were the people now living in the best of the council housing while the Bengalis were still based in the private rented sector. Over half the white population was employed in service industries or by the council – while two thirds of all Bengalis were still working in the clothing industry. A quarter of the white population were pensioners – there were scarcely any Bengali ones yet. The Bengali population was still preponderantly male – this was not so for the rest of Spitalfields. These very different population profiles did not make united political action easy. On top of this, there is no reason to expect that just because people come from the same ethnic background, they will share the same political outlook. As in any community, Bangladeshi individuals and groups reflect a spread of views right across the political spectrum.

But there have also been things in common. Most white council tenants had moved out of the slums. They understood the pressures of slum housing. They also continued to be far from happy with the housing they had been given. Some of it was pre-war, in need of major modernization. These were blocks with no lifts, no heating and sometimes no bathrooms. More of the council housing had been built in the bleakest era of the 1960s. The new part of the Chicksand Estate is a prime example. Potentially attractive maisonettes were unheatable – with bedrooms cantilevered out from the main structure of the building so that they had three outside walls, as well as floors and ceilings which were outside surfaces. The houses on the estate had been designed so that the roofs leaked perpetually, and the timber doors and windows warped and rotted.

Faced with their own poor housing and the surrounding squalor, many white tenants wanted to leave the area. But for those who wanted to stay, there were deeper concerns which they shared with the Bengali community. Many of them depended on Spitalfields' central location for work. They too had support networks of family and friends. They may not have been as poor as the Bengalis, but very few of them had any chance of buying a home of their own. They too would be vulnerable if Spitalfields were developed in the interests of the City. Like the Bengalis, they needed more and better public sector housing on their doorstep.

Yet until 1974 no Spitalfields-wide organization emerged. That summer, as local people grew alarmed at the way the area was declining, a mass meeting was called. Every staircase was leafletted. People were enthused and mobilized. Nearly 200 people packed the canteen at the Montefiore Centre – the planners came along and had to dodge the verbal brickbats. At that meeting Michael Myers, life-long resident of West Spitalfields and community activist, suggested that people should organize. He caught the mood. The growing momentum for action built over the previous weeks was shaped into the Spitalfields Community Action Group which set itself the task of rebuilding the area. Soon afterwards, local activists set up a Spitalfields Bengali Action Group. These new forces were galvanized by the GLC which picked out Spitalfields and the Hanley Road area of Islington as the subjects of a special project. The GLC reckoned these areas exhibited all the symptoms of what they termed 'deprivation'. With Spitalfields, it wasn't just a question of terrible housing and a derelict environment. As we shall see later, there had been plans drawn up by the councils to end the bad conditions. These plans had never got off the ground. The GLC's idea was to launch a partnership between all the statutory bodies and the local community to see those plans carried through, while at the same time giving local people some involvement in the programme.

This partnership, which was given no executive powers, was named the Spitalfields Project. Alongside the development programme, there was £1 million to spend on initiatives drawn up by local people. Immediately, it ran into hostile local opposition. Despite the rhetoric of local involvement, the decision-making body which was set up included only elected councillors. Local people were relegated to a 'Consultative Committee'. They fought for, and won, the right to have representatives on the full committee, which decided how money should be spent and monitored the development programme.

The Consultative Committee elected these representatives. Every local organization was entitled to seats on the Consultative Committee, which gradually broadened out to become a forum of local opinion. For the first time Bengali and white groups were sitting together, discussing the same issues and agreeing joint action. The involvement of Bengali groups accelerated after the fighting of 1978, which stimulated and strengthened their youth organizations. Because the Spitalfields Project had a wide brief and was looking at planning for the area from leisure to housing, from education to social services provision, the Consultative Committee not only developed a clear understanding of what was going wrong with Spitalfields, it also began to shape a much clearer idea of what was needed to put it right. Meanwhile the £1 million paid for initiatives taken by local groups and even set up new ones like the Spitalfields Housing and Planning Rights Service and the Kobi Nazrul Bengali Cultural Centre. As community involvement in the Project grew, the Spitalfields Community Action Group, which had been so important in the Project's early days, broke apart.

The Spitalfields Project ran for five years, until March 1980. When it ended, nothing had been redeveloped. But as we shall see, this bred anger rather than disillusion amongst local groups who had put so much time into trying to make the Project work. The Consultative Committee revamped itself as the Spitalfields Local Committee, more determined than ever to force through the plans that the area needed.

At its high point, this Local Committee involved over 40 organizations, more than half of whom attended meetings regularly. It fought for rented housing on several important sites, it represented local views on all important planning permissions. It fought planning enquiries. It sponsored the new health centre, improved social services provision for the elderly and for the Bengali community, worked to improve Allen Gardens and other leisure facilities, supported local youth groups and was deeply involved with the Community School. There was scarcely any area of local life it didn't touch.

It also distributed money provided by the councils – less than during the years of the Project but enough to give local groups real support. This was both a strength and a weakness. It ensured a high level of involvement from groups wanting money. It also meant that when the good years were over, those groups did not find it easy to keep any presence going without the money they had come to rely on. Once the Liberals took power in 1986 money was withdrawn from groups that didn't agree with them: in the case of the Spitalfields Housing and Planning Rights Service they made specific allegations about its political involvement. The new administration also severed formal links between the Local Committee and the council's committee structure. With many local groups also under attack, the Local Committee did not survive this decision. While it was possible to maintain a forum of unfunded community organizations in the late 1970s, it was not possible to re-establish this ten years later. To an extent this was because some groups were still being funded and didn't want to lose this money by getting involved in campaigns against Liberal policy.

Through the ten-year history of the Consultative Committee and Local Committee there were underlying tensions which shouldn't be minimized. White tenants on the Holland Estate tried to stop the Bengali Community School from being resited outside their flats at Denning Point. Some tenants on Chicksand wanted to stop the new housing at Davenant Street because it was being built for large Bengali families. But the success of the Local

Committee was that it not only contained these tensions when concentrating on issues which affected the community as a whole, but was able to support many initiatives which were clearly in the interests of small sections of the community. This wasn't just about careworkers for the elderly and equipment for youth groups – the Community School got resited, and the houses at Davenant Street were built.

It was this amalgamation of organizations – from mosque, church and synagogue, Bengali youth groups and white youth clubs, the white tenants' groups and the Bengali co-ops, the careworkers for the elderly and the support workers for Bengali pregnant women – which was the backbone of the Committee. In one combination or another it is these groups which have had to confront the pressures mounting up against Spitalfields. At heart it was a new community, wanting to see its children growing up and working in the area. Ironically, it had the very qualities the Labour administration claimed it was trying to recreate in Tower Hamlets. And those qualities made the Spitalfields communities very hard to beat.

The tactics

Those were the battlelines, and although there have been many skirmishes, the war goes on. There are three main areas of struggle: housing development, commercial development and methods of housing management.

Spitalfields has endured much already. Housing conditions were allowed to deteriorate until they were the worst in the country. No new housing was built to move people to. When slums were cleared they weren't replaced. Council housing land has been sold. Gentrification has been supported. Volume private housebuilders have been called in. Office developers have been welcomed with open arms. There's been virtually no support for local industry and employment. The homeless have been herded from one side of London to the other, some have even been thrown onto the street. The councils failed to take action against racist violence and no-go areas; they have tried to freeze Bangladeshi people out of the good-quality council housing, forcing them onto run-down, distant and hostile estates.

There has been no central committee plotting this. These tactics have been pursued at different times by the two different councils, and, in the borough's case, by both Labour and Liberal administrations. Sometimes the GLC and the borough council worked together, sometimes separately; sometimes with councillors themselves taking the lead, sometimes with officers acting under loose authority or completely on their own. Very few of the people who have been responsible for these policies would accept that they had been part of the war over this land. But all the tactics just listed must be seen together, because the cumulative effect has been to try and take Spitalfields away from the people who need it.

4 | Down with the slums

In 1967 there were still 5,000 people living in unfit tenements in Spitalfields. The councils had the power and duty to clear slums under the 1957 Housing Act. But they had no plans to let the slum dwellers stay in Spitalfields. Between 1965 and 1980 Tower Hamlets didn't build a single home in the ward; while the GLC only managed one tower block – at Denning Point – and a small estate of 100 maisonettes and flats on Hanbury Street. It was a simple equation. Five thousand people weren't going to fit into that space. Nor could they possibly be housed by waiting for flats to fall empty on existing council estates. If they were going to be moved at all, they would have to leave the area altogether.

Tower Hamlets' record remains unsullied. From the day the council was formed to date, it has never built a single house in Spitalfields. Indeed, only 7 per cent of all the 8,550 houses it has built are even in the E1 postal district, where the bulk of the borough's overcrowding is concentrated. So the housing disaster which Spitalfields became was no accident. It was created by the council's failure to build for its worst-housed people.

Without new housing, it's not surprising that the councils took 15 years to move the slum dwellers. It would have been longer but for the tenants themselves who, time after time, organized to force the councils into action. To begin with, tenants agreed to anything which was going to offer decent rehousing. But as the struggle wore on, people increasingly demanded rehousing inside Spitalfields itself. This demand grew as the early tenements were knocked down, and the land was lying idle which could have bedded the foundations of their new homes. But as that land-bank of demolished tenements grew, so did the realization inside Tower Hamlets Council that this was an opportunity to change the social make-up of the area. The Spitalfields community could be broken apart if this precious city centre land was sold and a new class of owners was drawn in.

The idea of 'improving' the area by breaking up the existing community and moving in a more respectable class of people was not new. In the 19th century, Spitalfields was deliberately split in two by a new wide road called Commercial Street. In concept, this was not dissimilar from the new boulevards of Paris, designed above all as a means of social control. Each side of Commercial Street tenements were built: to the east, Rothschild Buildings and Lolesworth Buildings; to the west, Wentworth Dwellings, Brunswick Buildings and Davis Mansions. They were put there to break up and replace the 18th century 'rookeries' of the area. The rookeries had housed the Victorian underclass, the poorest people of London, who were perceived as a threat to social stability, whose internal organization was little understood from the outside, and who could not be effectively policed. The Victorian solution was to demolish their neighbourhood, scattering the residents – they had no duty to rehouse them. In place of the rookeries, they built the tenement Model Dwellings with rents so high that only the most respectable of the working class could afford to live in them. A hundred years later, when places like Brunswick Buildings and Wentworth Dwellings reached their turn for demolition, the effect was not dissimilar. The new Bengali residents were also a threat. They were expected to disperse across the East End, while plans were drawn up to sell the site for private housing – once again drawing in a new and more respectable class of people.

Yet the next two chapters are a story of hope. Many people from the slums did win local rehousing. More significant, against the odds, much of that empty land now contains housing for rent at prices local working-class people can afford. This was a struggle that went from one

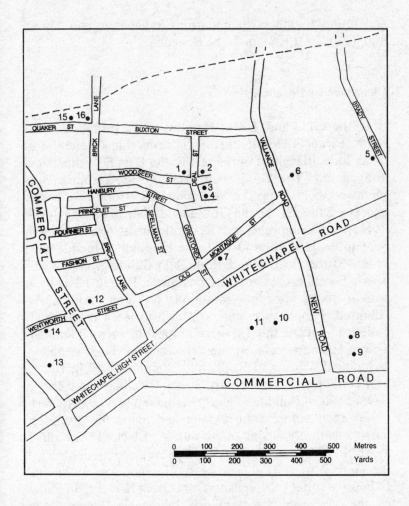

Albert Cottages 1
Albert Family Dwellings 3
Blackwall Buildings 6
Brady Street Dwellings 5
Brick Lane 16
Brunswick Buildings 13
Davis Mansions 13
Fieldgate Mansions 10
Great Eastern Buildings 15
Howard Buildings 4

Myrdle Street 11
Nelson Street 9
Old Montague Street 7
Parfett Street 11
Pelham Buildings 3
Rothschild Buildings 12
Sheba Street 16
Varden Street 8
Victoria Cottages 2
Wentworth Dwellings 14

4. Sites planned for slum clearance 1966–1981.

71

generation to the next, and from indigenous and Jewish immigrant East Enders to the Bengalis.

Clearance by the councils

Both the GLC and Tower Hamlets made promises about slum clearance. Despite this, Spitalfields slums were almost intact long after most of the rest of the East End slums had disappeared. The GLC, as a London-wide resource, was supposed to back up the local council's efforts in areas of high stress like E1. So the GLC added some of Spitalfields to its Stepney 'Comprehensive Redevelopment Area', while in September 1967 John Orwell, the borough council leader, promised the clearance of Rothschild Buildings and Wentworth Dwellings 'as soon as possible'. 'People have been patient about appalling conditions for long enough,' he admitted. People were going to have to learn more about patience – given the 15 years it took to move them all. Tower Hamlets took on the rehousing of 3,000 people – including 1,650 round Rothschild Buildings, 400 in Blackwall Buildings, 600 at Brady Street Dwellings and 250 in Great Eastern Buildings. The GLC agreed to house the rest.

But even before John Orwell had made his promises, tenants were organizing to get out. At Blackwall Buildings in April 1967 tenants had just won a seven-month fight to get the council to start the process of compulsory purchase. In February that year, tenants from Great Eastern Buildings by the Liverpool Street railway line, while fighting rent increases, were complaining of 'diabolical conditions' with greasy water regularly backing up into sinks, no repairs being done and infestations. As one tenant said: 'We are living for the day when we will all get out of these buildings.'

Admittedly things weren't helped by the incredibly high density people were living at. Victorian tenements had been packed as densely as possible to make the best use of valuable inner city land. They were not built by charities. They had to provide enough rents to give the 4 per cent to

5 per cent annual return which the Dwellings Companies promised their investors. This produced the austere blocks like Rothschild Buildings squeezed together and rising straight from the pavement, which we've already seen were anathema to the Victorian social reformers. Baron Nathan Mayer Rothschild put £10,000 of his own money into the buildings which bear his name, and they did at least house Jewish working-class people till they were demolished. But to give an idea of the density people were living at, less than a quarter of the number of people moved back on the Rothschild Buildings site when it was eventually redeveloped by Toynbee Housing Association with tightly packed terraced houses. With Tower Hamlets building no new housing whatever while tenants lived at these densities, Spitalfields rotted. As a group of council social workers put it in their 1972 pamphlet *The Great East End Housing Disaster*:

> On the question of clearance of slums, the planners appear to have been misguided in their selection of priorities. Large areas of Bow, where the standard of housing is good relative to other parts of the borough, have been cleared, while the tenements of Spitalfields are left apparently to collapse of their own volition . . . Whatever the reason, the continuing existence of seething, filthy, vermin-infested tenements such as Wentworth Dwellings is a public scandal.

So it wasn't the planners, or even Hitler's bombers, who got these slums cleared. The tenants had to do it for themselves. At Great Eastern Buildings tenants went through two public enquiries to get a Compulsory Purchase Order in 1976 and still the council didn't start rehousing. Tenants invaded the Town Hall. The *Daily Mirror*'s front page of 13th May 1976 ran the blockbuster headline 'THE UNACCEPTABLE FACE OF BRITAIN': there were buckets being used as toilets, mice scampering over sleeping children, and fungus rampant in the bedrooms. A year later, the Buildings were empty.

It was the same story at Brunswick Buildings by Petticoat Lane. Walls were collapsing, and postmen wouldn't deliver because of the sort of conditions which had been described by the *Morning Star* on 20th March 1974:

> The refuse collectors paid a long-awaited visit to clear the ten overflowing bins, but the dustcart, after squeezing through the tenement entrances, found its way blocked by parked cars and an array of Jaguars and Opels belonging to businessmen working nearby.

In 1976 the Brunswick tenants won their Compulsory Purchase Order and the promise of GLC rehousing, The pattern was repeated again and again – at Pelham Buildings, at Howard Buildings and at Albert Family Dwellings where the veteran Communist councillor Max Levitas supported the setting up of Tenants' Action Committees. But it was the two years of hard work by the tenants, backed by community organizations, which got everyone out.

1976 marked a turning point. The ward already had ugly scars across it where housing had been knocked down and nothing was being built to replace it. Some tenants started to argue that housing could be modernized instead of demolished. The GLC agreed to this in the tiny terraces of Victoria Cottages. But Tower Hamlets wouldn't listen when tenants from Brady Street Dwellings asked for the same. These tenements were built to high standards by the 1890 Industrial Dwellings Society, which later became a housing association. The flats were well maintained, but unmodernized. The Society wouldn't take on the decanting of 260 tenants to do the improvements so the council offered to knock them down. Though some tenants wanted to move because new flats were ready nearby, a group headed by Sidney Dempsey wanted to stay but was ignored. They put up a last ditch proposal to save the estate in 1977 but by then the rot of impending demolition had set in. Many flats were empty and smashed up – immediate repairs were needed to keep any hope alive. In April 1978 the council's Head of Secretariat wrote to the group:

Rehabilitation of such a block would be out of character with the adjacent new building and the whole development plan for the Selby Street area will provide a greater number of homes than will be lost in demolishing Brady Street Dwellings.

Six months later, once everyone had gone, the council unveiled a plan to build 365,000 square feet of offices on the site, which was to abut a massive new shopping centre. The value of clearing slums off the land was clear.

If Tower Hamlets was slow to rehouse the people where it had been forced to take action, it was desperate not to make any further promises to other groups of slum-dwellers – and there were many more people who should have been included in the slum clearance programme but whose housing was ignored by the Environmental Health Department. What distinguished these cases from the others was that they were mostly individual houses where tenants were unable to organize so effectively. This department knew that more slum clearance was impossible given the council's refusal to build new housing. Elizabeth Burney had already seen this going on in 1967 and described it in her book *Housing on Trial*:

> Tower Hamlets health officers admitted Brick Lane area to be their worst and most neglected district – which they say they must leave for at least ten years *because of the overspill it would create*. [My emphasis]

Conditions were so bad, however, that 29 houses and 39 tenements had to be added to the clearance list in 1971, and yet another 13 houses four years later, all between Hanbury Street and Casson Street. But nothing was ever done about these plans. None of the houses was ever cleared, scarcely a single room was even closed down. In 1978 the GLC surveyed all these houses round Brick Lane – over 90 per cent were unfit. Still the council did nothing. So the Spitalfields Housing Co-operative (whose role in Spitalfields will be described in the next chapter) offered to buy out one landlord – the tenants of these 27 houses and 12 tenements

75

voted for the take-over eagerly. In 1985, tenants, health visitors, education welfare officers, social workers and housing rights workers made renewed demands for action on the tenements of Hanbury Street. The health officers still refused to do anything which would mean rehousing for the tenants. They expected landlords, responsible for decades of neglect, to carry out necessary improvements.

The only big extra commitment that Tower Hamlets was forced to take on was again because of action by those in the slums, at Myrdle Street and Parfett Street in St Mary's ward. These were marked in Abercrombie's plan for immediate slum clearance in 1944. They are still standing today. The front doors of the cramped terraces open straight onto the pavement, with the basement windows set back just a few inches from the paving stones. Standing on a chair in the basement, one could touch the boots of people walking by outside. In the 1960s, a textile company had bought 30 of the houses and had left them empty. Squatters took over. Throughout 1972 and 1973, they were evicted time and again. But eventually, in a blaze of national publicity, they shamed Tower Hamlets into buying the company out.

Elsewhere, in the mid-1970s, Tower Hamlets deliberately went out to buy slum houses, threatening compulsory purchase if owners didn't agree. Spitalfields was left out of this policy – of the 145 houses bought between October 1974 and July 1976, only one was in the ward. By the 1980s they'd stopped trying to compulsorily purchase anything anywhere. In 1986 a blistering Ombudsman report savagely criticized the council's failure to act against Prince's Lodge, the slum hostel in Limehouse. Two independent surveys had shown scandalously unfit conditions for the 420 people crammed into 200 tiny rooms. But the council never even carried out a full inspection. The furore from the Ombudsman report forced through the sale of Prince's Lodge. But it has made very little difference to the approach taken on the 'houses in multiple occupation' in Spitalfields.

Even without buying up places, houses that are unfit could still be shut down – although once again the council has to

76

rehouse the tenants. The serving of 20 Closing Orders in Albert Cottages forced the owner to sell up for a housing association to take over in the 1970s. This showed how Closing Orders could be used constructively to improve conditions. But more recently health officers have hardly used their powers. In the two years from February 1984, only 13 orders were served in the whole borough. Seven were in Spitalfields – in most of these cases it was pressure from tenants, backed by professional advice, which led to action. This suggests more pressure might have closed more houses. It undercuts the health officers' claim that rising house prices had stopped them acting. Although it's true that, for technical reasons, Closing Orders are hard to use in areas of high house prices, the slums in Spitalfields hadn't reached these levels in the mid-1980s. The seven successful Closing Orders proved this.

So instead of combating the conditions, health officers are still directing their attack against the people living in the slums. Overcrowding is a criminal offence – people can be fined or even imprisoned for it. These sanctions can apply both to the people in 'control' of a building *and* to those actually suffering the overcrowding. Through the use of what have been called 'pyjama raids', officers would arrive late at night, count the number of people sleeping in each house and prosecute where numbers were over the set limits. 'We are in court every week,' the Chief Health Officer was quoted as saying in the August 1987 edition of *Environmental Health* magazine. When people have nowhere else to go, this just shifts overcrowding round from one house to another.

A more comprehensive approach is offered by declaring 'Housing Action Areas' where there are sufficiently large clumps of private housing in bad condition. This gives powers to grant money for improving private housing, while at the same time buying out recalcitrant landlords who won't co-operate. When the borough council was under Labour, the GLC suggested doing this, but didn't get support. The Liberals were also asked to take up the idea and refused.

They were worried this would be putting money in the hands of private developers – as we'll see, this hasn't worried them too much elsewhere.

Where they all went

Slum clearance meant a mass exodus of the people who made up the heart of Spitalfields. Some wanted to leave, it's true. But many didn't. The people of Rothschild Buildings went to the Ranwell Estate in Bow – so many moved that the local youth centre, Avenues Unlimited, opened a new branch there. From Great Eastern Buildings, tenants ended up on the Malmesbury Estate in Mile End and the Teviot in Poplar. The choice of where these communities moved to was simply dictated by the areas where the council was finishing new estates. Because of these mass movements Tower Hamlets argued that slum clearance wasn't breaking up communities. But at least Tower Hamlets offered its slum dwellers new homes. The GLC didn't, even though they did build new housing in Spitalfields. Howard Buildings was being emptied just as the new maisonettes on Hanbury Street were ready. Brunswick tenants were moving out when the Granby Estate just to the north was finished. The slum dwellers weren't considered 'worthy' of this housing, and instead were spread over older estates, sometimes as far afield as Becontree and Harold Hill. Yet as early as 1974 a survey carried out by the Spitalfields Community Action Group with tenants at Howard Buildings showed that a sizeable number of people would have liked to stay in Spitalfields.

Those who insisted on staying in the area didn't have an easy time of it. There was nothing on offer. They had to wait for something on the old estates nearby. If flats didn't come up quickly enough, Tower Hamlets tried to harass people out. They sent the bulldozers into Rothschild Buildings with five elderly tenants still there. With the threat of their fuel and water being cut, they held out for six months after the demoliton contract had already been signed. The playwright Arnold Wesker, who used to live in a street nearby, described a visit he made in the *East London Advertiser* during November 1973:

> The next time we went, they'd started to pull it down. There was noise, dust, rubble. We climbed up to to a first floor for an aerial view when, to my horror and astonishment, a tiny old lady stormed out of one of the flats. 'There's still someone living here,' she said to us and angrily asked us to go away. I couldn't believe they'd started pulling the building down while someone was still living there. That can't be possible. Whose callous indifference was that?

'We're all old. We all have roots in the area. Things like that matter,' one of the women said to Wesker. Some of them turned down nine offers before they eventually got the *local* rehousing they wanted.

Increasingly, the people who'd wanted to stay resented being forced out. By 1980, only two groups of tenants were still waiting for slum clearance – in Sheba Street/Brick Lane and Wentworth Dwellings. Sheba Street/Brick Lane was supposed to be part of the Great Eastern Buildings clearance. But while the predominantly white tenants of the Buildings had gone, the Bengalis of Sheba Street remained. Again, Wentworth was planned for clearance alongside Brunswick, but had been left. Once more it was Bengalis who were waiting.

Both groups dug their heels in, insisting on rehousing in the Spitalfields area. For the reasons explained in the last chapter, they had a lot more to lose by being forced out. Their determination was also based on the growing anger experienced by their predecessors in other slum clearance areas, and more immediately, on the trail-blazing successes of the Bengali squatting movement, which we will go on to look at in detail.

The squatters move in

Squatters smashed the council's housing strategy apart in E1. From 1970 onwards, right across London squatters were invading housing that had been left empty by over-ambitious council development programmes. Tower Hamlets was no exception. Although many of the early squatters were young, white and single, Bengali families were quick to join in. Some were homeless families who'd been rehoused on white estates, and had been punched and stoned back to E1 by systematic racist violence. Others were looking for places to squat to avoid this fate, as the council was offering them nothing through the waiting list, and they had exhausted the goodwill of friends and relatives who had been putting them up. These were some of the very first Bengali families to join their men in London.

Bromley Street, Aston Street, Whitehorse Lane, Belgrave Street were all taken over in East Stepney. Squatters moved into Adelina Grove near Sidney Street. Bengalis started moving into the houses won by squatters in Parfett Street and Myrdle Street. Squatters took control of Fieldgate Mansions – 30 staircases with eight tenements on each. Students mixed in with Bengali families as the GLC decanted the estate. The councils were losing control of their development programme. The cutting edge of the movement was an organization which called itself the 'Faceless Homeless'. They escalated the confrontation in 1974 by seizing a decanted council block in Bow called Sumner House, and held it despite everything the council could do.

The council was screaming that squatters were 'jumping the waiting list'. But the council didn't help its cause by setting up its own official system for jumping the list. Called the Housing Ballot, young couples 'won' a council house if their names were picked out of a Bingo drum. This ended any pretence that housing was being allocated according to need. If housing were allocated on the basis of need, Bengalis stood a chance – they were living in the very worst housing. The Bingo Ballot was a way of giving white working-class families, who weren't in the slums, an equal chance of housing.

This meant that Bengalis living in desperate, overcrowded conditions were being told this gave them no priority for council housing. So they had to take it for themselves. In the summer of 1975, the first mass Bengali squat in Spitalfields opened up the empty houses of Old Montague Street. Twenty-two adults and 50 children had put a roof over their heads. The squats had an electrifying effect. For the first time, through their own efforts, Bengali people were making housing freely available. Varden Street was squatted, Nelson Street taken over. As more squats were secured, everyone became increasingly safe from eviction. It was becoming too big for the council to deal with, although it did try a show of force against the Faceless Homeless in 1975, who, in response to the Housing Ballot, had seized a block in Corfield Street, Bethnal Green. The council sent gangs in to knock the block down with the squatters still inside. At night the demolition equipment was petrol-bombed. The squatters were given permanent rehousing as a Tenant Management Co-operative in Matilda House, Wapping. Although the council saved face by winning the land (which they then sold on for private housing) they had been sufficiently bloodied not to try the same tactics again.

After this, Terry Fitzpatrick, a face behind the Faceless Homeless, joined forces with people like Abbas Uddin, one of the organizers of the Bengali squats and later the first Bengali Labour councillor. In February 1976, with the support of the editorial collective of the magazine *Race Today*, BHAG was born. Bengali for 'tiger', this was the acronym of the Bengali Housing Action Group. Its first meeting united the different squatted streets and called for more – another block was taken, this time the recently emptied Pelham Buildings in the heart of Spitalfields. Now under one umbrella, Bengali squatters controlled a large chunk of the development programme. They were in a strong position to demand terms for proper council rehousing for its membership. Membership will always be loosely defined in a squatting organization, but at its peak BHAG was several hundred families strong, with a core of 150 in the four main squats.

BHAG took over anything worth squatting in no time. It had access to the know-how to rewire, refit lavatory pans, reglaze broken windows. But conditions were pretty dreadful, as one would expect from cleared slum housing. Things were run on the margin of health and safety. For example, one cable ran from the electricity board head to supply all 60 flats in Pelham Buildings. On a cold winter's night, the outside insulation of that cable would be too hot to hold. Terry Fitzpatrick nearly had his head blown off trying to replace the main fuse after the London Electricity Board had taken it away.

Despite the conditions, squats started to have a scarcity value. A 'waiting list' was set up for the 60 flats in Pelham Buildings. A market developed, with squats being sold on. This was the price of success. BHAG became so big, the fear of eviction so small, that squats became secure places to live. A couple of local drug-dealers even charged 'rent' for squats. When that wasn't paid, squatters' windows were smashed. Some squatters knew what they were paying for – and paid it just to get somewhere to live. Others were badly conned. But it undermined the movement – people paying money to move in needed money when they moved out again. BHAG stopped the profiteering, mainly by taking control of the housing itself.

The editorial collective of *Race Today* which had helped set up BHAG had become increasingly distanced from it. Members were concerned that BHAG as a provider of housing would lose its political direction. For them, 'all it could succeed in doing was recreating in a squalid ghetto block some of the feudal relations of the Asian village'. BHAG should have been:

A body of people who would promote the independent organization of the black working class to win, through a determined campaign, the physical, social space our community needed. We were not a group to make general moan about the neglect of the East End by the state's welfare authorities.

Race Today felt that BHAG's membership needed to be built round political demands and not simply round those of the Bengali squatters which could be defused by GLC offers of rehousing on derelict estates.

With nowhere new to squat, and conditions getting worse, some of BHAG's momentum was lost. Splits in BHAG developed. Patch repairs to the slums were peeling off, and BHAG had to demand council rehousing urgently. Here was a second generation of people asking to be moved out of the very slums which tenants had fought to be rehoused from only a few years before. But for the first time, the demand of rehousing in the relative safety of the E1 postal district was launched. BHAG was learning from the experience of previous clearances in demanding local rehousing, while it used strength in numbers to negotiate, as the Faceless Homeless had. It was able to draw on the lessons of both struggles.

In 1976 demands to the Labour GLC for rehousing had been summarily dismissed by Tony Judge, who was the Labour Chair of the GLC Housing Committee. 'If all immigrant groups put in a similar request it would be chaos,' he said. But as BHAG consolidated its position, the GLC must have realized its own weakness. It would not be easy to evict several hundred Bengali families who had nowhere else to go. The borough council's Homeless Persons Unit wouldn't be able to cope. Hundreds of houses would be left empty, for another generation of squatters to take over. The way to stop that would have been by smashing up the houses, and Lambeth Council had, in a blaze of publicity, come to grief at St Agnes Place trying that. The Tories who took over the GLC in 1977, however, came up with a London-wide amnesty for squatters – guaranteeing them all rehousing. The impossibility of their position in the East End must have been a key factor in this. BHAG voted to endorse the amnesty and was active in registering all the Bengali squatters it knew about. The GLC hired the Montefiore Centre for a whole day with a team of interpreters and the squatters poured through.

The new GLC co-operated with BHAG in trying to arrange local rehousing. BHAG drew up a list of estates where their members would be safe. Each estate was voted on by show of hands at a mass meeting and a list of 13 was given to the GLC with a guarantee from BHAG that no reasonable offer on any of those estates would be refused. Jean Tatham, the Tory Chair of Housing, seemed to take the point in a way that Tony Judge hadn't, quoted as saying in the *East London Advertiser* in June 1978:

> There have been physical attacks on Bengalis in areas of East London away from Spitalfields and it has been suggested that they need to live a a mainly Bengali area to obtain the protection which a large group of their people can provide.

An almighty row blew up when the Controller of Housing, Len Bennett chose to redefine this in a report written on 22nd May 1978 as 'setting aside a few blocks of flats in or near Spitalfields specifically for the occupation of people from Bangladesh, in collaboration with the leaders of the Bengali community'. This was leaked to *The Observer*, which on 6th June blew up the story into what came to be known as the 'ghetto plan'. It will be considered in more detail in Chapter 9; suffice it to say here that the plan was apparently defeated through united local opposition, and the rehousing of BHAG's membership continued with the GLC respecting the 13 estates BHAG had voted for. Superficially it appeared that the *Race Today* collective was right. When the rehousing was finished, BHAG was silenced. But their political demands were then taken up by others.

Sheba Street and Wentworth Dwellings

The slum clearance tenants of Sheba Street/Brick Lane and
Wentworth Dwellings were watching what BHAG was
doing. They were in a living nightmare. In November 1979,
there were 83 adults and 70 children living in the 80
inhabited rooms in Sheba Street. One of the houses was
described in the last chapter. Some houses had rat runs
through the cupboards where kitchen utensils were kept.
Children were bitten in their sleep – one girl had her lips
chewed. Food had to be kept in metal dustbins, otherwise it
would be eaten. One child died from infections caught from
the unhygenic conditions. There was no means of escape
from fires on the top floors. Three people were burnt to
death in two separate incidents in Brick Lane. In the second,
the cries of the two men in the garret could be heard in the
street below. The wife of one of them, Afia Begum, arrived
in England days later and, after a massive campaign during
which she went into hiding, she was deported because she
had no relatives in this country.

Conditions at Wentworth were little better. The five-
storey tenements faced each other across a narrow courtyard
strewn with the rubbish of the street market outside. The
tin baths hung in lines from the minute balconies, which
also had to accommodate the outside toilets. Wentworth
Dwellings and Brunswick Buildings may only have contained 300 tenements. But many were shared by three
or four men. Each had a family back home. Potentially
at least 600 households and some 3,000 people's future
housing depended on what happened in the rehousing
from the blocks. There are few Bengali families in
Tower Hamlets who don't have relatives who once lived
there. They contained the greatest concentration of
Bengali tenants in one place that there has ever been in the
borough.

In 1977, at the same time as BHAG started demanding
rehousing, the tenants of Sheba Street signed a petition demanding immediate rehousing for everyone in the

Spitalfields area. The next year Wentworth tenants got a Compulsory Purchase Order confirmed. They had high expectations – if squatters could win rehousing, why couldn't tenants go one better? Their committee was tougher than BHAG. It contained men like Alauddin and Osman Gani who surfaced in many a struggle later on. They named just eight estates where they wanted all empty flats kept for them. They left off BHAG's list anything they thought was poor quality.

The response from the two councils was very different. For those in Sheba Street/Brick Lane, Tower Hamlets housing officers were genuinely sympathetic. This wasn't an unusual response from officers on the ground. But they couldn't help. They were hamstrung by the wider policy considerations which had ensured that nowhere in the local area had been built to move the tenants to. The few Bengali families who'd been moved from the Rothschild Buildings area had been rehoused in two groups to give them protection and prevent isolation. But they'd been moved out to Bethnal Green and Arbour Square. People from Sheba Street refused to move so far. They just had to wait till flats fell empty. But with the old estates built for small families there were no flats for the single men, and no large houses for the big families. Some people had to wait ten years to move. The Brick Lane frontage wasn't knocked down till 1987. It is a measure of people's desperation that derelict rooms which tenants had moved out of were squatted again and again by families with nowhere else to go. They argued for housing too. The council kept drawing lines beyond which it was not prepared to rehouse people. And the remaining residents kept pushing those lines back, until most of them were housed.

At Wentworth, the 12 years between former council leader John Orwell's promise in 1967 and the GLC's buying of the estate had seen the buildings fall apart. As more Bengali women and children had to move in, so the pressure intensified to get everyone out. Despite the agreement with BHAG, GLC officers demanded that Wentworth tenants agree to move out across south and east London. The GLC District Housing Office claimed that agreeing to local rehousing would be trying to fit 'a quart into a pint pot' and insisted there was 'no possibility of rehousing from Wentworth being accomplished in the immediate area'. The committee refused to accept this – and the squeeze was on.

GLC councillors had little involvement in what was happening, while its officers had no sympathy with the need to keep this community together. Nor had they any intention of housing them all. When they went round the blocks to find out who was living there, they didn't use interpreters. They only got partial information about who was there. They then divided the blocks up into 'those with rent books' and 'the rest' – offering rehousing to tenants and nothing to anyone else, even though everyone was entitled to rehousing by law. If the dispossessed wanted anywhere, they could go on sleeping on the living-room floors of the rehoused rent-book holders. This division was usually quite unreal. Three or four men often put money together to buy a rent-book, but only one had his name on it. The rent-book holder was given a flat just large enough for his immediate family. Other residents were told by GLC officers that they should just move in too – even when there was no space and, in many cases, even when this would have recreated criminal levels of overcrowding. The Tenants' Committee avoided divisions by supporting everyone's right to separate rehousing.

Cases from the files of the Spitalfields Housing and Planning Rights Service show that offers came from as far afield as Lewisham. One family found it had 'accepted' somewhere it couldn't move to, after the 14-year-old son had been visited alone and had 'signed' for the flat. One man was refused housing altogether for the crime of using extra rooms on the same staircase when his family arrived. Eviction was threatened when offers were refused. But people still wouldn't budge. If the GLC had succeeded, the majority of residents would have been dispossessed. It never agreed the principle of separate rehousing. But as offer after offer was refused, and threats were ignored, it was forced to negotiate. In the end the majority was rehoused on the eight named estates although the committee estimated that 40 families were never rehoused at all. By 1982 Wentworth Dwellings were empty.

The end of the clearance programme

The slums were cleared; nothing was rebuilt. So the more houses were cleared, the worse conditions got. More and more people were being packed into fewer and fewer unfit houses. People's powers of endurance were extraordinary. No matter how bad conditions got, they would not move unless there was somewhere else in the area to live. BHAG, Wentworth Dwellings and Sheba Street proved it could be done.

A paradox developed. As the population went down, the levels of overcrowding went up. In 1971, 24 per cent of Spitalfields households were living at over one person to a room; by 1981, this had gone up to 28 per cent. This increase was concentrated in the streets where Bengali families were arriving – one terrace in Princelet Street which housed 77 people in 1951 had over 150 occupants in 1979. The more the men exercised their rights to bring their families over, the fewer streets there were to move them into.

The diminishing number of houses bulged to bursting – Spitalfields had waited too long for the promised rebuilding to start.

5 | Building on Brick Lane

To Spitalfields, the blitz was nothing compared with the devastation of slum clearance. There was corrugated iron everywhere. By 1980, 50 of the ward's 250 acres were derelict. If all this land had been used for housing, it would nearly have doubled the number of homes. Slum clearance suggests progress. But Spitalfields' status in the 1981 Census as the most deprived ward in London coincided almost exactly with the end of the clearance programme. Standing alongside it, making three of the six most overcrowded wards in London, were St Mary's and St Katharine's.

Dereliction bred both desperation and hope. The people of the slums had to walk past these sites every day. As they came out of Wentworth Dwellings, the site of Davis Mansions was in front of them. If they lived in rooms around Brick Lane, they had to walk past two massive empty sites, enough for 250 homes, each time they left the Lane or came back home. The ramshackle squats of Old Montague Street were wrapped round by derelict land. The overcrowded families in the pre-war council block at Wheler House could see the trees growing on Bishopsgate Goodsyard. The homeless staying with friends on the Chicksand Estate were almost completely surrounded by the graveyards of the tenements. And yet whenever anyone asked to be rehoused in Spitalfields, the councils said it was impossible – apparently there was no room.

Even the long-standing white tenants who had got somewhere decent to live were desperate. Their relatives and carers had moved away. Schools and shops had closed. The sites were eyesores, they bred vermin. Gangs took over the land and charged fly-tippers to dump rubble. Rubbish lorries revved and gear-crashed their way through the narrow streets and slag-heaps grew overnight. All this constantly reinforced the feeling that everyone was living in a dump.

The tenants and the homeless, Bengali and white, were united in demanding the immediate rebuilding of Spitalfields for the local people who were in most housing need. As Spitalfields had the worst housing conditions in London, it seemed only reasonable that new housing should go to *local* people. The figures supported the demands. In 1976 there were plans to put 1,274 houses on the land behind the corrugated iron, and it seemed this would meet the need. The Spitalfields Survey of 1980 reckoned 1,200 homes would be enough, while in 1979 GLC researchers were saying 1,600 – which included homes for many existing council tenants too. Spitalfields could house its homeless. The land was just sitting there waiting for the bricks and mortar. The shift in the Bangladeshi community – from migrants to settlers – didn't alter this. There was land for the families to live on.

Yet the councils still insisted that there would be no room for the homeless and they would have to move elsewhere. In the early 1980s, as the land lay empty, the stock phrases rolled out from the Director of Housing in every letter of refusal sent to people on the waiting list wanting homes in Spitalfields: 'Unless you widen your area of choice, I regret I can see no prospect of assisting you in the foreseeable future.' There wasn't any 'prospect of assisting', because the councils were looking for other ways of using the land. Effectively the Bengalis would be excluded from the area. Amidst the squalor of Spitalfields, St Mary's and St Katharine's, this wasn't a very easy policy to justify. A report to the councils' Joint Housing Management Committee attempted to do so in 1980:

The population of Spitalfields is likely to increase by 40 per cent in the next few years as the existing Bangladeshi dependants arrive from Bangladesh. If they are not to live in distressing conditions the Joint Housing Management Committee must continue to do all it can to encourage Bengalis to live beyond Spitalfields where they can be housed more quickly. This is not forcible dispersal. This is the same procedure used in dealing with every applicant, black or white, whose housing location demands cannot be met within a reasonable timespan.

But it *was* forcible dispersal. The report didn't even mention building new houses. This was a solution not allowed on the agenda. The idea of dispersing the Bengali community was an obvious follow-on from the previous slum clearance programmes, when many people had gone willingly. To justify it, the councils claimed that there were enough houses in the borough for everyone – people just had to move out of the overcrowded areas. The evidence of housing sufficiency was itself tenuous, but in any case it begged two questions: was that housing available to the people of Spitalfields, and, if so, did they want to move into it?

But there was a brief moment when the councils did appear to be trying to rebuild Spitalfields for its own people. In 1973 Labour was elected at the GLC, while a year later Paul Beasley took over as leader of Tower Hamlets, with his youthful and radical image still fresh. It was under this combination that the idea of the Spitalfields Project was developed.

Rebuilding wasn't easy because the slum clearance was not co-ordinated in the way that had once been envisaged for Comprehensive Development Areas. It hadn't left swathes of empty land. Instead there were nearly 50 sites and derelict buildings, each of which would provide an average of around 30 units of housing. This required co-ordinated planning. The Project would be the way of dealing with this. As Monica Myers from the GLC Policy Study Unit put it in July 1975:

> The programme envisaged was one where all agencies concerned, including the GLC, co-ordinated their activities in the area, and, where possible, gave priority to it in their existing programmes; remedial action would not be delayed by a period of research.

The GLC started out on the Spitalfields Project in 1975 committed to building four big schemes – Davenant Street, Howard Buildings, Hopetown Street and Wentworth Dwellings. Between them these were to provide some 400 units of housing. Tower Hamlets also had two major schemes – at Selby Street and at Thrawl Street. These would add another 450 units. Five years later when the project ended, not a single one of these units had been finished and only 100 of them – at Hopetown Street – were even on site.

The Project had apparently been a disastrous failure. But it was the politicians who were responsible. The Tories, who took over the GLC in 1977, never wanted this housing built. Nor, as it transpired, did Tower Hamlets' Labour administration. They were quick to line up with the Tories in undermining the whole momentum of the Project. Plans for the sites started changing without consultation or warning. The Project was turned into a charade. Council officers still came along to meetings with the local organizations, where they mumbled about technical problems like medieval plague pits, polluted ground, and financial problems about the schemes being too expensive. Then in 1980 the GLC announced the sale of the Howard Buildings land to private developers for a song – as we shall see later. The decisions these politicians made about the land show what, beneath the talk, their real intentions were.

Whatever happened to the new council houses?

The Labour GLC of 1973-77 seemed serious about rebuilding Spitalfields. Tower Hamlets Council played along. Throughout that Labour GLC, all the housing land sold by the borough council went to housing associations and not to the private sector. Toynbee Housing Association took the big site at Thrawl Street on Brick Lane, while Newlon Housing Trust took on the unfit little 'artisan' houses at Albert Cottages. In St Mary's, Springboard Housing Association took over houses in Varden Street which were still being squatted by BHAG. For several years from the late 1970s to 1983, Tower Hamlets distinguished itself by being the only council in Britain without a specific committee for housing. Succinctly, this shows the priority being given to building new council housing. Business was split between the Development and Health and Housing Management Committees.

With the next Tory GLC administration, even these committees ceased to conduct any housing business. A new Joint Housing Committee was set up to manage the entire housing stock of the two councils and to prepare the way for the borough council's takeover of GLC housing in 1985. This committee met for three years but was never recognized by staff unions. Its decisions were regarded as fairly meaningless, and the committee itself petered out. Meanwhile Tower Hamlets was beginning to take a harder line on selling council land as a Conservative government came into power.

The clearance of Brady Street Dwellings in 1978 has been mentioned in the last chapter. It formed part of the biggest site in the borough – the derelict 'East End' of Spitalfields with its railway cuttings and scrap yards as well as flattened tenement foundations. People wanted housing there. They said so in the Consultation of 1976. They saw the plans in 1978. Yet just a few months later, after secret talks and no tendering, this is where the council proudly announced it planned to sell the land for offices, a shopping centre bigger than Brent Cross and a few flats for single people. Sam Chippendale, of Arndale Shopping Centres fame, was in business. He had no-one interested in his offices, no retailers wanting his shopping centre, but he thought he had the site. If nothing else, he made sure the land has been known as the 'Shopping Centre site' ever since. He even came and met the locals where he rode out their sound and fury. People wanted houses; they even wanted better shops; but they could see that this scheme wasn't going to give them either. They were right. After six years of blight, the council started looking for another buyer. By then all the land in Docklands had gone – it was the only big piece of land left to put council housing on. The council chose not to.

Behind this site was another – big enough for 80 houses. The council didn't build on this either, claiming it could not provide 'value for money' because it had railway cuttings and viaducts in it. Housing co-ops and the GLC had both shown that housing could be built cheaply enough, but they were ignored. Instead, the land got wrapped in with the shopping centre site, waiting for a private developer. The council even planned to sell the houses in Parfett Street which squatters had fought for in 1974. But in the meantime, the squatters had formed the Sylhet Housing Co-op and, with GLC backing, they managed to buy the houses before they went onto the open market.

In February 1982 the council's Policy Committee endorsed a report which said that:

> Housing development in the Spitalfields ward will be outside the control of this Council as there is no suitable council-owned land in the area.

Despite the pace of the sales, this was never true. It still owned the land for the Whitechapel Shopping Centre which was 'not value for money' and its redundant works depot at Gunthorpe Street which was 'not suitable for families'. The depot was only 20 yards from the family housing being built at Thrawl Street by Toynbee Housing Association. Political commitment, not land, was the problem. As we shall see in the next chapter, its real interest was in selling its land for private development.

Between 1977 and 1981, the Tory GLC followed this route too. With George Tremlett as Chair of Housing, the Tories planned their own sales programme. The large family houses at Davenant Street were changed to smaller, more market-able units. By the summer of 1979 all detailed design work on their four big council schemes stopped. As houses came empty on council estates they were boarded up till buyers could be found. Families of eight living in two-room tenements in Wentworth, with raw sewage running down their walls, were told they couldn't be rehoused in Spitalfields because there was nowhere to move them to. Just a few hundred yards away, the cream of the GLC housing stock was standing empty for month after month as buyers fell through and new ones were sought. Once the GLC had established a market for the sale of individual houses on their estates, they planned the sale of their empty sites. Howard Buildings was first. In 1980 the Abbey National Building Society bought it for a private scheme. Had the Tories won the 1981 GLC elections, other sites would have followed.

George Tremlett was interviewed in the *Evening Standard* in July 1979 when the paper did an exposé on the 'streets of squalor' in Spitalfields. He blamed illegal immigrants for the housing crisis, although he couldn't provide any evidence (because of course there wasn't any). Tremlett knew the shortage in Spitalfields, he had seen it himself. He admitted it was becoming a source of national shame. But for him more council housing wasn't a solution. 'London has too many council houses at a time when the capital's population is shrinking,' he said. He agreed with Tower Hamlets: there was empty housing elsewhere, people should be forced to move into it.

Throughout 1979 one of the main tasks of the Housing and Planning Rights Service was to co-ordinate opposition to the sale of the GLC sites. It was a campaign that got local and national coverage. The GLC was put on the defensive. Crucially, they delayed selling the rest of their land until after the 1981 elections. The campaign, backed with survey information, also helped boost the support the Housing Corporation was prepared to give housing associations and co-ops.

Spitalfields had great hopes of the 1981 GLC Labour administration when it came to power. The Chair of Housing was Gladys Dimson, who had been active in one of the local housing associations and was well aware of local conditions. What's more, the GLC manifesto had made a commitment to protect all the remaining working-class communities in central London. Central London community groups had got the Labour Party to accept that they were under special pressures brought on by commercial developers. The GLC was to build rented housing and to stop office developments under its innovative 'Community Areas Policy'; Spitalfields was the only place where the GLC already had housing land – it could become the show-piece of the new policy.

Yet when the list of GLC housing schemes came out, there was nothing for Spitalfields. Again promises had been betrayed. The GLC was bombarded with complaints, spearheaded by the Local Committee. Yet a full year after the elections, local GLC councillor Ashley Bramall was still offering no hope of them building new homes. Housing associations started sniffing around, and GLC officers started suggesting that the GLC was going to sell the land. Spitalfields groups linked up with other organizations from around central London to expose the contradiction between words and action on Spitalfields. The GLC was shamed into admitting that its policy would mean little if it did not develop its own housing sites.

The community groups won the argument. GLC councillors asked its architects to pull out the drawings, and design work was at last restarted. The 69 houses planned for Davenant Street went on site in 1984, and the terraces of large houses were all full by 1986. Design work went on apace on the scheme for Wentworth Dwellings too and the first phase was finished in 1986 – 20 years after it had been announced. Seeing this housing going up after so many years of struggle was sweet success. But time ran out for the GLC, with two phases of the scheme still to be built. The site was passed over to the Liberals who soon gave up trying to finish it, and talk of selling the site restarted, even though the three phases were designed as a whole to include shops and stall space at ground level for Wentworth Street market.

Was the money ever there?

The other source of opposition to rebuilding Spitalfields came from central government. Spending on public sector housing was relatively high until 1976. The Labour government then cut it after the IMF financial crisis. But between 1979 and 1987 the Tories have cut even harder – spending on public sector housing is only a fraction of what it was in real terms in 1979 and it's still going down. Council building has almost completely stopped. In Thatcher's third term, not only will it be impossible for councils to build, it will be hard for them to hold onto what they've got. It is precisely this sort of land – very profitable to private developers – that the Tories want them to get their hands on. So although the drive for privatization has become more intense, they have always been hostile to funding rented housing.

But Tower Hamlets Council has used this hostility as an excuse for inactivity. Nothing was built in the 'good years' of the last Labour government when it could have got the money. This didn't just apply to Spitalfields: only one terrace of housing was built in the wards either side.

In the early years of Conservative government, the council didn't even bid for the money it needed. It asked for little and got less – and then in 1981 and 1982 it spent only two thirds of its tiny allocation. While the GLC was getting permission from the Department of the Environment to build housing at Davenant Street, Tower Hamlets didn't even ask for the money to build at Selby Street. It assumed, without even trying, that it would be turned down. When, under the influence of new socialist councillors, it made larger bids in the mid-1980s, its record suggested it couldn't spend the money. It's hard to say that central government funding was the problem when you don't ask for money and don't spend what you're given.

Before the Liberal administration took power in 1986, Tower Hamlets had abandoned any attempt at a housing development programme of its own. Its estimated expenditure on newly built houses in 1986/7 was only £800,000 –

scarcely enough for 20 units of housing. By that time it was too late. No matter how much money they asked for, the Housing Investment Programme was too small to finance much new building. The council was given just 10 per cent of its 1987/8 bid of £153 million, almost all of which was to repair existing estates. Private borrowing, in the manner of councils like Lambeth and Camden, would have been the only way of keeping a development programme going. Tower Hamlets did talk to a housing association about such a deal, using council land and private money, but further circulars from the Department of the Environment put a stop to it.

In December 1986, the House of Commons Home Affairs Committee reported on Bangladeshis in Britain. This report barely touched the surface of what was needed to improve conditions for the Bangladeshi community, but it did accept that housing was the major issue and that there should be an increase in money for the Housing Investment Programme, especially to build more large units. Even though this was a Parliamentary report, it wrung nothing out of the DoE.

This has meant that Tower Hamlets' housing investment has been concentrated on only the direst emergencies. With a lot of its stock built during the 1950s and 60s, when system building was at its worst, it is now literally having to catch the concrete falling from the sky. Tenants on estates like the Dorset and Cranbrook have lived with a semi-permanent corrugated iron structure round their tower blocks, built to prevent the falling concrete from splitting people's heads open as they go about their daily business. Remedying spalling concrete, defective slip bricks and collapsing balconies is an expensive business. It amounts to £4 million on the Cranbrook Estate alone – or a quarter of one year's entire Housing Investment Programme.

But even in this desperate funding shortage, the Labour council committed £4,950,000 of its allocation to finance Toynbee Housing Association to build 80 units of shared-ownership housing at Orient Wharf in Wapping. This money could have been used for council housing, but it wasn't. Its

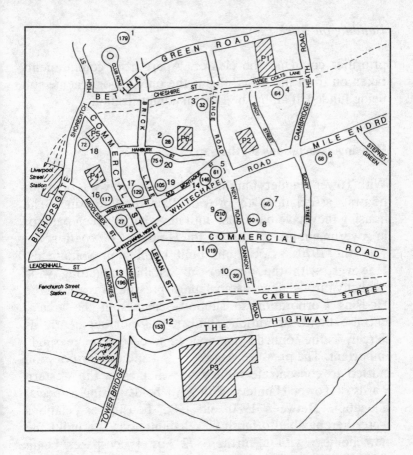

(50) Rented Housing Schemes (with number of units)

Adelina Grove 6 Co-op
Albert Cottages 2 HA
Ashfield St 7 GLC
Batty St 11 HA
Cavell St 8 HA
Casson St 20 Co-op
Cudworth St 4 HA
Davenant St 5 GLC
Fieldgate Mans 9 HA
Fleur-de-Lis St 18 HA
Folgate St 18 HA
Fordham St 9 HA
Guinness Est 13 HA
Hanbury St 20 Co-op
Heneage St 20 HA
Holland Est 16 GLC

Hopetown St 19 GLC
Myrdle St 9 Co-op
Nelson St 8 HA
New Rd 8 HA
Old Montague St 14 HA
Old Police Stn 18 Co-op
Parfett St 9 Co-op/HA
Peace St 3 Co-op
Ponler St 10 HA
Princelet St 20 Co-op
Royal Mint Sq 12 GLC
Spelman St 20 Co-op
Thrawl St 17 HA
Varden St 8 HA
Virginia Rd 1 GLC
Wentworth 15 GLC

Private Housing Developments

P1 Waterlow Estate
P2 Whitechapel Shopping Centre (proposal)
P3 London Docks
P4 Spitalfields Market (proposal)
P5 The Cloisters
P6 Abbey National scheme

5. *Main rented housing schemes built in 1980s and main private housing developments on land previously in public ownership.*

priorities could not be clearer. Apart from commitments taken on from the GLC, this is the only major scheme still being funded at all by the Liberal administration.

Housing associations fill the gap

With Tower Hamlets building nothing, the way was open for housing associations to provide 'fair rent' housing. The housing they have built has, until now, largely been paid for in government grants through the Housing Corporation.

In the 1970s associations built nothing in Spitalfields. However, with the disaster in Spitalfields getting wide publicity through local campaigning, pressure was put on the Housing Corporation to support schemes in the area – because the Corporation's budget was not cut nearly as fiercely as the council's, its money had become increasingly important. The pressure was successful and the Corporation started to concentrate money on schemes in the western wards of Tower Hamlets, with Spitalfields getting a special allocation. Between 1980 and 1986, housing associations were thereby able to finish 99 rehabilitations and build 182 new homes, with a further 172 hostel bedspaces being provided. Even though these schemes weren't tailored to local need, they did make a major contribution in alleviating that need. Sensitive allocations and good management partly compensated for the early bad planning. Most of the housing went to local people who needed it, and those people were happy.

But there were problems for the local groups trying to get the housing associations to develop housing to meet the needs of Spitalfields. Most associations are run by unelected Boards which are not democratically accountable. As charities, usually set up by social improvers, the Church or rich philanthopists, their boards of management often still reflected their origins. Few encouraged local involvement and, when they started working in the area, none had a Bengali representative. It was rare for them to discuss their plans with forums like the Local Committee before taking action. In the 1970s, the dangers inherent in this were highlighted with two associations – both Newlon and the Peabody Trust were used to promote office developments in West Spitalfields, as we shall see in the next chapters.

Another problem was that Tower Hamlets Council provided no overall direction or control of housing association activity. Eight associations started building in the ward, another four had schemes nearby, but there was little co-ordination between them. This failure, combined with the associations' lack of consultation with local organizations of what was needed, meant that virtually all their housing was for single people. Of the 172 hostel spaces and 281 self-contained units built by 1986, only a dozen had three or more bedrooms. There was no shortage of single people needing somewhere to live. But these developments only increased the pressure on the very large families who were being offered nothing by the council. Even with the small households there were difficulties – when Newlon's single people started families, they had nowhere in the area to move them to. The housing planned for completion from 1987 onwards shows more balance, and there are now just three major developers – Toynbee, Newlon and the Spitalfields Housing Co-operative.

Throughout, associations have been reluctant to take on the complications of buying tenanted places. They ignored the same housing that the council had avoided. The exceptions show how valuable this approach could have been. Samuel Lewis Housing Trust took on the tenement estate at Fieldgate Mansions on the other side of Whitechapel Road in St Mary's Ward. The Mansions, with their concrete yards between blocks at basement level, strung across with dozens of lines of washing, evoked the pre-war East End. The Trust had to decant and rehouse 671 people from 213 one-bedroom flats. Because the flats were small and overcrowded, they had to build new homes alongside their modernization of the tenements, housing the 'surplus' population in a quarter-mile radius of the original site.

Bethnal Green and Springboard Housing Associations have managed much smaller schemes in this way.

This method means no tenant will be moved out of the area. It preserves the existing community. It ensures that the minimum amount of housing is empty at any one time, as the modernization is done in small phases. It has given the tenants some control over the sort of housing they will be moving back into, although in the Fieldgate case, there have been major disagreements between the Residents' Association and the Trust. However, Fieldgate Mansions showed that, with a bit of planning, quarts can be fitted into pint pots. Six hundred and seventy-one people, who were crowded into 213 bedrooms, were rehoused at average housing densities in the immediate area of their choice.

But the most significant thing for the tenants in Fieldgate Mansions was that they had originally been squatters. The GLC had decanted Fieldgate as part of a clearance programme. It had been squatted largely by Bengali families, but also by young, white, single people. Samuel Lewis bought the blocks in 1982 from the GLC with a commitment to rehouse all existing licensees – the erstwhile squatters. The squatters of Pelham Buildings had demanded, and obtained, rehousing together in E1. But they had not stayed together, nor had they been offered good-quality flats. The people in Fieldgate not only succeeded in staying together in E1, but also got new homes in Ponler Street, Burslem Street and Cannon Street Road or new conversions in the street where they had been living. Things had moved a long way since Pelham Buildings.

However good the deal was for the people of Fieldgate, they did not get any choice about who provided it. Samuel Lewis spent three years working out the details with the GLC before they bought the blocks. The Trust has its roots in the paternalist housing trusts of the 19th century – and there was something of this spirit in the way in which it plunged into Fieldgate which it saw as its 'most daunting yet fascinating challenge'. To some extent, because of its style, Samuel Lewis commanded the respect of the Housing

Corporation and was therefore able to get an 'in principle' commitment to the many millions of pounds that the scheme would cost. But in the end, the tenants didn't choose Samuel Lewis, Samuel Lewis chose them.

Co-operative control

As described in Chapter 2, the Bengalis of East London came from a rural background which required each community to be very self-reliant, where villagers had to make and carry out their own decisions on the development of such things as schools. For them the remoteness and indifference of a state bureaucracy was nothing new. They had always had to organize much for themselves. It was therefore not such a big step for them to get involved in housing co-operatives where they could control and direct housing development to meet their own needs.

Co-operative housing gives control to ordinary people. Until 1988, co-ops were funded by grants in the same way as housing associations. However, with co-ops the money is controlled by the people who are actually going to live in the houses. In Tower Hamlets this has released a great potential. Co-ops have been able to buy the derelict land that has been staring them in the face for so long. Tenants in Princelet Street who've spent 15 years looking out on a slag heap of rubbish on the other side of the street watched their new homes grow there. They've been able to buy the land where *they* want to live and not where the council wants to put them. They've been able to design houses to suit their own lifestyle. Bengali women in Spitalfields have set down important guidelines about the way they want new houses laid out. For the first time men can arrange with a co-operative landlord to go home on extended trips to see families back in Bangladesh. They can trust the co-op to make arrangements so their homes will still be there when they get back. The shared experience of bad housing creates an understanding of the problems faced by individual members which no other landlord could provide.

Three groups of Bengali squatters, who took over streets of houses at the time of the BHAG, have now won their housing permanently by setting up co-ops. Most advanced is Sylhet Co-op which now owns the famous 34 houses of Parfett Street which had been fought over so fiercely in the 1970s. Modernization of these homes started in 1986. There are two others based in Commercial Road – Shahazalal and Mitali. This follows the pattern of the four co-ops in East Stepney and Adelina Grove where squatters became tenants. These four also have a sizeable Bengali membership. Combined with the one in Spitalfields, these co-ops will eventually house over 2,500 people. That is 6 per cent of the population of E1 and something like one in eight of the Bangladeshis in the area.

Spitalfields Housing Co-operative is unlike these others. Formed not by squatters, but by tenement dwellers of Wentworth Dwellings, its members saw a co-op as the way of stopping the GLC from moving them from one set of slums to another. With a co-op, they wanted to buy housing in their own chosen area, and not be forced to move where the GLC was demanding. Ten Wentworth tenants first met above a mini-cab office in Fashion Street in the summer of 1979. They were some of the worst-paid workers in London, with scarcely a penny of capital between them. They can hardly have imagined that within a decade their co-op would own the best part of £25 million pounds worth of property.

For these ten, it took too long to set the co-op up. They had to accept the offers of GLC rehousing they were trying to avoid. But, encouraged by Osman Gani, one of their number, and Ahmed Fakhruddin, a tireless community activist, some stayed on as a 'steering group' to keep the idea alive. In the winter of 1979 they spent many evenings visiting the privately rented terraces in Princelet, Hanbury and Spelman Streets which Tower Hamlets had failed to buy up in the 1970s. Through the cold evenings they went from room to room explaining the co-op idea. In these dimly lit rooms heated by paraffin stoves, with tenants sitting on their beds in their vests and lunghis, the debate developed. The tenants were convinced. They agreed to ask the co-op to buy the houses from their landlord. Seventy tenants in 21 houses and 18 tenements became the core of the co-op – only three of them were not Bengalis.

Conditions in this new portfolio were indescribably bad. Just six flats had baths or self-contained toilets. Most families, however big, had just one bedroom to sleep in. Landlords hadn't bothered with repairs for decades. Windows were rotten, roofs leaking, glass missing, plaster flaking. But however bad the conditions, the co-op came up against the old problem of tenants who had been forced to buy their rent-books for large sums – hoping to recoup this money when they left. The co-op couldn't allow rent books to be sold on. So people who had spent money buying tenancies were now going to lose it. From then on, new tenants were chosen by democratic vote and not by the payment of illegal deposits. This meant that there was a minority group who opposed the co-op takeover, some of whom continued their opposition after they became members.

There were clothing workshops both in these houses and in their backyards. It was this mixed use of buildings which had put housing associations off intervening in the private sector. In this case the community-based Spitalfields Small Business Association was set up. It borrowed money to buy the buildings and to then lease on the residential parts to the co-op. It then became responsible for managing the workshops, raising money to improve them, and dividing them off from the residential space.

Expectations had been raised – the co-op members wanted their new homes. This wasn't simple. To modernize them, houses had to be emptied – and the co-op had nowhere to move people to. What's more, because of the overcrowding, less than half the original tenants would be able to move back once the work was done. A lot more houses were needed quickly. Between 1982 and 1984 the co-op scoured Spitalfields for empty houses – it got some but not enough. There was little on the market. So it also bought six houses in Mile End for people who were happy to move there. (They were just in time – gentrification nearly doubled prices between 1985 and 1987.) It asked the GLC for land and got some. But this all took time while members waited on in their rotting homes. The co-op needed to show it could do something quickly.

Codrington House, a GLC block of 44 flats, was standing empty. It was structurally unsound, had baths in the kitchens and needed total rehabilitation. The money wasn't there to repair it, but the GLC was spending a small fortune for a 24-hour security guard to prevent another mass squat. As soon as the co-op formed, the GLC pushed this 'gift' at them. The co-op took it, seduced by the possibility of being able to house people immediately. Half the block was to be for decanting tenants from their slums and the rest for some of the 400 other people who'd joined the co-op's ranks with nowhere to live. The co-op had taken on the worst of the council stock and the worst of the private sector. It was a dangerous position to be in, and it nearly broke them.

The co-op couldn't manage Codrington House. Their tenants didn't want to decant from one slum to another. They wanted one move – straight into a decent new home. The flats reserved for them at Codrington stayed empty until they were all squatted on the same night by other desperate families. The other half of the block was given to families who'd joined the co-op with nowhere to live. Even these people could only put up with Codrington's conditions on a short-term basis. When it seemed clear the co-op couldn't move them out quickly, they wanted the GLC to take the block back. It was they who organized the squatting of the empty flats. They knew the co-op would not be able to manage the ensuing mess. Sure enough, the block was handed back to the GLC and all the occupants were given GLC tenancies, which were taken over by Tower Hamlets. The council was unwilling to commit itself to doing anything – even though 30 per cent of families were living at or above levels of statutory overcrowding. Five years later, no-one had been transferred and no modernization done, though at the time of writing negotiations had started with the Samuel Lewis Housing Trust to take it over.

The co-op had to make a second start. It waited for the conversion of the empty houses it had bought. The first families from Spelman and Princelet Streets moved into ready-converted homes as they had asked. It was an important moment. It was the first proof that the co-op really could rehouse people. Tenant involvement increased markedly, but it was still slow going. Rehousing would take ten years for the 80 original families, without land to build new houses on. The Labour GLC supported them by handing over three important sites: land at Peace Street for 32 large family houses with gardens, land for 14 homes opposite their houses in Princelet Street and the old Police Station in Commercial Street – a building that featured time and again in the tales of the East End underworld of the nineteenth century.

By 1984 the co-op was controlled by its tenants; and they'd got enough land to rehouse everyone living in their houses. But there were more problems. Peace Street was to be financed by the GLC. With abolition looming, the DoE squeezed the GLC's capital expenditure so hard that it seemed the GLC would be unable to finance any of the co-op schemes it supported. Several co-ops launched a joint campaign to safeguard the money. Only in the last week of the GLC's existence was the money secured in nerve-racking deals. A year later the Peace Street development went on site, was delayed again when the first builder went bust, but is scheduled for completion in 1989.

Despite these setbacks, by 1987 the co-op was responsible for around 40 per cent of the development programme in Spitalfields. By 1990, the co-op will be managing nearly 200 units of modernized housing. Some original tenants will have waited seven years for rehousing, which is a long wait. It raised questions about what the co-op should do next. Buying more tenanted property means more of the heart-ache of being a slum landlord facing out the increasing frustrations of members awaiting rehousing. It is the co-op's willingness to do this which has made it so attractive to the Housing Corporation for funding. And there are plenty more tenanted houses to buy.

But the co-op also has hundreds of members who aren't tenants. They've waited for years and are expecting the co-op to do something for them. This means buying more land and empty buildings. This is getting increasingly difficult as land values soar. But, as we shall see, the government may now be intervening to end this dilemma, by stopping the co-op from building any more housing that its members can afford.

The Whitechapel Community Trust

Since Sam Chippendale's attempts to develop the Shopping Centre site at Whitechapel, the site had been blighted. When the Liberals took power in 1986, the drive to sell the land went on unabated. Community groups saw that the only way of keeping the land for local use was by setting up their own company to compete with private developers. If tenants from the slum terraces could manage a £25 million housebuilding programme, this bigger scheme was surely possible. The Whitechapel Commmunity Trust was set up to involve the largest possible number of groups and individuals locally in drawing up a scheme.

A development of similar size, under community control, was taking place at Coin Street in Waterloo. After fighting a series of Public Enquiries the developers who wanted the Coin Street land had been defeated. Such tactics were well known to community groups; but the Whitechapel consortium was competing in the commercial market against development companies on their terms and this was breaking stony new ground. One of the Tower Hamlets groups involved – the Environment Trust – agreed to take on this work. They had to learn the rules of commercial development very fast as the council quickly invited outline proposals for the site.

The Community Trust involved 600 people from Spital-fields and surrounding wards. It held bilingual meetings to discuss issues such as the proportion of public to private housing there should be. Forty Bengali women organized their own meeting to decide their priorities for the site. A scheme was agreed. It would provide a shopping centre to meet local need, maximize the amount of housing on the site, and use the old railway arches for light industry. Many large retailers were interested. Prudential Assurance was prepared to put up £20 million, with the Housing Corporation and the Halifax Building Society suggesting they could fund rented and shared-ownership housing.

This scheme faced very stiff private-sector competition. Twenty-two developers originally expressed interest. Intense campaigning succeeded in getting the council to include the community scheme in its favoured short-list. The final choice was made between the Trust and a developer called Pengap. The private scheme was more prestigious – including a spiral moving staircase as the centrepiece of the shopping centre. There were echoes of Sam Chippendale. Pengap's costs were much higher than the Trust's – would retailers really come to an East End centre with West End rent levels?

But the biggest difference in the two schemes was in the housing proposed. The Community Trust recognized that this was the last chance to improve local housing on a large scale. It proposed 201 rented homes and 170 for low-cost sale to local people, using land and grant subsidy. Pengap offered just 58 rented units and 62 for sale at market price. Both schemes added 40 units for shared ownership. In all, the Trust wanted 411 homes, many for large families – Pengap just 160 with none having more than two bedrooms. This was the difference. The Trust would have housed 1,963 people – or a quarter of the ward's current population – against Pengap's 561.

The council's 'public consultation' only got 200 responses and although a thin majority was in favour of Pengap's shop design, there was a majority for the Community Trust's housing scheme. As well as these 200 responses, there were 600 people who had been actively involved in drawing up the community scheme. But by the time the council came to make a choice it was controlled by the Liberals. Their neighbourhood committee in Bethnal Green supported Pengap. That, combined with the results of the public consultation, won the day. The strategic importance of the site didn't get considered. Despite the local involvement in the Community Trust, Liberal leader Eric Flounders said that the Pengap scheme was 'rooted in people's everyday experience and desires'. The decision to support Pengap was taken at a special meeting called for 8pm on a Friday night, and the papers only got general circulation on the previous day. In the tradition of their predecessors, the Liberals had made a choice which would force more Bengali families out of the area. But the arguments aren't over. A succession of developers took the scheme on from Pengap, ending up with Trafalgar House. By the end of 1988, even Trafalgar House had given up. The land is up for grabs again. The ideas of the Community Trust have another chance.

Big houses

It hasn't just been the number of rented houses that Tower Hamlets Council has tried to restrict. It has also been their size. A large proportion of the Bengali families in the area need four or more bedrooms. Even when the rebuilding did start, it wasn't being designed for these large families. By 1985, with 600 new units built, only a handful had four or more bedrooms – and most of these were built by the co-op. We've seen how the mismatch of need and house sizes caught the housing associations short. It is still one of the main factors shutting large Bengali families out of council housing in the area. In 1987, of the 380 flats relet by the council in Bethnal Green neighbourhood (which includes Spitalfields) only 16 of them had more than three bedrooms.

So the Labour GLC and housing associations changed their programmes to build housing for large Bengali families – as happened at Davenant Street – while the Spitalfields Co-op designed large houses from the start. As a result many more big houses have been planned. They're about 30 per cent of the programme but, because they're so big, 60 per cent of the people housed will be living in them. The proportion is going up all the time because more five-and six-bedroom houses are being planned.

New houses with four or more bedrooms

	% of units	% of people housed in them
Built 1985–1987	31	51
Programme 1987–1990	27	60
Future programme	33	65

Tower Hamlets Council has tried to restrict the number of large houses being built. Under the Labour administration, the planners allowed the Abbey National Building Society private scheme at Howard Buildings to go ahead even though almost all the houses only had two bedrooms. So even if there had been a lot of Bengali families wanting to buy, few would have been able to squeeze into the mini-homes on offer. But, as the other public sector landlords came up with proposals for large houses, the council developed a new planning policy to restrict numbers.

To prevent overdevelopment, there are accepted guidelines on the number of people permitted to live on each acre of new housing. But Tower Hamlets also limited the number of *children* living in each acre. The co-op's Peace Street scheme didn't break the density guidelines, but the council claimed that too many children would be living in the street. The co-op had discussed the layout of these houses with the women members and had incorporated their design ideas.

But the council forced the co-op to change the scheme, reducing nine of the 32 houses to three-bedroom ones.

As far as the council was concerned, it seemed, families with six children could stay in one-bedroom flats because the child density would be too great if they lived in five-bedroom houses. They quote studies which show that lots of children on high-density estates cause vandalism. But the Spitalfields houses had gardens, and the children, despite living six to a room, had vandalized nothing. The inspector who assessed the council's policy at the Public Enquiry in 1984 commented that they had 'an unduly scant explanation for a very restrictive policy'. He recommended they reconsider it. They didn't.

What's been won

Back in 1976, 1,274 new rented homes were promised. By 1986, 805 had been built. Another 204 were to go on site between 1987 and 1989, while there are plans for 367 more. Despite the odds, Spitalfields has blossomed. From the end of the war until 1981, the population had dropped while overcrowding and bad conditions got worse. 1982 was the turning point. The decline was reversed. The population of 6,450 in 1981 had grown over the next six years to nearly 7,900. One and a half thousand more people are living in the ward. More shops and restaurants have opened. An extra primary school has started up to take on the increasing numbers of children. Most of the corrugated iron has gone. From Petticoat Lane to Vallance Road is an almost unbroken run of new housing estates. In much of that new housing live the old tenement dwellers who had their roots in the area. There is a new heart to Spitalfields. And this regeneration is far from over. Another 500 new homes can be expected over the next five years.

For those who have been rehoused, it's an end to overcrowding and squalor. Internal family stress and tensions are relieved. Children can study for exams. Women have the space – for themselves, for each other and for their families – which was always denied. Above all, the uncertainty of hanging on, in one insecure address after another, is over. A tenancy on one of these new estates can be a home for life. This new housing is all the more precious because it was the badly-housed of Spitalfields who made it happen. They defeated the forces trying to drive them out – the very forces which should have been there to help. In 1976, Bengalis with secure tenancies were confined to a few inter-war GLC blocks. By 1990, they will have the majority of secure and housing association tenancies throughout the ward.

Sixty per cent of this housing has come through housing associations and the co-op, as the table below shows. In 1976, Tower Hamlets Council was due to build half of it, but they never started a single house. To have got so much built in the teeth of Tory policy is a great triumph. But with even tighter controls now being brought in, the future plans are in great danger.

Despite the successes, there is still a vast unmet need. Many families haven't found a home in Spitalfields and are now homeless. Eleven hundred households are in temporary housing – 90 per cent of them being Bengali, and most still

New rented homes in Spitalfields since 1979

Developer	Completed by 1986		On site 1986/89		Future plans	
	Rehab	*New*	*Rehab*	*New*	*Rehab*	*New*
GLC	127	201	—	—	—	—
Housing assocs	99	182	19	19	—	247
Housing co-op	20	4	55	57	—	58
Hostels	8	164	—	82	—	—
Tower Hamlets	—	—	9	—	40	—
City Corporation	—	—	—	—	22	—
Totals	254	551	83	158	62	305
		805		*241*		*367*

wanting to live in and around Spitalfields. But that's not all. Apart from the co-op's work, conditions for the 300 families still in the private sector are untouched. And of the 200 council tenants who were living in statutorily overcrowded conditions in 1981, some have moved, but many live on in conditions where the council, as landlord, is breaking the law. And there are still families hanging on with friends because they have nowhere else to go.

In the 1970s it was predicted that building 1,200 new homes would end the shortage in Spitalfields. There are many reasons why the shortage is still there:

-   By the middle of 1988 only 850 homes had been finished. There are 550 to come – many of them large houses. Because they're bigger, the new houses will fit in as many people as the 850 units already built. Effectively the programme is only half way through.
-   Howard Buildings, the Peabody Estate, and now much of Selby Street has been lost through sales to private developers.
-   Not all the rented housing went to Spitalfields people anyway – some went to those in need from neighbouring wards, while the GLC brought in people from across London.
-   Few flats are coming empty on existing estates. Council house sales and worsening job and housing prospects elsewhere have drastically reduced the turnover of flats coming empty.

During this period, there have been changes in the Bengali community itself. Throughout the 1980s, Bengali families have been drawn to Spitalfields from the depressed north – industrial jobs upon which the Bengali community depended, in towns like Oldham, Scunthorpe and even Bedford, have gone. Often these families have come to stay with relatives in Aldgate, as they call it, while they look for work. The Bangladeshi population is a young one – in 1980 37 per cent of the population in the ward were under 20 years old, compared with 26 per cent in London as a whole. This would mean a very fast rate of new households forming anyway. But families are often still arranging marriages for their children with partners in Bangladesh. Traditionally, these newly formed couples would stay with the main family. But changing customs, the shortage of large houses, and immigration rules mean they often need to get a small place of their own. Finally, it's usually forgotten that all surveys underestimate the Bengali population. Households away on holiday in Bangladesh at the time of a survey or census should be taken into account when assessing the area's needs, because they still constitute a significant proportion of the potential population. They never are, and it is difficult to get accurate information about such households when they're not in the country.

The future

Under the last Labour government Spitalfields got no new housing at all. Ironically, new housing has been won under a Tory administration that has made it progressively more and more difficult to build housing for rent. Although, to begin with, Spitalfields alone was getting the benefit of this, both co-ops and housing associations have started working in the same way in the neighbouring wards of St Mary's, St Katharine's and the south of Weavers. This means there

New rented housing in City fringe wards since 1985

	Homes built 1985–7	Homes programmed 1987–9	Homes planned from 1989 on	Total
Spitalfields	203	241	367	811
City fringe wards	232	564	395	1191
Totals	435	805	762	2002

will be less pressure from nearby areas for the rest of Spitalfields' new housing, as the table above shows.

The Bengali community has consolidated itself in all these wards, which have many of the advantages of Spitalfields itself. Yet although they contain three times the population of Spitalfields, the number of houses built there between 1985 and 1987 was much the same as in Spitalfields. But now more than twice as much is being built in these wards as in Spitalfields, and plans have been turning into housing on the ground much more quickly. Of the 983 homes on the drawing board in 1985, half were ready to live in two years later.

Potentially, much more could be built. At July 1988 there were plans for another 762 homes – 367 of them in Spitalfields. Even this isn't the limit. There are five other big opportunities without even considering the Truman's Brewery site:

- The private development of the Shopping Centre site could be stopped. With the Community Trust scheme there can be a shopping centre *and* an extra 320 rented homes for 1,400 people on the site.
- There is now planning permission for offices on the Market site. There is housing to go with it – but 114 homes for 281 people will be up for sale.
- The land on the Goodsyard at Bishopsgate, just over the ward boundary, is not all good for housing – it is right on the Liverpool Street line. But there is enough room on the Bethnal Green Road side and at Pedley Street to house 200 people. The Liberals' Planning Brief for the site gives housing little priority, however.
- The Liberals themselves have listed 15 more housing sites for Spitalfields in their proposed revisions of the Borough Plan, but this would include getting rid of the park at Allen Gardens. Keeping the park, 100 homes for 300 people could be built on the other sites.
- Housing associations have outline schemes for another 100 homes in the wards surrounding Spitalfields.

Adding these to the houses programmed, Spitalfields could still provide another 1,100 houses for 4,600 people altogether. Doing the same sums for the surrounding wards would produce another 1,170 homes for 4,200 people there. There's still no reason for anyone to leave the area because there's 'no room for them'. This is a total of 2,300 homes for nearly 9,000 people. It's peanuts compared with the building programme in Docklands – not even 10 per cent of what's being built there. Docklands housing will be finished in less than a decade, proving that if the political commitment is there, such house building is no problem. For Spitalfields there isn't that political commitment. It's not that the people in the slums and hotels *can't* be housed in Spitalfields and surrounding wards. It's just that if the government and council have their way, they *won't* be.

There have to be limits to a programme of building rented housing when both local and central government are trying to stop it and there is no London-wide authority to appeal to. Spitalfields is showing signs of reaching the limits. There is still plenty of housing land that's available – the Liberals want to sell off as much as they can. We will look at their strategy to sell off Spitalfields next – it forms part of the onslaught they have unleashed on their own housing stock across the borough. It ties in with the government's intensifying efforts to house the rich at the expense of the poor. The 1988 Housing Act is designed to prevent anything being built in London for the badly housed, for the first time this century. Councils won't have the money to maintain what they've got, let alone build anything new. Housing associations and co-ops will lose some of their grants. They will be forced into expensive private borrowing – and therefore into building housing which the overcrowded of Spitalfields just cannot afford to rent. There seem to be few ways round the regulations. The Tories are expecting small co-ops not just to borrow private money, but to take on liability for contracts over-running their costs, and for long-term major repairs to their houses without any grant aid at all. Even if grants were kept at present levels,

117

the rise in land values means it would be very hard to build anything.

These constraints are already biting deep. Housing association and co-op activity is contracting. In 1985, looking beyond their housing programmes, they had between them outline schemes for 1,257 more homes in Spitalfields and the surrounding wards we've been looking at. By 1988 this had dropped to 762. Few new schemes had come up in those two years, while many of the 1985 possibilities had been snatched by private developers. The schemes that are left are small, on 30 different sites. Big sites, which are easier to develop, have been lost. So it's vital to hold onto the land that's left.

For the people still in slums and hotels, the longer-term prospects are really bleak. Housing programmes take time to enact. What's on site now is still the product of the campaigning of the early 1980s. Local organizations now stand alone against the private developers. Yet Spitalfields itself has changed. Lessons have been learnt in the long march to get the first 800 homes built, But that very success also meant that the hunger for housing has gone from the activities of many groups. Half the people living in the worst housing have been housed. That is bound to change the perceptions and priorities of the community as a whole. Cuts in funding and tighter political control by the Liberals, have severely hampered the activities of local groups on these issues in any case. This underlines the political importance of the network of housing co-operatives. Because they can be sustained through their members' rents, they have a sounder base than other groups. Their unhoused members continue to press for more housing to be built.

Realistically, however, these co-ops and housing associations are only getting more land for housing by doing deals with property developers, rather than by fighting against them. We'll look at the implications of this later.

Spitalfields can house many thousands more people. Who those people will be depends on the balance of political forces. Every development needs to be fought over. Even if the battle is lost, even if developers do steal land which has housed working-class people in Spitalfields for 200 years, it is still not the end of the struggle. No shift in power is irreversible. The private estates like the ones in the Wapping Docks already provide a fast turnover of good-quality housing. These could be bought up and rented to the homeless. It won't happen without a change of government, both nationally and locally. Even then community-based organization will be essential – 'sympathetic' local authorities, like the 1981 GLC Labour administration, did nothing until put under pressure. But Spitalfields isn't going to win on its own any more by special pleading. It must be part of a wider struggle.

6 | Spitalfields for sale

In 1981 only 67 people in Spitalfields owned their own home. This shows starkly the extent to which the population of Spitalfields was living on land which other people owned. With over 95 per cent of the population renting their homes, there can be few communities in Britain more directly at the mercy of landlords and developers.

Even some of the owner-occupiers had not bought their homes from choice. They had wanted council housing but been refused it. Without much ready cash, and with building societies not quick to lend on houses in the Spitalfields slums, large families often had to share small houses in terrible disrepair. Southall is the only place in London which parallels Spitalfields' levels of overcrowding. There, two thirds of the housing is owner-occupied – and Southall people certainly wouldn't choose to live in the conditions they have to put up with. These overcrowded owners are trapped – with no money to repair their homes and no priority for council rehousing. When people are desperate, they'll try anything. The story of George Hooper, who was convicted in July 1984 of obtaining money by deception from 79 Bengali families, is a measure of this. He'd simply shown them photos of a housing association scheme under construction and had persuaded them that by paying him small weekly deposits, they'd be able to buy the houses.

The 1980 Spitalfields Survey showed just 15 per cent of the population were even aspiring to home ownership. Half of these would only buy outside the area. Of the rest, many simply couldn't afford a mortgage. This left about

60 families who wanted to stay in the area and could get a mortgage. Against this number were the thousand households needing somewhere better to rent.

Even with families combining incomes together, Spital-fields could not follow Southall into owner-occupation. Incomes were lower – with 68 per cent of the population earning less than £80 a week in 1980. But opportunities were also fewer – much of the private rented housing had been developed by property companies in the last century. These companies either held onto their property holdings or sold them without breaking them up. Even when single houses came on the market they were in appalling condition. The few such houses being bought by the Spitalfields Housing Co-op were costing over £100,000 each to make habitable. Building societies aren't keen to give mortgages on houses like these. As a result, before the advent of the co-op, many private houses had been bought for cash by local business people who had then rented them out, carrying out the minimum amount of work to maximize their profit.

Rented housing was desperately needed. The councils promoted housing for sale.

The councils' sales strategy

Since the Tories won the 1979 General Election, every tier of government has been in favour of housing for sale in Tower Hamlets, with the exception of the 1981 Labour GLC administration. Yet the Joint Docklands Action Group in its 1987 report *Housing in Docklands* showed that in 1985 three quarters of the Tower Hamlets population had a household income below £8,500 a year. What's more, the gap between average incomes and average house prices has been widening far more quickly in the East End than across London as a whole. Between 1981 and 1985 house prices in Tower Hamlets went up by 115 per cent, twice the London average; and this was before the full effect of the redevelopment of Docklands could be felt.

Housing for sale is going to give very little housing to the existing population of Tower Hamlets. Instead, it must draw in a new and wealthier class of people. Once a market can be established on the edge of the City – which shouldn't be difficult in such a wonderful location – the process should start a momentum of its own, attracting in more people and increasing property prices so that run-down terraces become viable for gentrification. Even tenements can become acceptable studio flats, given the right environment. In the process, dereliction vanishes; unfit housing becomes bijou. For the council, the higher disposable income boosts shopping outlets, increases the value of housing through improvements, while the new East Enders won't be making the same demands on council housing and social services departments. To achieve this turn-round the council spends nothing, while in the longer term it actually makes savings. And the by-product would be that the Bengali families, who'd been privately renting the space, would be pushed out and forced to go elsewhere taking their problems with them. It's a well-worn pattern, seen all over central London and in other major cities. Housing for sale became another factor in the attempted displacement of the Bengali community.

To achieve this, the political parties had to manage the conjuring trick of getting people who can't afford to buy a home to vote for their policy of building housing for sale. One means of doing this was by presenting housing for sale as an antidote to the disintegration of the East End communities, where skilled people of working age have moved out to buy, leaving the elderly, unskilled and unwaged. The white families left behind are still living in council housing, only some of which is modern and little of which is well-maintained. Few people have gardens, virtually no-one has a self-contained house. To some extent because of this, the 'right to buy' has not yet been a great success in Tower Hamlets – less than 3 per cent of the housing stock has gone, with a trickle of 30 or 40 houses a month (out of 50,000) being sold. This may change as people find they can't move except by getting their discount and using it to buy something elsewhere. Certainly, more people are making enquiries. But even if they do this, there has been nothing to buy. The local authorities and housing associations, between them, owned over 90 per cent of the housing stock. Bitterness has increased with the ending of council house-building, which had offered the hope of transfers.

Building houses with gardens for sale seems to offer a way out. But people can't afford them. So in practice, both Labour and Liberal administrations in Tower Hamlets have fronted their sales policies by offering a very small amount of housing for sale to council tenants and people on the waiting list at subsidized prices. This very small amount of housing is given a massive hype – with every single tenant and waiting-list case contacted – creating the idea that it is freely available. In the early 1980s Tower Hamlets sold off dozens of terrace houses in Bow which had been bought in the municipalization programme of the 1970s but never modernized. They followed this with the sale of Riverside Mansions in Wapping. Tenants were decanted to new houses. Their old flats were sold to private developers who had to offer a third of them back to council tenants at discounts. Tenants bought at £26,500 and found that within weeks their flats were worth £65,000. People queued over-night in the streets for what the *East London Advertiser* called 'The Sale of the Century' with 'homes going for a song'.

This is the contradiction behind subsidized housing for sale. If the new owner can resell at market value, the difference between the purchase price and the market value is clear profit. Although the council controlled who got subsidized housing in the first place, they have never controlled the process any further. The second owner is someone who can afford the market price, cutting out all the people the subsidized housing was being provided to help. Yet the Liberals are trying to accelerate the sale of council housing. Under Labour, at least the tenants of Riverside Mansions were rehoused together in new homes. Such considerations no longer apply. Tenants at Bacton Tower and Burnham Estates in Bethnal Green found out through the local paper that the Liberals wanted to sell their homes. Lefevre Walk is going on the market too. Selling estates immediately increases the numbers of the homeless. As the council stock decreases, there will be more and more people needing to fit into what is left. Even if these estates are notionally sold at 'market value', this doesn't take into account the moving out of previous tenants who use up flats which could otherwise have been used to take families out of bed and breakfast hotels.

Yet even these sales are just the cosmetic dressing on the programme to provide central London housing for the wealthy at the expense of the existing working class. This has centred on the London Dockland Development Corporation (LDDC) which has generated an upheaval in the class structure of the borough that has no parallel. The LDDC took control of the housing land in the docklands wards. Originally the council was to be allowed to buy some back. But the LDDC succeeded in multiplying the land values by a factor of ten. Southwark was given £80,000 compensation for land which it was then reoffered for £1 million. Councils couldn't find this money during the years when council housing programmes were completely starved of cash. So the LDDC was happy to see unchecked private development – *Housing in Docklands* provides detailed information on this. During the 1980s, 70 per cent of all new housing in Tower Hamlets will be in Docklands and 87 per cent of that will be private. In the six years to March 1987, 9,319 homes were given planning permission in the Docklands wards.

By 1987, 2,300 private houses had been built in Shadwell and St Katharine's – with at least another 1,500 on the way. Most of this land had originally been planned as council housing. As such it would have transformed the housing prospects of E1, but not only have tenants been kept out, the LDDC's schemes to make some of this housing 'affordable' to local people have been even more laughable than the council's. No controls over resale of subsidized housing were enforced. Up to 20 per cent of these new estates are changing hands before anyone moves in. Businessmen use false local addresses to buy homes and sell them on. Some new residents of luxury housing issue rent books to their friends to show they are 'local' – they then qualify for the subsidized housing which they can sell straight on at vast profit. To make things worse, the council sold off the small amount of land – for 250 homes – which it had been allowed to keep. The Labour administration did two deals. In the first, land was sold to office developers who agreed to build council housing on the Isle of Dogs instead. In the second, developers were allowed to build private housing, handing back 90 units to the council as part of the deal.

Such an enormous transformation obviously has spin-offs – further and further afield across the borough housing for sale becomes viable. The original contradiction remains unresolved. The working-class families who aspired to such housing still aren't getting it. First the Labour and then the Liberal administrations weren't able to satisfy their electoral base. A new class is moving in with allegiance to neither of these factions. The increasing bitterness of disappointed tenants could well split two ways – with a more radical socialist opposition, and an increasingly right-wing Liberal administration using every ploy it knows to keep its support from slipping even further to the right.

Privatizing Spitalfields

These sales policies were tried and tested in Spitalfields, and in every case supported by the local authority. An example was that of the Peabody Trust, whose 63-flat estate on Commercial Street was the first built by the Donation Fund of the Victorian philanthropist, George Peabody. This was made up of small spartan tenements with much bare brick to prevent infestations in the plasterwork. He intended to see such estates of Model Dwellings built 'for the working classes of London' throughout the centre of the capital.

125

In the 1970s the Trust emptied the estate, got planning permission to build offices on a site it owned nearby, with the council making it a condition of the permission that the estate be modernized through its sale to private developers.

In 1982 the scheme was marketed as The Cloisters. It was a remarkable transformation: with enough money, any housing can be made attractive. A few flats were for shared ownership but most were sold outright as short-term convenience housing. Of the first 27 people to move in, no less than 18 had moved out again four years later. Soaring prices led to profit-taking – something the new residents were presumably well versed in. Tower Hamlets Council could have prevented this if it had insisted on the flats being modernized by a housing association. Though the Peabody Trust claimed it would be too expensive to do up for rent, profits from the office development would have paid for it.

There was no real attempt to pretend The Cloisters was going to house local people. This was not the case with the Abbey National Building Society's houses on the ex-GLC site at Howard Buildings. The houses were built by Barratts. Although perhaps best known for building the Dulwich estate which includes Margaret Thatcher's retirement home, Barratts specialises in low-cost volume building using standard designs. So in Spitalfields no thought was given to local need. Almost all the houses had only two bedrooms, and very small ones at that. Sound-proofing was minimal, gardens tiny. As the President of Barratt America was once quoted as saying: 'You give people 80 per cent of the space, 80 per cent of the lifestyle, 80 per cent of the goodies – but at a price they can afford.'

There was a lot of local publicity for the scheme, generating this sense that it was something for 'local people'. The reality was rather different. In 1981 the Abbey National claimed that much of the housing would be rented for just £25 a week on 'assured tenancies' outside Rent Act control. In fact only a handful of houses were rented, and at rents 50 per cent above what was advertised. The Abbey National also claimed at the time of building that 'our housebuilding programme, which we are pursuing without subsidy from any quarter, is and must continue to be related to what people can afford'. But there was a massive subsidy. The GLC bought the site for £667,000 and sold it on for just £165,000, a subsidy of £10,000 on each house built. The GLC also had to rehouse the people living there in council housing nearby. Abbey National didn't bear any of the financial or social cost of this. Hundreds of council houses had been used up to give Abbey National a clear site. Once the houses had been sold, the Abbey National proudly announced that 90 per cent of them had gone to local people from Tower Hamlets. But when pressed, it was admitted that the figure related to residents and not council tenants. The families who really needed to live on that land could only stand and watch as the removal lorries moved in the newcomers' furniture.

But the price was right. Two-bedroom houses cost £26,500 in 1981 and they received 600 completed applications. Few of them were from Spitalfields. Of the 104 houses built, only three went to Bengalis. Even if most people did come from Tower Hamlets, the Abbey National had no means of keeping it that way. After a short period people were free to sell at market value. And within four years over 40 per cent of the original occupants had done just that. Some of the resales are going to Bengali households – there are now 14 on the estate. Families are having to share and overcrowd in order to afford the mortgages. Two families have tried to get permission to build extensions, but this has been bitterly fought by neighbours as the houses are so tightly packed together that any further building would seriously damage the light to other houses.

This Abbey National scheme provided a blue-print. The Tower Hamlets Labour administration followed it up with schemes on their Waterlow Estate, divided from Spitalfields only by the Liverpool Street railway line and potentially a valuable source of rehousing. Once squatters had been bulldozed off part of it, 36 homes for sale were built at Finnis Street for prices similar to those on the GLC site. The sale of

127

the rest of the 1,000 tenement estate followed. Claiming each flat would cost £70,000 to repair, the council was happy to let Barratts buy it up. The tenants weren't consulted even though many wanted to stay on. As part of the deal Barratts had to return 90 flats for council tenants, but the work didn't start on these flats until they had made their profits from fixing up and selling the rest of the estate. The council has controlled who buys these 269 homes. The first homes in Wilmot Street, went, as the *East London Advertiser* described it, 'in a race that rivalled the Harrods sale for thrills'. But this is the end of council involvement.

The Liberal administration has stepped up the privatization of housing. To begin with, it is deliberately turning down chances to build rented housing. For the Selby Street site, there was money from the Housing Corporation ready and waiting, which the Liberals turned down. The Corporation was prepared to give the full funding for 78 rented homes there. The Liberals wanted most of them to be privately financed, to create assured tenancies – which would be too expensive for local people. The Housing Corporation's Regional Manager, Clive Turner, was furious and wrote a letter which was presented to the Bethnal Green Neighbourhood Committee on 9th May 1987:

> The development of 50 per cent of the single family houses on assured tenancies is unworkable within even the most elastic definition of affordable rents. I had hoped I would be allowed to speak to the Committee to avert the decision on assured tenancies as it was clearly made in complete ignorance of the facts.

But the Liberals didn't want houses with 'affordable rents'. They also asked for shared-ownership housing, which would be too expensive for local people. However, by February 1989 they were again faced with having to accept a higher proportion of rented housing because of problems in raising the private finance.

It has been the same story elsewhere. At Spitalfields Market, where they can influence developers to build rented housing, over half is going for sale. They even seem keen to turn some of Spitalfields' park at Allen Gardens into housing for sale. Where the Liberals have had a significant influence, they have allowed 226 of the 367 new homes in Spitalfields to go for sale. Of the 141 rented units, they don't intend to build a single one. They couldn't have followed more closely in the old Labour administration's footsteps if they'd tried.

The Liberals also decided to sell all the council's remaining housing land. Through the first half of 1988 they put the Wentworth site, Code Street, the Gunthorpe Street depot, Bell Lane and 3/5 Toynbee Street into the hands of estate agents for private sale. This is enough land to build at least 100 homes. It is hard to see how they can claim to be worried about a shortage of large houses for the homeless when they're selling the only land where those houses could be built, although there have been discussions with housing associations for the three main sites.

Elsewhere in the borough, the Liberals are getting rid of estates they already own. There was no proposal to do this in Spitalfields until the government announced its Housing Action Trust for Tower Hamlets in the summer of 1988. Generally these Trusts are being set up to privatize council housing, with the tenants being bribed to agree through an enormous injection of public money – only available if they vote themselves out of being council tenants. The six estates chosen were the Holland in Spitalfields, the Boundary to the north, the Berner, Solander Gardens and Shadwell Gardens to the south and the Ocean to the east. Of the seven estates with the highest proportion of Bengali tenants in the Tower Hamlets, only the Chicksand was omitted. Documents seized during a tenant occupation of the offices of the government's consultants, Peat Marwick McLintock, show that the plan was forcibly to move the tenants out of the estates on the City border, decanting them further east onto the Ocean Estate. In this way, a new wall of private development would have been established from the Berner Estate through Spitalfields to the Boundary Estate. The streets of private housing between these estates would have been revalued in the process – forcing out their private tenants too.

Tenant opposition to the Trusts nationwide has been remarkably united. The government first had conceded tenants a vote on whether they wanted a Trust on their estate and then dropped the idea altogether for half the estates originally intended, including the Tower Hamlets six. But there were other factors at work too. The overcrowding on the City fringe estates is so intense that the government consultants couldn't find a way of getting them empty. Nicholas Ridley admitted as much on BBC Radio 4's *PM* programme on 17th March 1989. Effectively it was an admission that the Trusts were never about tackling the worst council housing conditions in the country. They were about profit, and the profit margins just weren't there in Tower Hamlets.

The Liberals' role in this is significant. Leaked minutes of a meeting between Liberal leaders and the Department of the Environment, written by a council officer, showed that the councillors present agreed on these six estates. When the list became public and 500 tenants immediately packed York Hall to protest, the full Liberal group first denied its involvement and then issued a press release declaring 'total opposition' to the Trusts.

The Spitalfields Trust

The growth in owner-occupation in Spitalfields did not just come through the handing over of public sector housing and land. The ideal starting point for gentrification was in the core of 18th century town houses at the side of Hawksmoor's famous Christ Church on Commercial Street. It was an area which could become downright fashionable. This was brought about by the Spitalfields Historic Buildings Trust.

Founded in 1977, the Spitalfields Trust was concerned that over the previous 20 years, 90 of the ward's 230 Georgian houses had been destroyed. Its membership of middle-class aesthetes had in common their burning enthusiasm for Georgian architecture. They not only wanted to save the houses, they wanted to restore them to their 'former glory'. Their commitment to this was extraordinary. They would go to remarkable lengths. Finding dust marks on a plaster wall which showed the outline of a Georgian skirting board, they got new skirting made in facsimile.

But the reality of restoring the houses had a human cost. Most of the remaining Georgian housing was owned by property developers hoping to get office planning permissions. They were four- and five-storey houses, often still containing the long galleries with dormer windows on the top floors that were used for silk weaving. Some houses did still have wooden panelled rooms, delicate plasterwork and sweeping central staircases. But most had fallen into total disrepair. While developers waited their time, the houses either made privately rented slums, or were used as workshops for the clothing industry. The workshops had generally spread out of the backs of the houses to cover the walled gardens with sheds and back-extensions. The Trust's vision of the area was incompatible with workshop uses and public housing. The inevitable result of that was that Bengalis would not be working or living there. They would be replaced by owner-occupiers rich enough to afford the fine detailing of replacement Georgian internal features.

The Trust combined the enthusiasm of the 'new Georgians' with shrewd business sense. It started in 1977 with nothing, squatting two houses in Elder Street which Newlon Housing Trust was about to demolish to make way for rented homes. The Trust knew how to use the media, and a campaign fought from inside the buildings was successful in saving them. As a charity, it then started raising money for all it was worth – from covenants, interest-free loans, grants from bodies like the Historic Buildings Council and even the borough council. They raised enough to buy the buildings and pay off Newlon's abortive architect's fees of £13,000 and then went on to raise enough extra to fund the £74,000 restoration of the buildings to their 'former glory'. The Trust was then able to sell the houses at a profit of over £60,000.

The membership of the Trust was on the move. The Trust published a regular newsletter of available houses in Spitalfields, advising potential buyers to go through the secretary 'to avoid undesirable price competition'. The Trust itself intervened in the market to buy houses that were in need of 'saving'. By 1980 its buying and selling had been so successful that it was able to pay £250,000 for a set of workshops just outside the area. Apart from a small interest-free loan from Baring Brothers, this was financed from private sales.

The purpose of buying the workshops was to create workspace which could be used to move out more of the clothing firms which were still defacing the Georgian houses. To be fair to the Trust, its workshops were an improvement on previous working conditions for many machinists, and it managed to carry the scheme through while keeping the unit rentals relatively low, using secondhand materials. The completion of this scheme allowed all the Bengali machinists to be moved out of the Trust's 'prize' house at 27 Fournier Street, which was double-fronted with a curved central staircase. It was sold on to a member who, according to the newsletter, continued for some time afterwards to reside in another country.

The Trust's activities had created their own momentum. By 1981 it could report that 40 houses had changed hands recently, and the pace was accelerating. In all but exceptional cases, intervention by the Trust was no longer necessary. The next year saw the peak of £24,000 in donations, after which energy in the organization began to ebb. The speed of this transformation was helped by two things. The main property developer, Tarn and Tarn – owners of nearly 40 houses – lost an appeal against the council's refusal to give them office planning permission. They started putting them on the market, helped by a recession in the clothing industry which meant that many of the clothing firms had gone out of business and the houses were becoming empty of their own accord.

They wisely let the houses onto the market slowly, maximizing the profits from the rapidly increasing values which the Trust's activities were generating. As the Trust said of Tarn and Tarn in 1981: 'They are no doubt encouraged by the fact that residential values for such buildings have at last overtaken their value as workshop premises.' And there was plenty of money to be made. When the Trust had bought 5 and 7 Elder Street in 1977, it had paid £3,500 for them, on top of the abortive architect's fees. Seven years later, when two less distinguished houses – at 15 and 17 Fournier Street – came onto the market as derelict shells, they went for £250,000. That is some turn-round in property values. Once they've been restored, they're worth a fortune. By 1988, houses were coming onto the market singly in the £400,000 to £500,000 price range. Indeed, the process which the Trust set in train now seems to have got out of control, as its newsletter of September 1988 ruefully admitted:

> The trouble these days would seem to be not so much lack of money as an excess of it – at least amongst certain well-heeled purchasers of some of the finer 18th century houses, who, having paid several hundred thousand pounds for a derelict hulk, then feel they have a right to pull it about as they think fit.

The Trust's power to intervene in the local market was greatly enhanced by its purchase of 41 Artillery Lane. This had been a grocer's shop. The Trust was charmed, in a suitably Georgian way, by all the old wrappers and posters kept immaculately by the owners over generations. The shop was turned into an office, which Tower Hamlets gave planning permission for. In selling this and the clothing workshops (which had served their purpose), the Trust cleared £455,000. It used this money to buy ten further properties and sites surrounding the Spitalfields Market, mainly owned by the Market's landlords, the City of London. The land will provide new housing with Georgian facades for sale. Some houses will go to Trust members, while others remain in market use. Behind the Trust's thinking here, was the prospect of the redevelopment of the Market. This property holding will give the Trust a powerful voice in what happens – and in any event it will appreciate in value. The Trust was ready for the redevelopment, briefing its own architect to come up with a scheme including 'Georgian' post-Big Bang dealing floors for the City, so that the offices were in harmony with the three surrounding Georgian conservation areas. This scheme was not approved.

The Trust has always reacted furiously to accusations of gentrification. In the summer of 1983, the Trust wrote an angry riposte to *The Guardian* when an article implied this. Although *The Guardian* apologized, it's hard to see why. The Trust has taken three houses directly out of public ownership – the two in Elder Street, and one in Princelet Street owned by the council. The Trust knew that three households were squatting there, and that there were viable schemes to keep the housing in public ownership. It still insisted on the sale going through. It wanted to use the building as an extension to the 'Minority Study Foundation' next door. As people from ethnic minorities are forced to leave the area, it plans a permanent exhibition to show what those people's contribution to the area has been.

But the effects of gentrification are more profound. They are not just driving out the private tenants and clothing workers in the immediate area. They have created a market which is extending into the Victorian housing beyond the '18th century town'. Prices are rocketing. It makes other public housing schemes less viable, and it means there is more competition for each house that becomes empty. The asking price for Woodseer Street cottages is now over £200,000, while the Trust's City border site in Spital Square will further stoke the engines with neo-Georgian flats for sale.

If the Trust had merely wanted to save the architecture, it could have sold the housing it bought to housing associations and co-ops. It did actually do this with one terrace of

Victorian cottages, but remained unimpressed by conversions done by Newlon Housing Trust in 18th century housing. Although some panelling was lost, the tenants were happy enough. The Trust's position was spelt out in 1982:

> The fact is, of course, that many Spitalfields buildings are unsuitable for public housing. They cannot be cut up as flats without disfigurement – there is no doubt that their delicate features are best looked after by owner-occupiers.

No-one was talking about building more flats. The town houses were large – ideal for the large and extended Bengali families of the area.

More houses are now lived in – there are eight occupied in Wilkes Street where there was one ten years ago. But the population in Fournier Street, Wilkes Street and the bottom of Princelet Street has dropped from 152 in 1977 to 115 today. Where there were 100 Bengali people a decade ago, only 45 remain. Throughout, Tower Hamlets Council has supported the work of the Trust. Its planning policies insisted on returning the houses to single family use, with all workshops being stripped out – one member who actually *needed* a workshop appealed against having to do this, but lost – though the council had no strategy for replacing them elsewhere. It gave the Trust money for repair and replacement of Georgian features. It sold the Trust the only housing it owned in the Conservation Area. Above all, it refused to take over the houses owned by Tarn and Tarn. When the council won its battle to prevent Tarn and Tarn turning them into offices at the Public Enquiry in 1980, it insisted that public housing schemes were viable, and said it would be prepared to carry them out. It never did. Instead it wanted a run-down area turned round without public investment. In the process, the people who lived and worked there have been turned out, and a new Spitalfields middle class has been born. Yet it was the Bengalis who were the true heirs to the buildings – they would have been the people able to keep the houses in the mixed use for which they were built, with both living and workshop space.

135

Local demand for ownership surfaces

During the 1980s the proportion of owner-occupiers in Spitalfields will have multiplied five times over – at least 15 per cent of the population will be owning their own homes by the next Census. So far, this enormous growth in owner-occupation has been successful in driving out local people, housing only a handful of the wealthiest.

Despite this, there is a growing demand from within the community from people who want to own their own homes. Certainly it is far greater now than in the survey of 1980. It is centred round successful business people and the increasing numbers of educated Bengalis who for the first time have been able to find professional employment to match their qualifications. But these people cannot afford the market price of the large family houses locally – which would be the only ones suitable for them. For the reasons given above, they too are often not interested in the 'right to buy' their council flats which are usually too small, often in poor condition and sometimes on run-down estates. So they move out to areas such as Upton Park and East Ham where they can afford the mortgages. They appear to be drifting eastwards following the migration of the Jewish East Enders before them. But many are resisting this. Spitalfields is still important to their families – providing all the benefits enumerated earlier. What's more, their position and influence in the local community are weakened if they are living outside it. In a different way, they are raising the question which had taxed the council. How damaging is it to a community if this class is constantly being creamed off and poured into neighbouring boroughs to become home-owners there?

In 1984 a Spitalfields Home-owners group was formed to demand subsidized housing for sale to local people. They argued that this unmet need could only be dealt with by using some of the remaining vacant land to build large family houses for sale. Ironically, their confidence in putting this forward had come largely from the experience of the

Spitalfields Housing Co-op. Many of the members of the group were involved in the co-op and had seen the way in which the co-op had been able to take over derelict land and develop it. Ideally they would have liked the co-op to develop the housing for sale – but this is something which could not be fitted into the co-op's aims.

The group began to compete for land destined for rented housing. Their justification for this was that once the new housing was ready, they'd move out of their council housing, leaving it to someone who needed it urgently. Effectively this creates a system where those who can afford it get houses, and those who can't stay on the old estates. But local business people have another reason for needing to own their homes. Most are very short of capital to develop their business. None has any collateral, against which to borrow. Owning a house bought at a discount might allow them to borrow money to invest in their business – which might mean not only higher profits but also more jobs.

They concentrated on two sites. One was the Shopping Centre, where they insisted the Community Trust scheme should include subsidized housing for sale. The other was council land on the edge of Allen Gardens Park which was big enough for 14 family houses and which the Spitalfields Housing Co-op had been trying to buy. They wanted the land cheap, but they came up with a way of preventing this subsidy from simply going into the hands of the purchaser. Resale was to be controlled. If the houses were built at two thirds of their market value, the resident would only own two thirds of the house. The remainder would still be owned by the development agent. When people left they wouldn't be able to cash in their subsidies – making it possible for other local people to buy. This depends on a non-profit-making development agent – in this case the Spitalfields Small Business Association. Their share of the housing would have created an asset base which would have helped raise money to develop small businesses. The Liberals looked at the idea but decided to put the site on the open market.

Fighting the sales

The danger of the Spitalfields Home-owners group is not so much the small amount of housing for sale that they want for themselves. Their existence and their pressure politics are legitimizing the Liberals' desire to speed up the privatization of housing in the borough. Neither they nor the badly housed will benefit from such a speed-up.

The successful extension of housing for sale in western Tower Hamlets over the last decade has created several very powerful interest groups already. There are the new Georgians. There are the City executives. And then developments on the scale of those in the Wapping docks are bringing in a new professional class of families with children. They have already seriously disturbed the property market although their effect on Spitalfields has not yet been central because the community has won so much land for rented housing. But this will change. More of this kind of housing is planned – both on the site of the Market and next to the Shopping Centre. The Thatcherite policy of submerging the problems of the inner cities with owner-occupiers is already having significant successes. One of Labour's safest seats in London in 1983 was Newham South. With the completion of much of the Docklands housing, it had become a marginal seat just four years later.

Effectively, this is what the Labour council tried to do to Spitalfields but failed. The Liberals are trying again. This time they will have the force of government behind them. They have shown with their early estate sales that tenants unwilling to move will be no obstacle to their plans. The 1988 Housing Act will now make this process much easier by giving private landlords the right to buy council estates and by restricting housing investment to those estates where sales are planned. This doesn't just apply to the estates affected by the Housing Action Trusts. The housing market has now developed to the point where such estate sales could be enormously profitable in Spitalfields. They could also be used as a much sharper weapon in any attack on the Bengali

138

community. The prospect looms of enforced decanting of Bengali families who would be spread thinly across the borough until their problems 'disappear', while their flats are sold off under the excuse that there is a local demand for owner-occupation. The spectre of the slum clearance programme could well return with a vengeance.

Attempts to provide low-cost housing for sale to local people must be seen in this context. Spitalfields cannot afford to be divided about the type of housing it needs. A united campaign for low-rent housing must be sustained. What subsidies there are must go to build for those in greatest need. There are still so many in need precisely because so much housing has been sold. Rented housing in the Wapping Docks could have taken a lot of the strain off Spitalfields. Instead, 3,800 extra houses have actually intensified the housing crisis in E1. Two hundred and fifty more families have already lost homes to owner-occupiers in the Spitalfields developments for sale. Local people wanting to buy must recognize that these sales haven't helped them either – they have been priced out. Local battles for the sites will simply allow outside interests to take everything. If the Whitechapel Community Trust is able to build the Whitechapel Shopping Centre scheme, it will meet local demand for low-cost home-ownership. To campaign further for this type of housing will be dangerous, to say the least.

7 | Space invaders

Outside the Providence Row Night Shelter men and women used to wait every evening. This is one of the few places where you can still get a bed for the night when you haven't got a penny to your name. It was a queue of desperate people hoping for somewhere in one of the unmodernized Victorian dormitories which are administered by the nuns of the next-door convent. The nightly unlocking of the doors opened up a world for the streetdwellers of London which has changed little in a hundred years. Recently, the system changed – you can book in at any time of day. But there's still a queue just down the street at the convent door, where soup and blankets are handed out to those who arrive after the Shelter is full. For years there have been plans to modernize the Shelter, but so far nothing's happened.

Across the road is another building of much the same size. Finished in 1988, it has glaring blue windows framed by a high-tech structure which contains office suites. Eighty yards away is yet another new block which in 1987 had an annual rental of £1.4 million. That would be enough money to build a home for the whole queue of homeless people round the corner at Providence Row every year.

There is nothing more startling in Spitalfields than this poverty rubbing up against the gleaming new buildings of Europe's biggest financial institution – the City of London. Spitalfields developed because it was outside the City – the Huguenot silk weavers avoided the restrictions of the Guilds which operated inside its boundaries. Now the City wants to move onto the land of the people it kept out.

It would seem the most uneven fight, between Britain's poorest and most recently settled residents and some of the world's most powerful financial institutions. There is little the City has to offer the people of Spitalfields – the more money there is invested in the area, the poorer its residents become. Until now the City has made slow progress, despite the encouragement given it by the borough council. Until now. The so-called Big Bang threatens to change all that.

What the developers want

The boundary between Tower Hamlets and the City stretches from Liverpool Street Station to the Tower of London. It wasn't just silk weaving that established itself outside the restrictive practices of the City. The London Docks were built to relieve the chronic congestion in the Pool of London – caused by the City's insistence that ships unloaded there so that the City could collect its dues. So it's a very old boundary, rigidly enforced, which led to the growing division between the financial institutions on one side and manufacturing and trading on the other.

The City reached its peak population around 1850. Relatively speaking, its decline from being the most populous square mile in the world to the uninhabited landscape of office blocks was fast. The working-class housing was pulled down, without the residents being given anywhere else to move to. The City workers were increasingly able to travel into their work. So the City institutions had room to expand within their own boundaries. This continued after the war, first with the redevelopment of what had been bombed, and then with the movement into high-rise blocks.

Computerization was heralded as the weapon which could break the Central London office market apart. New technology implied several things: fewer staff could do the same work; clerical and computer functions could be decentralized to cheaper sites; improved communications meant firms were less dependent on being in Central London generally.

141

But these arguments don't fully apply to the City, with its three main interrelated functions of banking, stocks and share dealing and insurance. Insurance firms that once were a few yards from Lloyds can now afford to be a few hundred yards away. Dealing floors for the Stock Exchange are more spread about the City. But the Exchange isn't going to work with one dealing floor in each major British city, or even in each London borough come to that. And while some banking functions have been moved out, the big banks seem reluctant to move too much too far. The NatWest Computer Centre was sited on the Old Goodsyards behind Leman Street in St Katharine's ward. Even the planned new mega-banking centre at Canary Wharf on the Isle of Dogs is not being started without the Docklands Light Rapid Transit Railway being rammed through underground until it stops dead right under the gold vaults of the Bank of England itself. To work, the City still needs people in close proximity to each other, as well as computers, even if it is able to move some of its clerical functions further afield.

If the City needs to expand, it may take over Fleet Street but it's making slow progress in cutting through the Law Courts and Covent Garden to the West End. The river is less of a barrier than it was – Citibank has offices either side with computer link-ups and a boat shuttling between. North is possible, as the 4 million square feet on what used to be Broad Street Station are proving. But East is best. It's both the nearest and the cheapest. The Stock Exchange and the Lloyds Building are both within 600 metres of the Tower Hamlets boundary. That boundary, so zealously protected, has also been a boundary in property prices, which until recently, has been low on the Tower Hamlets side.

So Spitalfields and St Katharine's wards have found themselves in the front line against City expansion. Things started quietly. In the 1960s many of the Georgian houses in the Elder Street and Artillery Lane Conservation Areas, which had provided rented housing, were taken over as small offices. Some of these firms weren't even City-orientated; others were small insurance and investment consultants. Only two big blocks were built — Rodwell House, and Cromlech House above the 'Big Red Building' of the radio advertising jingles and other shops in Petticoat Lane. Cromlech House even included much industrial space.

The second phase followed as the property market began to pick itself up after the crash of 1973. Big insurance firms – including Minets, Hogg Robinson, Sedgewicks and Frizzells – all decided to move across the City border. At the same time as cutting overheads, this allowed people like Minets to rationalize and shed staff as they moved. Alongside this movement into purpose-built space, speculation started. St Katharine's ward took the brunt of both the move by insurance firms and of the speculators. But Spitalfields was not immune. In the 11 years to the end of 1983, 88 per cent of all new office space granted was in these two wards. One hundred and ten new office developments had been approved.

In Spitalfields, during the middle and late 1970s, small office permissions continued to be the norm. Between 1973 and 1977, 24 were granted, all in Conservation Areas, averaging just 8,000 square feet each – or the size of two large town houses. But Frizzels also moved into new space in Elder Street, and permissions started to be granted for speculative developments. The Central Foundation School for Girls was moved out and the buildings pulled down. The old Police Station and flats above were earmarked. The demolition of the tenements at Brady Street Dwellings was heralded by the news of a multi-storey office block to replace them.

But none of these schemes was built. Through the early 1980s, new developments almost dried up as the table overleaf shows.

The number of new schemes seemed to be tailing away. Tower Hamlets Council's own survey of empty office space suggested it increased on the City fringe by 35.8 per cent between 1982 and 1983. A general orthodoxy was growing that the supply of offices in the central City area was

143

Planning permissions granted

Ward	1978/79 (sq ft)	1980/81 (sq ft)	1982/83 (sq ft)
Spitalfields	616,000	82,000	26,000
St Katharine's	1,057,000	669,000	399,000

outstripping demand. 1983 was the first year in a decade when less than £2 billion had been invested in real estate institutions nationwide.

Almost overnight the picture changed drastically due to two new factors – the 'hot-house' effect of the takeover by the London Docklands Development Corporation in the riverside wards and, more significantly, the impending Big Bang in the City of London. The scale of change is staggering. The largest office scheme in the Docklands area is at Canary Wharf. Ten million square feet of commercial space is going up. If this same area was built as housing, it would make some 6,000 homes – enough for a town the size of Hertford. Canary Wharf will include the tallest building in Europe, will take 2 per cent of Britain's entire annual output of structural steel, and demands a skilled workforce so large that they are having to call in builders from all over Europe. To work, it needs not only the Docklands Railway, but new roads to smash their way through the existing Docklands communities to the City. The Reichmann brothers, who are developing this with over £3 billion of their own money, have already made it work in New York. They built something almost as big on the wrong side of Manhattan and persuaded American Express to move there, buying out all their existing Manhattan space. Where American Express went, others followed. Similar incentives are now being offered to get the Midland Bank to move to Canary Wharf. A golden pathway has been laid between the City and Canary Wharf. Banks and others are buying up space along the line.

This is not disconnected from the Big Bang. But the more immediate pressures on land as a result of the Big Bang will be felt nearer to home. The deregulation of the New York stock exchange resulted in something between a doubling and a tripling of the turnover in shares. More share dealing meant more office space. If the Big Bang follows this pattern, London still has a long way to go, and there are already 70 million square feet of offices in central City locations.

The immediate effect of this is a remarkable explosion in the price of prime office space. Between 1982 and 1986 the price of prime City space changed little, moving up from £30 to £35 a square foot. In 1987 this almost doubled to £60, with the City District Valuer predicting the first £65 a square foot rent before April 1988. Suddenly this transforms the profitability of office development. If developers were making money before, they can now make mints of it. Greed for these unheard-of fortunes lies behind the rebuilding of the City.

After the Big Bang, the number of 'market makers' on the Stock Exchange has risen from five to 25. Each one of these firms needs its own dealing halls – a basic 150,000 square feet of space. This is only the kernel of its operation: more space will be needed – the amount depending on the width and complexity of its other work. The Americans rushed into the London market after deregulation, but the Japanese didn't. Even now, their cautious financial institutions are still weighing up the new London market. If they come in, with the concomitant increased demand for floorspace, other market makers could well be pushed out, reducing demand yet again.

The withdrawal of market makers may have some influence on the amount of office space needed. What is more of a determinant is the volume of share dealing itself. Computers can make deals with each other, the whole process can be vastly speeded up. But at some point each deal has to be recorded on pieces of paper, people need to hold share certificates, tax officers need records to look at.

145

Predicting future volumes of share dealing can be tricky, especially after the crash in share prices in autumn 1987. A year later, the volume of trading was still well below the levels recorded before Black Monday.

The volume of dealing is something which can vary enormously from month to month. But planning, developing, building and letting offices takes years and even decades. Potentially this brings much greater volatility to the central London office market. Without notice, a demand-led market for space could suddenly find itself oversupplied. Nothing underlined this more vividly than the collapse in the value of the big office developers like Rosehaugh and Stanhope when the Stock Market started to slide. While the Stock Market overall lost 24 per cent of its value, the big developers' shares went down by over 50 per cent. Uncertainty in the market has a multiplier effect on the developers.

With the resulting volatility, development becomes a gamble. The way to improve the odds is to hold land with existing office planning permission, and to have the know-how to put up new office space at lightning speed. For the developers, Spitalfields is the ideal place – a blighted bank of land which can be 'harvested' in the quickest possible time.

There is a counterbalance to this. Traditionally office rents have always been at their highest in the very heart of the City, and have tapered off the further away they are from the centre. This has changed. Office space built for the new technology era needs five-foot voids between floors for cables and ducting which is accessible to engineers at times of break-down. Minutes of lost trading is money lost – while faults are traced the show must go on. This space doesn't exist in office blocks built ten years ago, let alone inside the classical porticoes of Threadneedle Street. Thus the new space becomes the most desirable, and commands the highest rent, even if it isn't central. The City understands this. In a desperate attempt to keep the heart of the operation inside its boundaries, the City is being pulled to bits and rebuilt. The Corporation handed out planning consents for 15 million square feet of new office space in 1986 and 1987 alone.

But putting five feet between floors has other implications. Office space is measured and paid for in square feet, not cubic feet. To get the same square footage of office space on a given plot of land you have to build higher, or if that's not allowed by planning regulations, then you need a bigger plot of land. Office blocks need to be 50 per cent taller, or to stand on 50 per cent more land to accommodate the same square footage as they did 20 years ago. The Canary Wharf building, which will stand 200 feet taller than the NatWest Tower, will actually have fewer storeys. Horizontally and vertically, this puts more pressure on Spitalfields.

Central office blocks built 20 years ago are dinosaurs. Those built in the 1970s are on the verge of extinction. The great post-war office redevelopment around London Wall, the phoenix from the blitzed ashes of the City, is itself being ripped apart. From the new ashes come the very wonderful creations of the 1980s. The same process is at work in Spitalfields. The first wave of post-war office development is about to be razed. Cromlech House and the 'Big Red Building on Petticoat Lane' will go. Rodwell House is planned to follow. Office backwaters will be moving, so to speak, onto the Grand Canal, with rents to match. Such are the margins of profit, offices like London Life on Bishopsgate, just five years off the drawing board, are biting the dust.

Development in Spitalfields minimizes the amount of banking being lured to Docklands. That's why the City Corporation, owners of Spitalfields Market, wants to see it redeveloped, even though the Market is profitable and is expanding. It all helps its bid to make the City the world's prime financial institution. New transport plans also put a spotlight on Spitalfields. In 1988 the idea was mooted of extending the East London Branch of the Metropolitan line – south to Dulwich and north to Dalston, while in early 1989 Paul Channon, Transport Minister, announced the spending of £3 billion on public transport in London, including the linking of the British Rail system between Paddington and Liverpool Street by tunnel. Commuters from West Oxford will be sitting at their desks in Spitalfields less than 90 minutes after leaving home. The point where these two routes cross is on Brick Lane. On one side are the derelict Bishopsgate Goodsyards, on the other Truman's Brewery. Grand Metropolitan has just announced the Brewery is to close. Spitalfields was once a fringe location. Now it will be prime space. The Goodsyards, the Brewery, the Market, the Shopping Centre and Whitechapel High Street make 50 acres of development land – 20 per cent of the ward. If the bulk of that became offices, Spitalfields as we know it would no longer exist.

Whitechapel High Street has already seen big developments by the insurance firms. But nothing compared to what is now proposed. Roy Sandhu of Roy Manufacturing owns a site opposite Brick Lane. In 1986 he came up with the suggestion of a 60-storey block with a semi-circular frontage facing back towards the City. Called Central House, it would have been taller than any existing building in Britain, with its architectural inspiration coming from the Manhattan skyline. The planning application, which was outside the council's office guidelines on almost every count, came in only weeks before the 1986 local elections, and was eventually withdrawn. A revised application is still expected. On the other side of the street, plans have been reshaped for a series of blocks which would rip out the City of London Polytechnic, several clothing firms, the Whitechapel Baths, as well as the present shop frontages. In early 1989, new planning applications had been put in which covered half the site. Further schemes were being worked up on the rest, all of which are designed to fit together like the pieces of a jigsaw.

For decades there have been rumours about moving Spitalfields Market out, following on from the demise of Covent Garden and Billingsgate. Nothing happened till now. The present developers, London and Edinburgh, are the first to get the consent of the City Corporation which owns the site, the first with planning permission, the first to get the agreement of many market traders, with a suitable Waltham Forest site to move them to. The Market has been there for 400 years and its right to exist is enshrined in statute. The government is in the process of annulling the statute. Soon only the state of the office market is likely to stand between the developers and this El Dorado.

London and Edinburgh also won British Rail's competition for the redevelopment of the Goodsyards, divided from Truman's Brewery by the railway tracks into Liverpool Street. In July 1989 London and Edinburgh and Grand Metropolitan announced they would develop the two sites together, building over the tracks and creating 20 acres of prime space.

In this climate it is not surprising that when Trafalgar House took over the development of the Shopping Centre site at Whitechapel they wanted to change tack. A 426,000 sq ft triangular mega-office block became the centrepiece of their 'shopping' scheme; when winning the tender, Pengap had insisted a shopping centre was viable in its own right.

These examples simply highlight what is happening. They are not an exhaustive list of Spitalfields development sites. If these were all built, it would bring over 4 million square feet more office space into the immediate area, as the table below shows. Between 1973 and 1983, permission was granted for 924,000 square feet in Spitalfields, of which nearly half was never built and has been re-included in the present applications. The present plans for the ward mean a six-fold increase in the amount of development potentially compressed into a much smaller time-scale.

Add to this what is happening in St Katharine's ward. The workshops of Mansell Street have disappeared. One entire side of the street is re-emerging in the polished marble and granite taste of the new developers. Prescot Street is being gobbled up, while 400,000 square feet are under construction on the site of the Royal Mint. Combined with the space in Spitalfields, this amounts to some five million square feet being built or planned. The City itself has 25

Space invaders

Major potential office schemes in and around Spitalfields

Scheme	Status	Size in sq ft
Rodwell House rebuilding	Has planning permission	188,000
Cromlech House rebuilding	Has planning permission	80,000
Whitechapel High St	Seeking planning permission	218,000
——"——	Under consideration	200,000
Spitalfields Market	Has planning permission	885,000
Shopping Centre	Has planning permission	425,000
Central House	Seeking planning permission	1,250,000
Bishopsgate Goodsyard	Outline scheme	1,000,000
Aldgate Exchange	Seeking planning permission	307,000
Total		4,553,000

million. Thus the eastern fringe is becoming a significant part of the whole redevelopment of the City. Yet all this is only just keeping pace with the Isle of Dogs which itself has another 25 million square feet underway.

Past developments have seriously undermined the fabric of Spitalfields society. The new wave could be devastating. But as with the tidal waves in the Bay of Bengal, there is nothing inevitable about it. In both places, proper planning can prevent the damage.

What development is doing to Spitalfields

The City rid itself of its working-class population nearly 100 years ago. It would like to do the same to Spitalfields today. The west of the ward is already seriously depleted.

The council denies that this is because of office development, but the facts show otherwise. The Census shows that in the 1950s the borough's population dropped by 11 per cent, while remaining relatively stable in Spitalfields. But over the next 20 years, West Spitalfields lost 57 per cent of its people, while the population of the borough as a whole

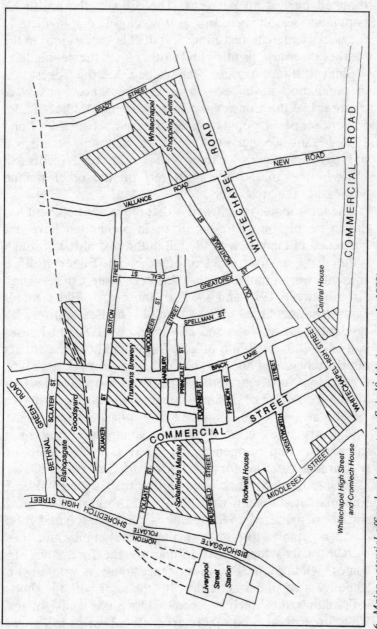

6. *Major potential office developments in Spitalfields (as at early 1989).*

151

dropped by just 16 per cent. The drop in the borough's population wasn't surprising as it was losing employment in the docks and manufacturing. Spitalfields kept its jobs in the Market, brewery, printing and clothing, yet the people left.

Slum clearance has also been blamed. Yet the biggest falls in population have been in areas where no slums were cleared, like the Conservation Area around Artillery Lane; 66 per cent of the population disappeared between 1961 and 1984. Meanwhile, surveys have shown that most people will not leave Spitalfields willingly – 40 per cent of residents still work in the area, while most rely on the other unique advantages the area offers.

The inescapable conclusion is that office development has driven people out. The big drops in population have not happened in tandem with the fall in the rest of the borough – they have been at times of office boom. Eighteen office consents were granted in that Artillery Lane Conservation Area between 1975 and 1984. In the nearby Elder Street Conservation Area, there were 18 houses entirely in residential use in 1956 and no offices. By 1980, 11 houses had been converted into offices. These had been the streets of privately rented housing. Not only were most of the office applications concentrated in the Conservation Areas, a higher proportion of planning applications was successful.

Take away the housing, take away the people, and the whole structure of local services collapses. Local food shops close and re-open as take-away fast food joints or restaurants catering for the lunchtime City trade. Older residents still remember Wentworth Street as the local East End market, bursting with life – with kosher meat, halal chicken slaughtered on the premises, plenty of fish and good cheap vegetables to buy. Now the market comes and goes with the City's lunchbreak. Gone are the food stalls. In comes high fashion clothing and fancy goods, now taking up 85 per cent of all market space. It's the same with the shops – Franklin's the butcher becomes Ossie the jeans. In the High Street there's no supermarket. Woolworths has gone; Boots has gone. The continuing vitality of Brick Lane to the east is a reminder of what Wentworth Street once was. It's a yardstick of what offices have done to the western City edge of the ward. But even in Brick Lane there are warning signs. The owners of the two most successful food supermarkets have started investing, not in more local retailing, but in the property market.

Three schools have disappeared. All West Spitalfields children have to cross a major trunk road to get to school. Doctors' rolls drop – and then surgeries have to move. The Commercial Street post office closed down. Pensioners have to walk into the City to cash their giros, crossing the Market and getting their feet tangled in the netting and packing cases of rotten vegetables. Holland Estate has to be virtually barricaded with metal gates to stop City workers using residents' parking space. This loss of services creates its own pressure – for those who are not young and fit, daily activities become a growing struggle. Even walking the streets becomes subject to the ebb and flow of office workers.

The effects of office development are not confined to sites where development is happening. The expectation of getting more office consents and the increase in land values mean that all land in the area is affected by the pall of office development, and rentals are increasing. As a result land stands empty, waiting for the right moment in the office market. The Central Foundation School for Girls and Brady Street Dwellings were knocked down in the late 1970s; ten years later the sites were still derelict.

But blight is more insidious. As developers buy up land, they keep existing users on shorter and shorter leases to ensure that they can be evicted when the price is right. Surveys have shown that clothing firms in Whitechurch Lane and on Whitechapel High Street were not investing as heavily as they could afford to do, because they were on short leases and unsure of the future. Nothing will now be invested in the infrastructure of the Spitalfields Market, even if London and Edinburgh don't tear it down as soon as they're allowed to. Because there's an outstanding office planning permission the land is almost priceless. Yet its very value means that nothing will be spent on the Market buildings now on the site – it is only valuable so long as the Market buildings are destroyed.

The Fournier Street Conservation Area is a powerful example of this process. While office permission was sought for some of the houses, the number of people living in them dropped from 107 to nought. Clothing firms went in on very short leases; no repairs were done. Some houses actually collapsed. Others were shored up. A key factor in the Inspector's decision to disallow offices in Fournier Street was his concern that this would increase land values in the area.

The effect on land values of office development dictates the use of every piece of surrounding land. The sale of Bishop's Court in Artillery Lane and reletting of space on Middlesex Street in 1987 showed rents moving through the £40 a square foot barrier. If a three-bedroom council flat were let at the same level, the rent would be over £920 a week. In Wapping, Swedish developers were prepared to pay £20 million an acre for office land. If farm land were this price, it would cost the equivalent of the government's entire national housing budget to buy just one small-holding. If there is any chance of offices being built on land, its value will be so great that it will be impossible to use it for any other purpose. To stop land reaching these absurd values, it is important that the planning authority is clear about where it does and does not allow office development.

Even if land is designated for industry or housing, nearby offices still have an effect. The developers of Spitalfields Market have included industrial space in their scheme. By their own admission however, the space will command rentals which are much higher than anything the local clothing trade can afford. This means not only that the trade is shut out of the Market site, but the industrial rentals there will also start pushing up prices in neighbouring streets. These streets are the heart of the clothing industry, based there because industrial rents were so low. Thus an office development on the Market could easily undermine the clothing industry, even though it isn't actually going to involve the demolition of many workshops. It encourages owners of industrial land to sell up. Land values must have been a factor in Grand Metropolitan's decision to close the Brick Lane brewery.

Similarly, residential property prices have shot up. Housing associations and co-operatives have to follow tight cost guidelines set down by the government. As prices go up, it becomes harder to get the government to accept that their schemes are 'value for money'. The shared-ownership housing planned for the site behind the Shopping Centre was conceived when the land was worth £500,000 an acre in 1986. The scheme no longer looked possible when, in early 1988, the site was revalued at £1.38 million an acre. And in the summer of 1988 the Spitalfields Co-op couldn't afford the £494,000 a developer was prepared to cough up for some shops and the remaining 24 slum tenements in Hanbury Street. Shopkeepers were immediately faced with massive rent increases. Less than a year later, the successful purchaser offered the same portfolio back to the co-op without any improvements at £1 million!

The council's justification

This is not an inevitable process. In theory, the council still has sufficient planning powers to confront such develop- ment. It hasn't tried to use them, because the Labour administration courted the developers, while the Liberals have been happy to live with the progeny of that courtship. It was clear to anyone prepared to look that the community is being decimated. Because the Liberals let it go on, the development process becomes another weapon in the attempted break-up of Spitalfields and the dispersal of the Bengali community. The council would deny this vociferously, claiming that office development is bringing three benefits to existing residents of the borough –

employment, a higher rate base to improve services with, and community facilities paid for by the developers. But none of these benefits can be substantiated.

Employment is the key issue. If office development brought jobs it would be a blessing. But it doesn't. Spitalfields residents already have 300,000 jobs within walking distance of their homes. There's probably nowhere in Britain with such a large number of jobs within such a small geographical radius. And yet the 1981 Census shows that in London only Ordnance ward in Newham had a higher rate of unemployment than Spitalfields' 22 per cent, and only Ealing Northcote had a greater proportion of semi-skilled and unskilled workers.

Between 1973 and 1982 10,000 new jobs came to Tower Hamlets – 9,000 of them in banking insurance and finance. This was to be expected from the 3 million square feet of new office space that had been built. Yet the rate of unemployment in the borough went up, the proportion of residents having to work outside the borough increasing from 44 per cent to 49 per cent.

There is a gross mismatch between the skills needed by the expanding City and the skills available to the Spitalfields' unemployed who already have office blocks at their front door. Building more at the back isn't going to give them office work. Locally based training programmes, with adequate child care provision, would give unemployed women some chance in the City jobs market. If those jobs were available to them, the economic prospects for the Bengali community as a whole would be greatly transformed. In a Southwark survey, unemployed women asked for training, childcare and transport to give them an opportunity to work in the City. They did not want offices brought to them – they understood the damage to their communities that would ensue.

Yet the Labour administration in Tower Hamlets mocked its electorate by 'bringing office blocks to the people' without training people to work in them. The Liberals have started asking developers to provide small training packages

– at Canary Wharf and Spitalfields Market for instance – which will benefit a few local people. But by continuing to grant massive office consents, the Liberals confuse the disadvantages of office development and the advantages of office employment, just as the previous administration did.

In almost all the big new developments, the pattern has been for the incoming firm to bring its own workforce. Because new buildings take new technology, this often means the firm can use the move as a way of making people redundant rather than as a job creator. This happened when Minets Insurance moved to Leman Street. It is happening in the moves to the Isle of Dogs: a 1986 survey by local residents there found just 30 local people employed in the entire Enterprise Zone. The exception to this rule was possibly the moving of the NatWest Computer Centre to Alie Street which was quoted at the Borough Plan Enquiry in 1984 as an employer of local school-leavers, but no figures were produced to prove it.

More offices meaning fewer jobs is no contradiction. Between 1961 and 1981 office space in the City went up by 25 per cent while the number of jobs went down by 16 per cent. With rents so high, firms keep their headquarters' functions round the City, moving clerical and technical functions further out. This means office space is increasingly executive and high-technology orientated. Executives and computers mean more space and fewer people. This particularly hits employment opportunities for women who are disproportionately highly represented in the clerical tiers of these organizations.

When put on the defensive, the council has argued that even if local people aren't getting the white-collar jobs in these offices, the developments are so big they are bound to create many hundreds of service jobs – in catering, cleaning, delivering mail etc. Although this is obviously true, it ignores the service jobs that are already there on the ground in the buildings that exist today. Spitalfields Market, for example, needs cafés open throughout the 24 hours, there's casual work from the traders, daily street

157

cleaning and so on. All these jobs will go when offices come.

The second supposed benefit is a higher rate base to improve services. The Labour administration never ceased to be seduced by the very high rates office tenants pay. These can only be spent locally if the government allows it. But rate income by itself is never enough to cover costs. All local authorities rely on central government grants to help provide services. If income from rates goes up, grants go down. So it was always a weak argument. But as the Tories have exerted more and more central control over local authortity finance, the argument has lost all validity. Once the poll tax comes in, the government will be administering a centralized, unified, commercial rate system, with the income distributed nationwide.

In the meantime, there are serious side-effects for the borough's working-class residents from high rateable values being placed on new offices. Housing next door to such places is considered to be more desirable – and its value goes up too. Regardless of the quality of housing, Spital-fields has become an expensive area, which its working-class population cannot afford. Although the poll tax will break this connection, office rates will not save Tower Hamlets residents from paying a high poll tax.

Finally, the council's trump card in justifying offices has been that offices bring 'planning gain'. Section 52 of the 1971 Planning Act gives councils the power to oblige developers to pay for some 'community benefit' along with their commercial scheme. These Section 52 agreements, as they are known, have been the council's pride and joy. Senior planners have even travelled to European conferences to boast about them.

So the council sells office development by claiming that it also provides public housing, community centres, open spaces and so on. But these arguments are a travesty of the planning process. If these things are needed, the land should be zoned to provide them. They can't be squeezed onto the edge of office developments – they should be there instead of them. The land won't accommodate both.

Indeed, Section 52 agreements have often been the means of *getting rid of* community facilities. The Central Foundation School for Girls went to Bow; the Half Moon Theatre to Mile End; clothing jobs were supposed to be moved from Commercial Road to Bethnal Green. There are plans to move the Whitechapel Baths out and the Spitalfields Market to Waltham Forest. Who needs these things moved – local residents or the developers? The council has constructed deals which rip out these community facilities.

The real beneficiaries are the developers. However mistaken the idea of planning gain, if the council were interested in using it to benefit the local working class, people would be consulted over its use. Until the massive Market development, this never happened. The council thought it could decide for itself what the 'community' wanted. One developer paid for repairs to Christ Church used subsequently for cultural events by the new Georgians. Planning gain of £200,000 was paid to the Whitechapel Art Gallery for offices at 52 Commercial Road. This deal got through the development committee by one vote – that cast by Paul Beasley, a Trustee of the Art Gallery but not acting improperly as he did not stand to gain personally.

In some cases, Section 52 agreements have deliberately promoted private housing for the wealthy. Fifty exclusive flats went up on Mansell Street to house needy office executives. Most scandalous was the case of the Peabody Trust, where 63 rented flats were turned into studios for sale as the planning gain for the new office next door, even though Peabody had first built the block precisely to ensure decent rented housing was provided for working-class people in central London. Other Section 52 agreements simply weren't honoured.

However, some rented housing has been built under Section 52 agreements. Newlon Housing Trust led the way in the early 1970s. Its Chair of Trustees was director of two property companies; two other Board members also had property interests, some of which used the link. Newlon got houses for next to nothing. Developers got four office

159

planning permissions. The 1974 Housing Act eventually made it illegal for developers to hold positions on the boards of housing associations in this way.

Newlon separated its activities from those of the developers, but still continued to negotiate housing gain from office developments. The association has ended up with over 50 units of rented housing in West Spitalfields and the Fournier Street Conservation Area. This can't be sneezed at – it provides homes for local people who were previously desperate for somewhere to live. But it's no gain to the housing stock. All the houses Newlon brought back into use had been residential before. The offices which were built in Folgate Street and Blossom Street as a result of these deals had previously been homes and workshops. So the Section 52 deals have led to a reduction in the amount of housing. The planning department, which seems to have problems with the fundamentals of arithmetic, still call this an increase.

More disturbing is that land values are now so high, associations and co-ops just can't afford to build anything *unless* they make deals with developers. Spitalfields Housing Co-op was offered land in Spelman Street by a developer wanting to build offices in Bishopsgate. The deal fell through. But at the next attempt the co-op was offered two 18th century houses in Folgate Street. This will be the first large family housing to rent in West Spitalfields in decades. But that isn't the full story. These very same houses had been modernized ten years previously as part of a planning deal then. They'd stayed in private hands and had been left empty. So when the co-op took them on, this was the second deal on the same two houses. The houses are only going to provide homes for one set of people, but they've provided office planning permission for two sets of developers.

This underlines how useless many of the deals in the 1970s were. When housing was built, much of it remained in the ownership of the developers. They didn't want it. It either stayed empty, or was used as a convenience by businessmen who needed the occasional City stopover. This doesn't happen now because Newlon, the Co-op and Toynbee Housing Associaton have formed a triumvirate: all ready and able to strike deals with developers in exchange for rented housing. As a result Newlon is building in Puma Court and Toynbee hopes to tag flats onto the back of an office planned for Whitechapel High Street. But the Spitalfields Market proposals have upped the ante. The developers are offering 238 homes on the site: 124 for rent (including the 22 there now) and 114 for sale (with 16 at subsidized prices). Eight hundred and forty people would be housed – 70 per cent of them in the rented housing which has the larger units. This housing would be shared between the triumvirate.

Unlike previous deals, however, the developers will build the houses as well as providing the land. This means the associations would have housing outside the government's grant controls. The rents would be pure profit which can be ploughed into other rented developments. The population increase could go a long way towards restoring demand for local services – because no housing would be lost, and much more built. The developers don't stop there. They offer a children's play area, a crèche, a community centre, a fashion marketing centre (included after pressure from the Spitalfields Small Business Association), a law centre, nine shops to meet local needs, £2.5 million for industrial and environmental improvement, £50,000 a year for five years for training – as well as open spaces, shops, small business units and a 'Covent Garden' type area for the new office workers. The training money was tripled and the environmental money doubled by the Parliamentary Commons Committee which decided to revoke the Market's statutory right to exist.

Development on this scale poses political problems. A fashion centre is needed. People have waited ten years to convert Allen Gardens from raw pasture into a park. Above all, the members of the co-op are desperate for the large family housing. Other means of funding these projects have been destroyed by the government – this looks like the only way of getting them off the ground. The developers can afford to provide these things and buy off opposition. Commercial rents will give them an income of at least £500 million over ten years. Community benefit worth £20 million is small change against that income – never mind the increase in capital value of the scheme. But with a development that size, and rents that high, land values in Spitalfields would go wild. Accepting the 'community benefits' is accepting long-term damage. If the scheme goes ahead, no-one will be able to move in Spitalfields without the permission of a developer. People needing housing will have to wait till developers want offices. The Market jobs will go; the clothing industry won't be able to sustain itself against these new rent levels. Meanwhile the area could be blighted while the developers wait their time.

Opposition to the development has been divided. The local Labour Party, taking the long-term view, co-ordinated the campaign against the scheme in Parliament. From this work has emerged a new campaign grouping: 'Save Spitalfields from the Developers'.

Much the same dilemma faces the community living round King's Cross, where the biggest development in Europe is planned. It could bring over 2,000 homes to rent. There, community groups seem more willing to accept the 'new realism' and try to reach a deal, rather than oppose the principle.

Council policies

The Labour council widened its office policy when it brought out its Borough Plan in 1983. This allowed offices anywhere within 400 metres of a 'major transport interchange'. Tower Hill, Aldgate and Liverpool Street were deemed such interchanges, spreading 'hope value' for office development all the way up the western edge of the Borough. It also brought the threat of offices to new areas like Bethnal Green, Mile End and Whitechapel. However, no office permission was supposed to be given where there was existing industrial or residential floorspace. But developers didn't have to worry. Having laid down these guidelines the council cheerfully ignored them. Industrial space has been lost – for example, at 17–19 and 63–65 Prescot Street and at 52 Commercial Road, where 120 jobs were affected.

Housing land has gone as well. In Wapping, the council sold its own housing land to let Citibank in with 600,000 square feet of offices – hundreds of homes were lost. But worse was to follow. The offices weren't even built. This was land which was sold on to the earlier-mentioned Swedish developers prepared to offer £20 million an acre. Someone made tens of millions of pounds just by signing a few pieces of paper. That money was made directly at the expense of the badly housed of Tower Hamlets. Tower Hamlets agreed to this, despite breaking both their primary safeguards – the land was zoned for housing and it was much more than 400 metres from a 'major transport interchange'.

The message was clear. The 'protection' given to housing and industry in order to allay local fears, was worthless, and the council meant it to be worthless. Developers only had to push and they would receive. Even when planning conditions had been imposed, they sometimes seemed confident of getting them overturned. In July 1980 *The Sunday Times* announced the plans of Polly Peck to build an office at 153 Commercial Road, worth £9 million but costing just £2 million to build. Because it was outside the council's office zone, it was hard to see why the office was valued so highly. Polly Peck had to sign an agreement to use the offices themselves or for other firms providing industrial employment in the area. The Liberals released Polly Peck from their agreement on payment of just £300,000 towards some housing association schemes.

The Labour administration seemed pulled along by the vision of the borough unfolded by Paul Beasley through his five years on the board of the LDDC. Major schemes were rushed through even faster until Beasley was no longer able to carry the administration with him, when Central

House came up for approval. The application offered virtually no planning gain, involved the demolition of many clothing workshops and showrooms, broke the council's development density levels and was so large that the council would normally have consulted the public about it. Beasley called an extraordinary meeting of the Development Committee just weeks before the 1986 local elections after which he knew he would not have any part in the administration. But the application was withdrawn.

The Liberals haven't wooed the developers as Beasley's administration did. But they haven't had to: interest in the land is so much higher now. Not until the end of 1988 did they consider rethinking the office policy they had inherited. In the meantime, decisions have continued to undermine existing policy. Houses in Parliament Court, last used for light industrial space, and Leyden Street, used as residential, will become offices. As at October 1988, they had not agreed to renew the planning permission for the rebuilding of the Providence Row Hostel. Instead they are suggesting the hostel might move off the site and be rebuilt elsewhere with the money made from selling the land to a developer. This hardly ties in with a policy which protects existing residential space – but maybe the council doesn't want the single homeless trooping through the prestige redevelopment of the Market site in search of a bed for the night. Indeed, the council's general policy is to push the single homeless out of the borough by cutting down the number of bedspaces available to them.

The Liberals are not getting in the way of the big developments. When they consulted about the alternatives to the Market, they only offered two choices, both of which were massive office developments. They amended the Stepney Labour neighbourhood's planning brief for the sites round Central House, to ensure tall office buildings would be acceptable. They supported Trafalgar House putting offices in their Shopping Centre plan. They are happy to see the Goodsyards site go for offices – although their planning brief for the Brewery now specifically excludes offices and seeks to return the area to its traditional street pattern.

The response of Spitalfields

Fighting offices has united Spitalfields people as nothing has since the slums were cleared. Virtually no-one in the ward wants more of it eaten up by office space. But stopping offices is no easy task. It took community organizations the best part of a decade to defeat Greycoats who wanted to develop the rest of the South Bank at Waterloo – and organizations there had the support of the GLC and the two borough councils throughout. That support made a lot of difference because the planning policies for the area clearly favoured what the community wanted. In Spitalfields things were different. The council and community were at logger-heads. Despite this, community organizations used the planning process to the full in opposing the council. Consultation is built into planning law. Anyone can object to planning applications, anyone can appear at Public Enquiries, anyone can make comments on District Plans. But the local authority doesn't have to take any notice.

Objections were lodged systematically by the Local Committee and the Spitalfields Housing and Planning Rights Service as each new Spitalfields office application arrived. If the council supported the application, it still went through. If the council was unhappy about the details, it would use the community organizations' objections as an added justification for refusal. Objections never changed the council's mind.

Community organizations also fought their corner at Public Enquiries. Twice, in 1980 and 1983, the council and community were apparently on the same side. Both times the developers were defeated: the Fournier Street Conserva-tion Area was kept as housing; some of Artillery Lane was preserved as clothing workshops. These appeared to be important victories, with Inspectors' reports endorsing principles which local people held dear. But they were short-lived. At Enquiry, the council committed itself to modernizing many Fournier Street houses for council tenants. In the event, it encouraged the 'new Georgians' to take them away from the homeless who needed them. In Artillery Lane it simply gave planning permission which it had previously refused.

This was devastating. The Enquiries showed that the council's guidelines were sound and could prevent the worst excesses of development. But by consistently breaking their own guidelines, they created precedents which meant that the guidelines could not be used again at future Enquiries. Developers would just have to point at all the exceptions that had already been agreed, and Inspectors would nod the development their way.

Failing at that level, the long-stop for the community was the Public Enquiry into the council's statutory Borough Plan. But a carefully argued case, presented jointly by seven community groups, cut no ice with the Inspector. He supported the council's planning policies – washing his hands of the problem that they didn't observe their own safeguards and guidelines. It was up to them how they implemented their policies, he said. With the Inspector taking this view, the planning process becomes pointless. However bad the council's policies, they were nothing like as bad as the reality of unfettered office development. Yet the people most immediately affected by these breaches of planning policy are given no legal powers whatever to prevent the abuse.

Nowhere is it truer than in the planning process that if participation changed anything, they wouldn't allow it. Such participation, especially arguing a case at Public Enquiry, is very demanding. It is also very one-sided. Developers have inexhaustible supplies of money, experts, legal back-up and time. Community groups can only fight with their own energy and commitment. However cynical of the planning process, once entered it is a remorseless tread-mill.

Progressive disillusion with this has been compounded by the Tory government. Effectively, it isn't just in Docklands that they have got rid of planning controls. Even when Inspectors are unhappy about office development, they are now overridden in the Department of the Environment at

Marsham Street. Inspectors didn't support the development of Hays Wharf. It went ahead. Even the LDDC has refused some offices which would block out the Tower of London and Tower Bridge. The developers only have to squeal to Marsham Street – and the permissions come in.

So the fight against offices was never contained by the structures of planning legislation. In Docklands, the Joint Docklands Action Group already had a tradition of campaigning against office development. From the late 1970s, the Local Committee and the Housing and Planning Rights Service (SHAPRS) generated reports and press releases against the developers. It was one of these – *What's Happening to West Spitalfields?*, published in 1980 – which caused Tower Hamlets Council in conjunction with the GLC to cut SHAPRS' funding at three weeks notice. It meant that for a time energy was diverted into simply keeping SHAPRS afloat.

SHAPRS got enormous support in this fight for survival through the autumn of 1980. Angry pickets hurled abuse as the councillors walked up the Town Hall steps to try and vote the organization out of existence. But loyalty to the organization was based much more on its housing work than on its confrontation over the council's office policy. This points to a weakness in the campaigning against office development. Although community activists readily accepted the arguments against offices, there were always more immediate and easier issues to organize round. Why fight a developer for a few houses when there are acres of empty council-owned housing land lying empty? Only occasionally did anger erupt, as when the Whitechapel Art Gallery's 'planning gain' meant 120 clothing workers going down the road. The Liberals were eventually successful in closing down both the Local Committee and SHAPRS (which had survived Beasley's attempts to cut it). It took the Market proposal to reassemble a coherent campaign to Save Spitalfields from the Developers. Based entirely on voluntary effort, without funding or workers, it had its work cut out to cover the ground.

For a time in the early 1980s, a more effective challenge to council policy was mounted by Spitalfields' alliance with the Campaign for Homes in Central London – CHiCL. There was nowhere quite like Spitalfields, but the remorseless pressure from office developers was affecting all the working-class communities left in central London – from Pimlico to King's Cross, Docklands to Battersea. These groups gave support to each other at the big Public Enquiries with London-wide significance – like Coin Street and Hays Wharf, opposite the Tower of London. But their main strategy was to get new London-wide planning policies adopted which would protect remaining working-class communities in the central area from further commercial pressure. The 1981 Labour GLC started revising the Greater London Development Plan. From this emerged the 'Community Areas' policy, nurtured by CHiCL and designed to protect the central London communities. The GLC could block the largest commercial developments, fund organizations in the Community Areas, and promote developments which would strengthen those communities. It started to do all this and was abolished.

The abolition of the GLC was essential to the Tories precisely because policies like this were in danger of working. The priority given to Spitalfields through this policy had meant that local pressure was successful in getting two housing sites developed. It also brought money for other things – notably the Asian Women's Centre and Davenant Community Centre. But most important, it meant the strategic planning authority was lining up alongside community organizations in the fight against more offices.

Now there is no strategic planning authority for London. Instead all power rests with the Department of the Environment. Their March 1989 Draft Guidelines for Strategic Planning in London are terrifying. If adopted, these Guidelines would override any council trying to control business development, while they single out the City's eastern fringe as an area where office expansion should be encouraged. Borough councils will be obliged to take account of these guidelines in their local plans. If they are adopted, planning is over; market forces will reign supreme.

8 | Unpicking the seams

Work has been the magnet, drawing people into Spitalfields. The big employers of 100 years ago have survived until now – Spitalfields Market, the clothing industry, the brewery, Liverpool Street station and the City. The street markets are still alive – Wentworth Street, Petticoat Lane, Brick Lane. They have all profited from the endless supply of unskilled and semi-skilled labour which Spitalfields has had to offer. Yet that paradox remains: London's second-highest area of unemployment is where there are the most jobs. This puts great responsibility on the local authority. First it should protect and expand the areas of work available to the workforce. Secondly it should be working to break the community's dependence on badly paid unskilled work.

Tower Hamlets has, until recently, done little about either of these things, while its planning policies have attacked the main sources of work available to the Bangladeshi community in clothing and catering. Without work, the Bengalis' central reason for being in the area would be taken away from them. The economic underpinning of their community would start to collapse.

Clothing

Central to the integrity of the Bengali community is the clothing industry. We've seen the complex web of inter-dependency there is between the Bengali workforce and the industry. Two thirds of all Asian people living in Spitalfields work in clothing. Despite a whole generation growing up

170

around the sweatshops, Bangladeshi people have been unable to break their dependency on the industry. Neither have they been able to get any real control over the processes. Few have made it to become manufacturers or wholesalers in their own right. At best, they have been able to keep small firms going, which have been reliant on orders passed down to them by the manufacturers. At worst, they have been in and out of work in the endless seasonal cycle which means that in the low season production can be as little as a quarter of what it is at its peak.

The only significant change which the Bangladeshi labour force has brought about is the growth of the leatherwear sector. Teddy boys and Rockers were around as the Bengalis arrived in the East End. For the first time leather was a down-market fashion. The new workforce was quick to fill the gap. It is now a major part of the clothing sector in Tower Hamlets. Such is its pre-eminence in the British leather manufacture market, that, nationwide, 98 of the 229 manufacturers listed in Yellow Pages in 1982 were in Tower Hamlets. Most of those firms were in three clusters, one in the heart of Spitalfields, one centred on Weavers ward to the north and the other in St Mary's to the south.

The clothing industry in Tower Hamlets appears to be in a state of permanent crisis. Thirty-four thousand people in Stepney and Poplar worked in clothing in the 1930s. Today there are probably no more than 7,000. Men's tailoring has gone almost altogether. What remains is mostly women's fashion, clothes for catalogue firms, and leatherwear. Exact numbers are hard to come by. In 1981, only 4,600 people were still recorded as working in the industry in the whole borough. But homeworkers never appear in these figures – employers don't recognize them as employees, while the workers themselves don't want the taxman to take anything of the tiny amounts they earn. Because demand varies with the seasons, numbers employed also vary wildly from month to month. The Spitalfields Survey in the summer of 1981 – which certainly didn't pick up many women homeworkers – estimated 1,000 people were working in clothing in the

171

ward. But even taking this into account, Spitalfields has a predominantly male workforce – which is unusual in the London clothing industry generally.

With these fluctuations in the workforce, there are fluctuations in the firms themselves. Nigel Perry, in his 1982 report for Tower Hamlets Council on the leather industry, went to meet 14 firms which had been trading two years previously – only five were still in business. Some firms go bust, others go into voluntary liquidation to avoid paying debts – mostly to the Inland Revenue. They then start again under another name. This isn't so difficult when 83 per cent of clothing firms in London employ less than 25 people. This myriad of small firms, going in and out of business, taking people on and laying them off, is the heart of the industry.

The constant crisis is dictated as much as anything by the structure of the industry. Retailing is increasingly controlled by big firms. To the traditional High Street names of the 1970s, Principles, Benetton, Next and others have been added in the last few years. The new shops have made headway with 'designer' wear – often it's the label that counts. Traditional firms have had to fight back. Although more of the market is in fewer hands, there's a greater emphasis on wider ranges of well-designed good-quality clothes. Because they're big firms, they can afford computers which feed back sales figures from the shops to tell them with almost daily sensitivity which lines are selling and which aren't.

So although the retailers are big, they don't need to order long runs of clothes. With a wide range of design they can watch what's selling and reorder what's successful. This way they keep to a minimum the amount of capital tied up in stockpiles. Stockpiled fashion clothing is always dangerous, as fashions change, making stocks unsaleable.

The increased emphasis on short runs of fashion clothes should be good news for Spitalfields because its survival has depended upon its ability to respond instantly to the immediate demand and short runs of the high fashion business. The future should be assured. But unless the industry is restructured, the network of Spitalfields work-shops just won't be able to meet this new demand.

Between the High Street retailer and the sweated labour of women in their Spitalfields homes is a pyramid of wholesalers, manfacturers, contractors and sub-contractors. Not every item of clothing goes through each layer of the pyramid. But, commonly, a manufacturer designs a garment and provides the cloth to a contractor who cuts it, makes it up and trims it. (The small firms these contractors run are known as 'cut, make and trim', or CMT for short.) The contractor can then sub-contract any part of this, and the sub-contractor may farm out to homeworkers for lining, overlocking, button-holing and suchlike.

Internationally, profit margins in the clothing industry have gone down over the last 20 years. Big producers have made big redundancies. With profits being squeezed anyway, this pyramid structure in London is a disaster. At each level, profit must be extracted. Very few local Bangladeshis are more than CMT contractors. These CMT firms are all competing against each other to get manufacturers' orders. They cut their prices to the bone to get any work at all, and most of the profits stay with the manufacturer.

Wafer-thin profit margins mean poor wages. The Low Pay Unit was suggesting as late as 1984 that three quarters of homeworkers were still earning less than £1 an hour. In 1986 average factory rates were £92 a week for women and £130 for men. Most Spitalfields workshops pay well below this average. But any average doesn't show up the likely periods of unemployment between seasonal peaks of demand. Because most workers are self-employed, there's no holiday pay, no contract, no National Insurance contributions, no safety net, no union. Instead, more money is lost to accountants who have to sort out each worker's tax for the Inland Revenue. The poverty of Spitalfields is enmeshed in this sweated trade.

Working conditions are no better than the pay. Work-shops are set up anywhere. Old sheds with no natural light

173

except through leaky skylights, unused storerooms above shops and restaurants, and tenement basements are all homes to the machinists. In October 1983, five Punjabi women were burnt to death in such a place above a betting shop in Mile End. The only means of escape was a steep, narrow, wooden staircase from the first floor to the street. Afterwards the Health and Safety Executive published a report on conditions in the industry. The unions said it was a whitewash. Even so, of 100 London workshops visited, 31 had dangerous machinery, 38 defective steam plant, 39 electrical faults and 41 had other fire hazards. Fifteen of the workshops were structurally unsound, and a large proportion didn't have a proper toilet or place to wash.

These conditions aren't just bad for the workers. They're bad for business. Production is inefficient in bad space with old machinery. The most skilled workers will be drawn away to places which can offer better pay and conditions. Fewer skilled workers means less ability to compete for high-quality, better-paid work. Profits are cut yet further.

The fragmentation of tiny firms leads to further problems. The sub-contractors and outworkers are all self-employed, working on piece rates. Each person stitches together a whole garment. In this set-up there's no space for in-house training. People learn as they go along. A highly skilled machinist may be producing excellent women's coats, while his nephew sitting next to him, just out of school and learning the trade, is putting his first efforts into that same batch of coats. Yet there may be dozens of these small sub-contracting workshops all working on the same order. When the coats are all collected together by a manufacturer and sent off to the High Street retailer, their quality could vary enormously, even in the output from the same sub-contractor.

Fragmentation at the bottom with a few big retailers at the top means power is all in the retailers' hands. A mass of CMT firms all undercutting each other ensures the retailers have absolute flexibility – they don't have to deal with the labour problems of the seasonal variations in demand, while they know they're getting their clothes made at rock-bottom prices. The advent of new technology means that this old system doesn't suit the retailers as well as it used to. The small CMT firms never have the capital to afford the computer-aided design technology needed for the service the retailers now expect.

The lack of capital is particularly acute in Spitalfields. Remember that people started working in the industry 25 years ago with the intention of making enough money to go back to Bangladesh for good. Those few who have made money have invested it in land back home. While this may benefit the family there, the children here are faced with taking over a small business now desperately in need of capital investment, with no collateral against which to raise it.

A further difficulty in raising capital is the seasonality and volatility of the industry. Colossal peaks and troughs in production between the autumn and spring fashion seasons make financial planning difficult, and make it harder to maximize the use of expensive machinery. In the leather trade there is only one season – winter. Yet there is no way of planning production for one winter on the basis of what happened the year before, even if all the people you supply are still placing orders. After two hard winters, the mild winter of 1987/8 was ruinous – orders for leather outerwear declined drastically. Nigel Perry's survey found that most leather firms had no business plan for more than *two weeks* ahead. Seasonal fluctuations are now less attractive to the workforce too. Working in blistering conditions for four or five months, 16 hours a day, seven days a week in order to make enough money to survive the rest of the year was never a picnic. It had its compensations while the families were in Bangladesh – it gave time for holidays. Now the families are here, things are different.

Until recently the industry just demanded human flexibility – the gruelling long hours interspersed with stretches of unemployment which meant Spitalfields always had the workforce to respond to any new order, however urgent, however big. Now the retailers want more. Changes in design are ever more frequent, re-ordering ever more urgent. Computers are needed to help with design, to change design, to plan how to cut cloth so the minimum is wasted, even to help with sewing. This is an industry where computers aren't fundamentally about putting people out of work, they're about speed of response, variety of design, cutting down on overheads. With computers, short-run fashion clothing can be made nearly as cheaply as mass-produced stuff. However sweated the Spitalfields workforce becomes, they will be hard put to provide this flexibility without computers.

This means the work will either go to larger firms elsewhere in the country, or it will be taken overseas. The Pakistani leather wholesalers are placing more orders back in Pakistan. Wages there are even cheaper, the apprentice-ship system guarantees high quality and made-up jackets can be flown over quickly.

Unpicking the stitches

Throughout London, local authorities have been looking at ways of safeguarding the jobs in the clothing industry, while at the same time improving pay and conditions. Tower Hamlets has an Industrial Development Office, and its staff have been trying to find ways of supporting the industry locally. They're not getting very far, and this isn't surprising. We've already seen that encouragement of office development is putting land values far beyond what the clothing industry can afford. This means that an industry that is already under-capitalized won't be able to develop purpose-built workshop space. The permissions given to turn workshops into offices suggest that the council is not concerned enough about the industry. As was shown in the last chapter, safeguards protecting industrial space have been rendered worthless by the council's breaches of its own planning policies.

All this encourages clothing firms which do start to make money to re-invest not in the industry but in the property market. This is no idle threat. In the E1 postal district there are only four clothing manufacturers employing more than 50 people. Polly Peck and Roy Manufacturing are using the profits from the industry for property speculation. This is being helped along by the government's changes to what are known as 'use classes'. The use of a building cannot be changed to something in a different class without planning permission. But the Tories have just included offices and light industrial in the same use class – which means permission no longer has to be gained to turn clothing workshops into offices.

Although these policies attack the industry generally, Spitalfields appears to have been singled out. From 1979 the Labour council worked to designate the area immediately to the north of the ward as an 'Industrial Improvement Area'. This is where the Industrial Development Office has put its grant money – both to help clothing firms with the rent, and also to subsidize modernization of workshops. Despite representations, they refused to extend this Improvement Area to Spitalfields even though many more of the workshops are concentrated there. Instead, the Labour administration supported policies which have deliberately driven the workshops out of the mixed-use buildings where they have traditionally been housed.

The Spitalfields Small Business Association on the other hand, set up just after the Industrial Improvement Area was declared, has tried to keep the mixed use of houses and workshops in Hanbury Street and Princelet Street. In this way, men can use their sewing machines in the workshops at the back of their gardens. They can take the children to and from school, do the shopping, pop home for lunch and generally keep in touch with their family in the way that they are used to. The planning department has tried, and fortunately failed, to get the Association to move its workshops elsewhere. Given what's happened to land prices, the workshops must stay where they are or cease to

177

exist. Spitalfields doesn't fit neatly onto a map where each land use is coloured separately – shops, houses, workshops don't divide up in the way planners are taught they should.

Even if Spitalfields were the wrong place for the clothing industry (which it isn't), there's no sign of the council – under either Labour and Liberal administrations – planning for it anywhere else. They haven't built workshops elsewhere. Labour left it to the Greater London Enterprise Board to come up with a plan for new industrial space in the Brick Lane Improvement Area. This was an ambitious idea, trying to draw into one space lively designers and local producers. When the Liberals took power they scrapped the plan altogether, even though they weren't putting the money up. Instead it was proposed to turn the derelict acreage which it was going to stand on into 'open space', which would placate the 'Liberal' vote on the nearby Granby Estate. The message is clear.

Given this framework, the Industrial Development Office of the council hasn't much room for manoeuvre. It has tried getting export orders to give firms work to carry them through between seasons. It has given grants – but rent grants are fairly fruitless when office planning permissions are driving rent values up. It has tried to get better training initiatives underway. Until now, the council hadn't been prepared to put up the money that would be needed to do this well.

If the council had any real commitment to the industry, there would be ways of helping it. Other councils are now supporting a strategy of targeting help on larger firms that are viable, that have a coherent business plan and that recognise unions. The biggest success with this approach has so far been with the firm of Mark Anthony in Haringey, which employs 200 people, with 200 more working for subcontractors on site – where quality control can be sustained. Pay and conditions are above average, though not brilliant. There's a crêche and a union office. Success with a small number of large firms will create more jobs than all the work with the small contractors of Spitalfields. It also makes best use of limited council money and time – council investment is easier to monitor.

But it doesn't really help Spitalfields with only four large firms, at least two of which are happy to invest profits in office development. The small firms will never prosper as they are. But as they employ over half the Bangladeshi men of Spitalfields, they can't be discarded either. Methods of co-operation need to be developed to do two things at once – ending the dependency of local contractors on the big manufacturers and wholesalers, while creating units of production that can profit from computerization. This involves drawing together good designers and local producers who can then jointly market finished products direct to the retailers. The middlemen would be cut out. Profit margins would increase, opening the way to all the advantages of the bigger producers.

This solution is expecting a lot. Small firms used to undercutting each other will have to co-operate, or even merge, and share machinery. They will have to work with designers in a partnership they have no experience of. They will have to start marketing, when that has always been left to firms many tiers above them. They will have to plan ahead, when they've been used to surviving from week to week. The women at home will need training to move into the new more highly skilled workshop jobs. The fashion marketing centre in the redeveloped Spitalfields Market would help but the space won't be used unless there's money to staff and run it.

Neither the Labour administration nor, until recently, this Liberal one showed much sign of wanting to tackle the industry's problems. Yet they know very well that if the local clothing industry collapsed, the tap root to the local Bangladeshi economy would be severed.

Cooking the goose

In the clothing industry, Bangladeshi people can look for jobs inside their own community. The same is true in catering. The 'Indian' restaurant may seem a staple of most high streets. But the industry is still expanding in several ways which benefit the people of Spitalfields. Firstly, restaurants are now viable in towns that never had them before. High streets that used to have just one restaurant now often seem to be able to absorb two or three. As new restaurants establish themselves, relatives from Spitalfields are often called on to help out. Then in Central London the successful up-market Last Days of the Raj in Covent Garden has become the patriarch of a family of such restaurants, as well as being the source of many imitations.

More rich people are eating Indian food and are expecting, getting and paying for higher-quality meals. From being a cheap eat, 'Indian' restaurants are increasingly cashing in on the wave of nostalgia for the British Raj, pandering to it in the overall experience they aim to give people when they come for a meal. It all means more jobs for cooks, bar staff and waiters.

Brick Lane has itself become a 'cult' place to eat. People come from all over London for the 'experience' of eating there in the evenings, while at lunchtimes more and more City workers make the ten-minute walk for a Brick Lane curry. This is one area of the local economy which *has* benefited from the expansion of the City. In a dozen years there's been a transformation. In the mid-1970s only the Clifton was a serious restaurant. There was a scattering of formica-topped cafe establishments catering for local trade. Many of them have made the transition into smart restaurants, many more have started up. Around the heart of Spitalfields there are now around 30 'Indian' eating places, nearly half of which have opened in the last three years. A council survey of these and 14 other food outlets submitted to the Bethnal Green Neighbourhood Committee in March 1989 showed that they employed around 200 people. Most lived locally and at least half had got their jobs through family or word of mouth.

Working in the restaurants has advantages over the clothing trade, but the basic pay and conditions aren't among them. Pay can be as little as £80 a week, with waiters being expected to pick up the rest in tips. Although not to be relied on, tips are sometimes lucrative. However, basic pay is now much higher in eating places near the City. Hours are anti-social, and most places are open seven days a week, so time off is sporadic. But seasonal fluctuations aren't so significant, continuity of employment is reasonably secure. As the expectations of the quality of Indian food have risen, so has the importance of the chef: almost always a man, a good chef can now demand a high price for his services. But not all restaurants have good chefs, not all pay good money.

Setting up a restaurant in Brick Lane is nothing like as expensive as in the West End, yet it can open up with the 'goodwill' of London already on the doorstep. As capital is in short supply, many restaurants are opened by partner-ships of friends or relatives – sometimes these people run the restaurants, sometimes they employ others.

Just as Brick Lane was developing into this unique attraction, the planners stepped in yet again. They claimed that restaurants were taking away valuable retail space. So during the second half of 1987 they recommended refusal of planning permission for restaurants at 73 and 78 Brick Lane, and of fast food joints at 11 and 41 Wentworth Street. There are two inconsistencies in this. Firstly, it is the planning department itself that is responsible for most of the loss of retail space. It insisted on the demolition of 11 shops at 97-115 Brick Lane. All the shops at the north end of Brick Lane are being run down deliberately – planning policies exclude these shops from the Brick Lane shopping area completely. At the Bethnal Green end, the Lane now looks semi-derelict. The department has also allowed shops to be turned into offices in the Artillery Lane Conservation Area. Secondly, its justification for offices has always been that they generate service jobs in places like cafes and restaurants. Indeed, the council survey showed that office development had helped the restaurant boom. Its review of policy on Brick Lane in early 1988 did finally recognize the employment value of the restaurants, but it still wouldn't recommend a restaurant at No 73. It stopped another at No 53, because of loss of industrial space, while allowing wine bars in old industrial space in Artillery Lane.

Brick Lane is actually an excellent shopping centre for the Bangladeshi community. To prove this, a small survey of outlying estates was done by community groups in 1984. Most Bangladeshi families in Poplar and Bow still came back to Brick Lane to shop every week. Undeniably, it isn't so good for the white population. Especially in West Spital-fields where much of the housing has been stripped away, the remaining white people are such a small community they haven't got the purchasing power to support the shops – like butchers and fishmongers – they need. Stopping restaurants won't bring these shops back, while suggesting that restaurants are the reason why these shops have gone appears as a classic divide and rule tactic. In fact; the council survey showed that the restaurants bought most of their ingredients from the local shops.

In general then, planning policies have worked against both the clothing and catering industries – the only two sectors where significant numbers of Bangladeshis are employed.

The council keeps its own doors bolted

While the council has planned against the clothing and catering industries, it has done little to open its own jobs to the Bangladeshi community. Even before the Liberals took over, the council advertised itself as an Equal Opportunities Employer. But there's still little sign of a policy that will change the profile of the workforce. No records are publicly available of its ethnic composition.

Under enormous pressure Bengali professionals are moving into the front lines of social services and housing. These front line placements often mean that it is Bengali employees who have to face the Bengali anger about the failures in council services. Their number on the interview desks is not reflected in the management behind them. Then where are the Bengali building workers? Dustmen? Drivers? Receptionists? Swimming pool attendants? Clerical workers? Cleaners?

With the council's failure to employ Bangladeshis, it is not surprising that it hasn't made this an issue with other employers in the borough, or with the City firms moving in. Truman's Brewery in Brick Lane is a good example. It employed 700 people, but virtually no Bangladeshis – who are not prevented by their Muslim faith from working in such a place. Jobs went from father to son, and anyone applying for work used to need two referees already working there. In 1971 Truman's was taken over by Grand Metropolitan, which doubled the area used by the brewery and halved the workforce – an investment in plant, not people. Most of Wilkes Street and some of Woodseer Street have disappeared in the process, with a loss of housing and workshops. The council doled out planning permissions for all this without Truman's having to compensate the local community – least of all through a local recruitment policy. The Labour administration would appear to have been well placed to put pressure on: George Desmond was both a Labour councillor and a Truman's shop steward – in one memorable day turning up for work in the morning, and returning after lunch as Mayor, in his garb, to open one of brewery extensions. In retirement he became a Truman's publican. But Truman's headed off any attempts to influence the way it expanded – there was always the threat of pulling out of the borough altogether if it couldn't get what it wanted. Yet having got the land it wanted, it is going to move out of the borough anyway.

Local training initiatives have been set up. The Training Forum set up courses in both clothing and catering, and tried to attract local women to learn there. Tower Hamlets Advanced Technology Training has been providing courses which would equip people to compete for the jobs the City has to offer. The Liberals have cut funding to both these organizations which, serious in itself, also jeopardizes money coming from the EC. Otherwise, Bengali men and women are beginning to gain access to medical, teaching, social work and nursing training courses. But so far, numbers are tiny.

However, by the beginning of 1989 the Bethnal Green Neighbourhood Committee was showing signs of taking training and the local economy more seriously. It adopted a training policy which, among other things, aimed to set up a training centre and crêche to meet local needs, and to involve developers in negotiations over providing local jobs and funding training programmes. It is also looking at the needs of local industries – starting with the restaurants and the furniture trade.

The government, worried about the potential volatility of an area with an unskilled workforce and so few people with any stake in its business activity, has put in one of its Task Force teams to 'improve people's employablility' and to encourage small businesses. It has given money to existing training initiatives; it has suggested turning Brick Lane into a Bengali equivalent of Soho's 'Chinatown'. But it is not going to be part of its brief to confront the fundamental issues facing local industries.

So after 25 years' work, the Bangladeshi employment base is still dangerously narrow – relying almost exclusively on clothing and catering businesses which they themselves control. The council can't be held responsible for this – it doesn't control the jobs market. But planning policies have worked against these industries, while council employment practice has been no example. The Bangladeshi community has won permanent housing. But this isn't enough on its own if unemployment becomes permanent too.

9 | Breaking the bounds

We've seen how housing and commercial *development* have put pressure on Spitalfields. But, with nearly 90 per cent of the housing stock owned by local authorities and housing associations, a much higher proportion than anywhere else in Britain, it's just as important to look at the way that housing was *managed*. Councils had direct power to control the movement of almost the entire population. Given what's gone before, it isn't surprising this power was used against Spitalfields. There were three main intertwining strands, which this section of the book deals with: the way housing was allocated (Chapter 10); the way the homeless were treated (Chapter 11); and – the strand this chapter deals with – the way the existence of racist violence determined where the council placed people. These were the three factors in the attempted break-up of the Bengali community so that it would be dispersed thinly across the borough's worst estates – estates which the councils had decided should be its homelands.

Racist traditions in the East End were not invented by the local councils. But the way housing was managed allowed racist violence to develop to the point where it became very difficult for Bengali people to exercise any choice about where they wanted to live. This made it all the easier for the councils to force Bengali people onto the estates which had been set aside for them.

There was nothing inevitable about this process. Things could have been, and in some cases have been, very different. Despite tensions, racial harassment on Chicksand and Holland Estates, for example, is extremely unusual.

And although the tenants' associations have mainly been run by white tenants, they have a proud record of winning improvements to their estates which have benefited everyone. On both estates Bengalis were more heavily concentrated in the oldest blocks; and on both estates the improvements started with these blocks – major re-landscaping on Chicksand, and complete modernization on the Holland – before works started on Denning Point and the new Chicksand where more white tenants lived. They are successful, popular, multi-racial estates. Racism has not been abolished, but equally it has not been allowed to dominate. It's an environment where Bengali women have relative freedom of movement, where children can play outside without fear. This has been achieved in no small part through forums like the Local Committee, through the meeting of groups and individuals, and through debate and argument about the right of *all* local people to live on the estates. Above all, nearly everyone, Asian or white, is living on the estates because they have *chosen* to live there, and have not been forced into it by council housing policy.

Custom and practice

Communities across Tower Hamlets have been uprooted by slum clearance, have seen the younger generation move up and away, and are now confronted by Docklands homes they've always dreamt of, but cannot afford. So people feel defensive, want to keep what is left of family and friends, and resent how they've been marginalized in the 'new East End'. They want to make sure there is council housing for their families to move into as their children grow up. The GLC owned most of the E1 estates. As a London-wide body it could bring in new tenants from anywhere. Communities defended themselves by insisting that the best housing was given to the tenants who'd been there longest. As people move on in life, they will want to better themselves – no-one wants to get stuck at the top of a walk-up block, if that's where they landed when they first moved into council housing.

A substantial body of tenants would justify this concept of a 'fair' housing system as this woman does in a letter to the *East London Advertiser*, written in August 1982:

> Over the years and with a growing family, we have gone from one estate to another, a little better each time until five years ago when we moved to the Glamis Estate. It took me 27 years to achieve the best but I appreciate it because I've also had the worst. Would the Asians from Shadwell Gardens [an estate of 1930s walk-up blocks] appreciate a place like mine if they had one? These people seem to be quite happy living in their own environment: after all, it's what they have made it . . .

> Please try and remember there are still English people living in the East End and we have always been here. So fair's fair. Let everyone work their way up the housing ladder and prove they deserve the Glamis and Exmouth estates.

The white tenants who resented Bengalis being given the new houses at Davenant Street would have said much the same. Yet there are concepts here which can be traced back for over 100 years, to the builders of the first East End working-class tenement estates. Sydney Waterlow, whose company built the Waterlow Estate which has already been mentioned, said of his housing policy in 1866:

> The wisest plan is to meet the wants of that portion of the working class most worth working for – those earning £1 5s to £2 per week; and that as the pressure on this class is lightened, and better accommodation provided for their use, the class immediately beneath them will shift into the quarters from which they gradually migrate; that this will be repeated until at last the lowest of all – those comprising what may emphatically be called the lower orders, and who are least likely to appreciate the comforts of a decent home – will slowly, but surely receive their share of the benefits enjoyed proportionately by those above them.

187

These are standard 'Victorian values'. By constantly building new housing, you create a 'housing ladder' up which people climb throughout their lives, always keeping their relative class position. The writer in the *Advertiser* hardly dissents from this. Although she nows sees it is possible for people like her to move from the worst to the best housing, she agrees with Sydney Waterlow that 'the lower orders' ('Asians') are unlikely to appreciate 'the comforts of a decent home' ('a place like mine').

She is a class above the 'Asians' and her housing should reflect that. In July 1983, another letter in the *Advertiser* from a tenant on the Tarling Estate takes the argument a stage further:

> We're sick and tired of priority treatment being given to coloured people who have not lived in the East End for long. Our children are being forced to find homes outside the borough and our families are splitting up as they watch a steady stream of coloured people moving into flats and houses.

The real issues are there – children being forced out, communities being broken up. The problem is that 'coloured people', who have been able to climb over them, are getting out of their rightful place at the bottom of the ladder because they 'have not lived in the East End for long'. The logical extension of this is the position of organizations of white tenants like 'Fair Play' which demanded a 'whites first' allocations policy. Once again the *Advertiser* gave them plenty of publicity – so much indeed that it provoked a protest picket outside its offices in the summer of 1984. But take the argument one step further still and you reach the position held by a tenant on the Lincoln Estate in Bow, which she expressed at a public meeting in July 1984 to discuss violence against Bengali tenants on the estate, and which was reported in the 1984 Annual Report of the Community Alliance for Police Accountability:

> I'll tell you what you should do – you should put all these people [the Bengalis] in Fairfoot Road – and I'll drop a petrol bomb on them.

Although with the last quote we have reached the most extreme position which only a small minority would agree with, there are two points to remember. Firstly, she was making no idle threat. Bengalis were petrol-bombed out of their home in nearby Electric House, just one year later; while a Bengali council officer narrowly escaped being deliberately run over by a car leaving that very meeting. Secondly, the justification for petrol-bombing is still based on the theory of a housing ladder. It's just that, for the petrol-bomber, the people who get out of their place on the ladder should be murdered to restore order.

The housing ladder perpetuates the Victorian concepts of the respectable working class and the lower orders. It engenders division and competition between the badly housed. By putting the people you have chosen to discriminate against in the worst housing, it perpetuates the myth that these people actually *create* bad housing conditions. The system will only work at all, so long as there is a constant supply of new housing coming on tap, into which the people at the top of the ladder can move. This was true until the end of the 1970s, but, as Thatcherite policies have taken their grip, the supply of new housing has dried up. Movement stops. People who haven't got a foot on the ladder are never going to get housed at all. Those at the top have nowhere to go either. Frustrations and resentment build up. Hence the frantic attempts to provide housing for sale that these people can afford – like the revamping of the Waterlow Estate itself. But not enough people *can* afford this extra step. The system becomes inherently unstable, with the thwarted ambitions of the people at the top and the desperation of the homeless people unable to get on at the bottom. The system ensures that people on different rungs of the ladder will start arguing amongst themselves, rather than recognizing their common enemy – the State – which has coldly decided to stop providing affordable housing for the working class at all. Racism is a vital catalyst in these divisions.

But for the Bengalis, the ladder presented further practical problems. It didn't recognize the 20 years they might have already spent in the borough before even asking for council housing. It didn't recognize housing need – council housing allocated on the ladder principle simply wouldn't be able to target rehousing on those in the worst conditions. Then there was a higher proportion of large Bengali families who weren't going to fit into the existing mix of council housing – which was almost exclusively of small flats. They'd never get anywhere at all, unless large new houses were built, and they were allowed to move into them. Clearly the ladder was not a tenable basis on which to allocate public housing.

In theory, this wasn't a problem. Neither Tower Hamlets nor the GLC used the housing ladder system to allocate housing. Instead allocation was done according to need. 'Need' is a difficult thing to define. How do you compare the needs of a family of six renting one private room that has no kitchen or hot water with a single-parent council tenant in a one-bedroom flat on the top floor of a block without a lift? Both families will be desperate. On the other hand, it would not be sensible to leave a pensioner couple in a four-bedroom flat which they were given 30 years before when they had five children. A wise allocations system will be able to respond to all these very different needs, *including* the needs of the people who wrote those letters to the *Advertiser*. Their needs are just as real as everyone else's; but their needs shouldn't override other people's.

It isn't easy, and no system is perfect. The systems published by the GLC and Tower Hamlets had their faults, but they certainly gave the badly housed of Spitalfields high priority, alongside the homeless and tenants in urgent need of transfer. Essentially they recognized that it was people's immediate housing conditions that gave them priority for rehousing. The length of time people had already spent in council housing was not, officially, of much importance; nor was the way that people 'kept' their homes. In theory the system accepted that Bengali people had the *same* right to housing in the East End as anyone else.

Potentially this meant there would be a major clash with those tenants, already living in good housing, who believed in the housing ladder. When Bengali families, living in appalling conditions in slum clearance areas, started knocking on the council's door for rehousing, many of them qualified for the empty flats which were right next door to people who had taken '27 years to achieve the best'. Yet there was no confrontation. On estate after estate the Bengalis never arrived. Especially in the homes built *after* Bengalis had started applying for housing, there wasn't a Bengali face to be seen.

GLC officers – the inside view

The absence of Bengalis on the good-quality GLC estates was not surprising. Although the GLC *officially* allocated its housing according to need, its senior housing managers were still faithful to the housing ladder principle. Len Bennett, the Controller of Housing until 1982, had himself grown up in Poplar. When he left the GLC at the end of July 1982, he wrote a letter to the *East London Advertiser* complaining about 'outside elements' stirring up dissatisfaction inside a Bengali community which would otherwise have been quite content with the housing it was living in. It started:

I recall my happy childhood days in Poplar when there was no obvious 'class' distinction – we were all poor and we all lived in poor housing. With our peculiar Cockney humour we looked forward each week to a penny bath at Poplar Baths.

On marriage we were glad of a room in mum's house with all mod cons in the back yard: two rooms in somebody else's house was idyllic progress up the housing ladder. We waited interminably for the borough or the LCC to make us an offer of accommodation which was rarely declined because to get an offer was like winning the Irish Sweepstake. Many tried to shorten the process by telling 'The Housing' that 'mum has chucked us out', knowing full well that the polite response from

191

these shrewd housing officers of local origin would be: 'Then tell your mum to chuck you back again because we have nothing for you.'

These principles persisted: council housing is a privilege which people have to wait their turn for and where there is a shortage of such housing there are always people who will lie to get it. In a letter to the Spitalfields Project in March 1982, he saw the housing ladder as an inevitability:

The effect of most housing schemes [on people] whatever their ethnic origin is that they come into the public rented sector via the older properties.

Effectively this meant he was preventing Bengalis from moving onto the newer estates in Spitalfields and the surrounding wards of E1. Instead they would be forced to move onto old estates in parts of the borough where they did not want to live. He justified this in the same letter:

The Joint Management Committee [of Tower Hamlets and the GLC] has consistently said that the foreseeable solution to the housing problems of the Spitalfields residents lies in the public stock beyond the E1 area and is following the earlier policies of both councils in doing all it can to encourage movement to other areas of the borough. It must be understood that other areas of the borough have the same or similar conditions and the Joint Management Committee's concerns must be for Borough residents as a whole.

If you can't follow the logic of this, it's not surprising. On the one hand he's coming up with a 'solution' to the housing crisis in Spitalfields. On the other, he's denying there is a crisis. These were the contradictions of allocating housing on the housing ladder while trying to justify actions on the grounds of housing need.

So, on the ladder principle, the GLC systematically offered Bengalis the oldest estates, But while they were carrying out this policy, some officers were telling the public that Bengalis were having the best reserved for them. This was dynamite, bound to mobilize racist militants. Len Hudson, one of the assistant district housing managers, wrote in January 1983 in *London Town*, the GLC Staff Association journal, of the white tenants of the East End:

> What are their feelings likely to be as they see scarce resources channelled to helping minority groups, preference given to such groups by law in the competition for the increasingly few jobs available, 'positive discrimination' ensuring that minority groups get a disproportionate share of better-quality local authority housing?

These views were nourishment to the National Front. Peter Mitchell, its Waltham Forest candidate in the 1983 General Election, regurgitated them:

> Many councils now operate a 'Blacks First' policy. This was admitted by Len Hudson who wrote in January 1983 edition of *London Town* magazine that Pro-Black, Anti-White housing policies are driving whites to 'Trot off and vote NF'.

Hudson was a senior officer, confident enough to put these views into print. He was never disciplined, let alone dismissed, by the left-Labour GLC administration. His views were repeated over the counter. White tenants asking about specific empty flats were told they couldn't have them 'because they're reserved for Bengalis'. Such tactics were inflammatory. The suggestion that this ethos was prevalent in the department generally was backed up by Dr Deborah Phillips, an independent researcher who was asked by the GLC to study the allocations process in the GLC Housing Department during 1984. She confirmed there was a 'widespread belief that Bengalis are now getting priority treatment and a disproportionate amount of scarce financial resources' and that there were suspicions that 'Bengalis are using allegations of harassment to achieve a quick transfer to a better property'. An internal memo explaining why Bengalis weren't on the Exmouth Estate commented that there were 'difficulties which result from housing families who enjoy a different social and culinary style in blocks with internal access and where the aroma of more savoury cooking tends to permeate the immediate area'. Most damning, she said:

> A disturbing level of racist comment and joking was witnessed by the researcher. Bengalis in particular were commonly stereotyped as dirty, trouble makers, and causing problems on estates . . . Several officers . . . offered remarkably similar solutions, that is, to put all the Bengalis together in E1 and to allocate them to poorer estates; their view was that they would turn them into slums anyway.

We seem to be back once again with the ideas of Sydney Waterlow. Yet without interpreters, even the well-intentioned GLC officers frequently misunderstood what Bengali tenants were talking about. Combining these factors, the Housing Department's approach often had echoes from the British administration of the Raj, which is where, of course, more of the roots of this racism can be found.

Dividing up the borough

By keeping Bengalis off the better estates the GLC confirmed and reinforced the beliefs of the racist tenants. Keeping good estates white was clearly the way the system was *supposed* to work. At first, there was no resistance from the Bengali families either. While numbers were small, they were made offers on the old estates in and around Spitalfields. Getting permanent housing in Spitalfields at that time was so precious that its quality was a very secondary consideration. Also, after the street battles of 1978, the estates became a place of relative safety. Old Chicksand, old Holland and Wheler House in Spitalfields started filling up, as did the Boundary to the north, and the

Berner, Shadwell Gardens and Solander Gardens to the south. By and large, it was these estates which the government wanted to turn into a Housing Action Trust.) Although most of the flats on these estates were later modernized, they then had no central heating, no fitted kitchens, 1930s sanitary ware and suffered from condensation. Obviously, on the ladder principle, the people who'd been in these flats previously were expecting something better, and moved out when they were offered it.

By the late 1970s these old estates were nearly full of Bengali families. They were a majority of tenants in Wheler House, on the old Chicksand and in Shadwell Gardens. None of these tenants moved on up the ladder, so flats came empty less often. At the same time many more families started arriving to join their men. The GLC had to find somewhere else to put them. The Bengali families themselves wanted to move out onto the other estates surrounding Spitalfields. Dozens, then hundreds, then thousands of application forms were being filed in the Housing Department asking for 'Stepney', 'Aldgate', 'E1 postal district only', 'Spitalfields', 'Brick Lane area', 'Chicksand or Berner Estate'. The combinations were endless, the message the same. But each time they asked, they got the same letter back – 'If they weren't prepared to widen their area of choice there was little hope of housing them.'

Yet inside their area of choice was a massive spread of estates which Bengalis had scarcely set foot in. Although Spitalfields was being stripped of its housing through slum clearance, there was still a plentiful supply of housing in the surrounding wards. Precisely because the building programme was being sabotaged in Spitalfields, surrounding estates became an increasingly important potential source of rehousing. This arc of estates ran from Virginia Road, Granby Street, Hereford and Avebury in the north to the Cleveland, Exmouth, Mountmorres, Pitsea and Glamis in the east, and South Quay by the London Docks and St George's in the south. It was a massive resource. Including

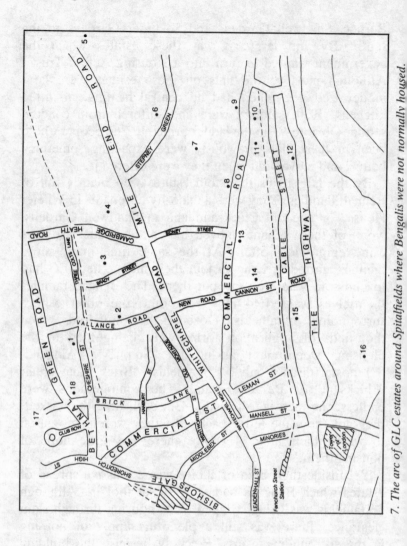

7. The arc of GLC estates around Spitalfields where Bengalis were not normally housed.

Barnado Gardens 10
Bigland 14
Cleveland 4
Collingwood 3
Exmouth 8
Fulbourne 2
Glamis 12
Globe Wharf 5
Granby 18
Hereford 1
Mountmorres 9
Pitsea 11
Rectory Square 6
St George's 15
South Quay 16
Stifford 7
Virginia Road 17
Watney Market 13

new estates being built at the time, it amounted to some 5,500 homes, with several hundred of them coming empty every year.

Without new homes in Spitalfields, the councils could either move Bengalis into this surrounding arc of good housing, or they could try and force them onto more of the old walk-up blocks scattered round the borough. The first GLC attempt to disperse Bengali families in the mid-1970s ended up with those families moving back, after merciless harassment, to squat flats in Stepney. They had no protection, and the GLC refused them transfers on the grounds of harassment. At that time such a ground didn't even exist on a GLC computer that included 200 possible reasons for people wanting to move.

Although it wouldn't be easy for Bengalis to move into this surrounding arc – racists were certain to take action against them – many families were clearly prepared to take this on. They would be living in the area they wanted – with work and support networks at hand. But they were not prepared to defend themselves on estates which they would never have chosen, if they had been the most peaceful in the world. Despite this, the GLC drew up a list of four or five 1930s estates across the borough, which they wanted to move Bengalis to, putting them in a dangerous new environment while at the same time cutting them off from their sources of work and support. These estates included Bow Bridge and Coventry Cross in Bow, Burdett in Limehouse and the Ocean at Mile End. No consultation was undertaken with the Bengali community about this choice, although the GLC did get the agreement of a fundamentalist Muslim group, Da Watal Islam, to the setting up of a prayer room on Coventry Cross. Because the GLC knew these estates would be unpopular, they could only move onto them families who had no choice about where to live. These were the homeless who were waiting for rehousing in temporary places or in hotels, and who were told they would only get one offer of permanent housing – otherwise they would be homeless again, and no-one would help them then.

The level of attacks was terrible. A survey of 32 of the first families on Coventry Cross showed that all but four of them had been attacked, 59 per cent of them were unemployed, and – most significantly – all but four had been given no choice about moving there. Coventry Cross had been their one and only 'offer'. Refusing it meant homelessness again. Len Bennett described this 'success' in a report of 1978:

> An interesting development has recently taken place, however, in the housing of Bengalis . . . as a number of them have accepted alternative accommodation on the Coventry Cross Estate in Bow, E3, which is an area which they have previously refused and it may well be that because sufficient Bengalis have moved in there, they feel that they have obtained 'safety in numbers'.

There is no recognition here of the coercion, nor of the violence unleashed against the families, nor the fact that many people lost work by moving away from their source of employment.

Sue Davis, a community worker based near Coventry Cross, helped fight for the rehousing of these families. In some cases, she itemized every single attack, and sent details in writing to the GLC. She kept a record of the response. The District Housing Office just refused to accept the evidence put in front of it. The reports were either untrue (why hadn't it been reported to the police?), exaggerated, a misunderstanding, children having 'fun', or not racist because not all the perpetrators were white. On one famous occasion it even wrote a letter to assure a tenant that a lit, petrol-soaked rag pushed through the letter box was 'not an incendiary device'.

In just one case she succeeded in getting agreement to a transfer. This family had been hit, had virtually had their front door busted in while they were inside, and had their washing taken from the line and then returned alight through the letter box. As usual GLC officers denied anything was happening. After two years of these attacks,

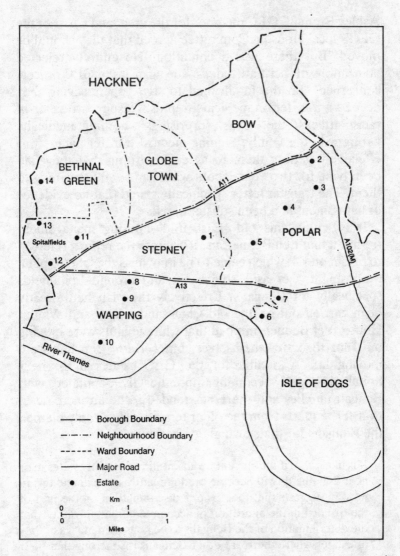

Boundary 14	Ocean 1
Bow Bridge 2	St Vincent 6
Burdett 5	Shadwell Gardens 8
Chicksand 11	Solander Gardens 9
Coventry Cross 3	Wapping 10
Holland 12	Wheler House 13
Lincoln 4	Will Crooks 7

8. GLC estates in Tower Hamlets usually offered to Bengalis.

Ashley Bramall, GLC member for the area, and Chair of the GLC's local Housing Committee agreed that they should be moved. But there was a condition. He entirely rejected 'allegations of racist attitudes made against the GLC officers concerned'. So the family had to sign papers saying they needed a transfer on medical grounds. Despite two years of racist attacks, there was, surprisingly, nothing medically wrong with the family. Signing medical transfer papers was effectively getting them to agree in writing that they had been lying for two years about what had been happening to them. The transfer letter specifically stated that no evidence of harassment had been substantiated.

It is within this old 'East End' housing management tradition that Len Bennett in 1978 wrote the report, referred to in Chapter 4, which came to be known as the 'ghetto plan' proposing to set aside blocks in and around Spitalfields specifically for Bengalis. Effectively the plan had already been carried out on the old Chicksand Estate and Wheler House. Yet Bennett implied that white tenants were moving out, not to better themselves, but *because* Bengalis were moving in: 'A number of the GLC estates in or near Spitalfields [are] becoming quite heavily populated with Bengali families and there has tended to be an increase in transfer requests from the older tenants.' He openly blamed the Bengalis for their own ghettoization:

It is likely that if the current trends continue certain estates in or near Spitalfields will become predominantly Bengali and this in no way suggests that there is any discrimination on the part of the Council in the allocation of accommodation but rather that the determination of the Bengalis to be housed in blocks of flats or estates where there are other Bengalis is so strong that their wish is creating the sitation which until recently was considered undesirable, namely the creation of an exclusive area for a certain racial group.

But such a ghetto can only exist where an ethnic minority is both living in the worst housing *and* is forced to stay there because it isn't given any other choices. Peter Shore, the local MP and Secretary of State for the Environment at the time, understood this. He called in Horace Cutler, then leader of the Tory GLC, and demanded that Bengalis be given a 'proper and real choice'.

It was a choice which the GLC was refusing to give. The Bengali Housing Action Group demanded rehousing anywhere on the 13 estates it named, many of which were of good quality and had remained a hallowed white preserve. This was the Bengali community's first attempt to define where it wanted to live, and the 'ghetto plan' was there to head them off by confining Bengalis to specific blocks.

But these blocks were never named. This left white tenants afraid they'd be forcibly transferred to let Bengalis in. They'd seen enough friends and relatives forced out already. They were the ones who'd hung on. They didn't want to fight that battle again so their anger and hostility was predictable. It was a dangerous time to rouse it – these were the weeks of Altab Ali's murder and the smashing up of Brick Lane. Bengali groups were equally afraid for the opposite reasons – if blocks were to be set aside, they would only be the worst that could be dredged up, while, with the level of violence being what it was, such blocks would be almost indefensible. Most groups, Bengali and white, took a principled position in favour of multi-racial estates.

The plan was discussed at what has come to be known as the 'ghetto meeting' of June 13th, 1978. Over 500 local people turned up to put their views to Jean Tatham, the Tory Chair of Housing. The meeting was held under the blaze of television lights in the Montefiore Centre in Hanbury Street, with hundreds of people being locked out because the numbers inside were on the point of breaking fire regulations.

The meeting is remembered for its apparent unanimity. Ahmed Fakhruddin from the Bengali Action Group forced his way to the front of the hall waving a paper spelling out the group's opposition. Bill Kelly, Chair of the Chicksand Community Action Group, recognized that this was in line with what his tenants were demanding on the Chicksand

Estate. The meeting was taken by storm. Everyone was against the plan and together they got it scrapped. What was agreed instead is still a matter for debate. But at the time it seemed Bengali people had won the right to rehousing in the area they had chosen.

The politicians were confused. At the meeting Jean Tatham claimed she'd been misunderstood. She said: 'We are talking about 300 Bengali families spread over some 3,500 flats in the area of their choice.' But that is precisely what Len Bennett's report was *not* talking about. He wanted designated blocks and no choice. Horace Cutler, then GLC leader, started out thinking Len Bennett's proposals were the demands of the Bengali community. Even Ken Livingstone, by then Labour's housing spokesman, and the Labour group were slow to oppose the plan because it took them time to untangle the confusions too. So suspicions the affair had stirred did not die. At the council meeting where the 'ghetto plan' was 'officially' buried, white tenants from Holland Estate shouted from the gallery that they were living in the dustbin of London, and that the GLC was doing nothing for the white community. Although the GLC voted that the 'housing stock under GLC management will be allocated solely on the basis of housing need and that it neither has been nor will be organized on a racially segregated basis', the policy of disparate ghettoes continued regardless. More families went onto Coventry Cross, St Vincent's, Will Crooks and Burdett. The white estates of Stepney stayed 'clean'.

Tower Hamlets Council didn't have the same choices as the GLC. It had built virtually no housing in Stepney anyway, and was reliant on the old estates built mostly in the 1950s. Its housing department did not have such a prevalent racist ethos. Bengalis were offered housing on some of the Stepney estates. Officers even produced material to counter some of the moves by racists to exclude Bengalis. But local councillors had a lot more control. They could deluge lettings officers with what are known as members' enquiries. These were often specific requests to house named indivi-

duals in particular flats. In this way, the largest Stepney
estate, at Sidney Street, was difficult for Bengalis to move
onto in any case, because Sidney Street was a refuge for
many of the elderly Jewish people who'd been moved out of
the tenement estates and few people moved away.

This meant that Tower Hamlets was soon facing the same
problem as the GLC. There weren't enough empty flats on
the old Stepney estates. Nothing new was being built.
Officers could either demand that the better GLC estates in
Stepney be opened up, or join in the attempts to disperse the
Bengali community. They chose the latter course. Tower
Hamlets' attitude became clear in 1983, when community
organizations had built sufficient strength to force the
first allocations of new housing to Bengalis (which will
be detailed later). These allocations met with violent
resistance from racist tenants. Bernard Kilroy, Tower
Hamlets Assistant Director of Housing, commented:

> The experience heightens the need for avoiding any kind of
> 'white cordon' of estates around E1 where strains created by
> housing shortages so easily make ethnic minority families a
> scapegoat.

His solution to avoid this 'cordon' was not to confront the
racism on these estates, but instead to do just what the GLC
had been trying:

> To make other areas of the Borough more acceptable to
> Bengali families (by ensuring a sense of security, a provision of
> community facilities and perhaps local work).

Like the GLC he was effectively supporting the 'white
cordon' by trying to move the Bengalis beyond it. Although
that was his proposal, he ensured neither security, nor
community facilities, nor work, before placing the first
Bengali families on his chosen estate – the Teviot in Poplar.
Unlike the GLC, limited consultation was carried out with
community organizations who advised that no-one should be

forced onto the estate against their will. Community workers there, in touch with local white youth, warned that moving Bengalis onto the estate would be a disaster. Despite the warnings, 14 families were moved into the two oldest blocks in the spring of 1984. As at Coventry Cross they were homeless and had no choice. The violence was unprecedented. In the first few weeks they suffered 46 racist attacks, many on children. People were hospitalized. Even community workers visiting the families were threatened.

Violence then flared up when homeless families were moved onto the Bethnal Green Estate. Thirteen recently arrived families suffered a total of 57 attacks in early 1984. Gangs of between 20 and 50 youths roamed the courtyards. People needed escorts to get in and out of their houses. At the same time the GLC decided to open up another of its estates – the Lincoln in Bow. Twenty-five families were scattered across 1,200 homes on the estate and the same levels of violence ensued.

The police were no protection. The Community Alliance for Police Accountability (CAPA) was set up in the early 1980s by a group of local people who knew from their own experience there were massive shortcomings in the way the East End was being policed. CAPA monitored the way the police dealt with attacks. In their Annual Reports they show that police were usually slow to arrive in answer to 999 calls, often gave the impression that Bengali callers were wasting their time, usually said there was nothing they could do, didn't take proper statements, and didn't use interpreters. Most important, they took no action even when, as CAPA reported on one occasion, a Bengali man was shot at in the presence of a police officer. If arrests were made, it was often of the people under attack, while assailants went free. It isn't surprising Bengalis didn't often call the police for help.

Unholy alliance

Yet even this violence pales compared with what happened when offers on the estates in the 'white cordon' were eventually made to Bengalis. There had been warnings. The 1973 Labour GLC, with Tony Judge as Housing Chair, had attempted to move a few Bengali families onto white estates without success. Then in 1982, Nayor Ali and his three children were allocated a house on the Glamis Estate – they were the first Bengali family to move on. In fact the allocation was a mistake. Nayor Ali's wife was English, but they had separated. When the GLC found out the mistake, they told him the Glamis Estate house was too big. They tried to withdraw the offer, but he'd already signed to accept. They offered him two other old flats, the same size as the new house, while still insisting the new house was too big. But he was the legal tenant.

So he tried to move in. Before he moved, dogshit was put through the letter box, and the keyholes waxed up. On the morning his furniture arrived, 15 women blockaded the way to prevent anything being moved in. An Alsatian was padlocked into the back yard of the house. When friends came to give Nayor Ali support, some were hit, and one knocked to the ground.

As more families tried to move onto newer estates, these 'reception committees' became a regular feature. By September, they had been recorded on Collingwood, Mountmorres, Ocean, Ranwell, Stifford and Exmouth Estates. Unlike the case of Nayor Ali, the 'committees' were usually successful in preventing people moving in through their intimidation. On Exmouth things went further. A flat was smeared all over with graffiti, pig's trotters were left hanging over the door. In a remarkable move, 53 tenants signed a petition asking the GLC not to house more Bengalis on the estate, because they said *they* were afraid of further violence if more families moved on. The clever wording didn't avoid a prosecution by the Commission for Racial Equality, as the petition was putting pressure on the GLC to discriminate – and the tenants had to undertake not to breach the Race Relations Act again.

The council could not rule out the possibility that one or more of its employees was colluding in this. Only with good inside information could the tenants have organized their committees to meet prospective tenants in the right place at the right time. But the housing policy went deeper, as the Housing Rights Service explained in 1983 in a written submission to the GLC for their report, *Racial Harassment in London*:

> It encourages white tenants to feel that it is 'their right' to have exclusive access to the best housing and that they alone are 'entitled to it'. It appears to them that the local authority itself is saying that race, and not housing need, is the criterion which gives you the key to rehousing. The first Asian tenant on the estate then appears as an aberration of the system, and smashing their windows and firing pellets at them will be rationalized as a way of ensuring that the housing system returns to normal.

Because GLC officers wouldn't credit accusations of such attacks, the violence was encouraged. The Labour GLC councillors took their time to challenge this. Their report on harassment, eventually published in 1984, relied heavily on input by community groups and those who'd suffered attack. It accepted that officers in Tower Hamlets often thought Bengalis used accusations of harassment as a way of getting transfers. Suspicions of lying were recorded on a quarter of all tenancy files where tenants asked for rehousing on the grounds of harassment. Yet to confront the attackers involved a wholesale reappraisal of council housing strategy. Racist attacks were not going to go away simply by 'dealing with the perpetrators', when the housing policy itself was a leading perpetrator. What they did suggest was a more rigorous procedure for dealing with harassment. But it was for the wrong reasons:

> With little prospect of a transfer and a council policy directed at building up permanent Bangladeshi communities on estates

outside the E1 area, it is clearly essential that firm action be taken to prevent further harassment.

The GLC was still supporting a dispersal policy, still going to make transfers difficult, and still wasn't going to let Bengalis make their own choices about where they wanted to live.

The report discussed the problem of how to 'open up' estates to Bengali people when white tenants were prepared to 'defend' them with violence. But it didn't mention the prerequisite – finding families wanting to do it, knowing the risks. If people don't want to move onto new estates, they will ask for a transfer before the first brick is thrown, let alone after the sort of violence described here. Their way round this was 'cluster allocations' – moving a group of families onto an estate together. But unless these people all knew and trusted each other, could call on outside organizations, and could see that successful work was being done to build support for them *inside* the estate, there was no safety in numbers – as Coventry Cross, Teviot, and Lincoln had proved. When seven of 14 new houses on the Piggott Street Estate in Limehouse were offered to Bengali families who'd never even met each other, they all refused them. This was a wasted opportunity: with the right preparation, there *were* families prepared to take the risk.

Neither council ever suggested working to break the racist ethos on the 'white cordon' estates. Yet this is not such an impossibility. Not all white tenants are racists. A minority can often control an estate, especially if the children of that minority feel free to harass black families at will – and it is often children who are responsible for the violence.

Racist attacks – part of the land war

Racist attacks are so often described as a 'disease' or 'cancer'. But they are part of a war, like all wars, about territory. Although not centrally co-ordinated, the intimidation is designed to terrorize Bengalis and other peoples from ethnic minorities out of areas which racists want to keep for their own. Some of the ground in Canning Town, Newham is held in this way. Loyalist techniques which have driven Nationalists out of whole areas of Belfast have not been so different. In both cases divisions required by imperial Britain are still at work.

Mosley's Blackshirts often used random terror tactics, with the *Daily Worker* reporting such incidents as a child being thrown through a shopwindow in Petticoat Lane and a car petrol tank being smashed open and lit in a crowded Mile End Road. The violence against the Bengalis is more personalized, directed to undermine each individual's confidence in his or her ability to survive. Although racist violence isn't confined to people's homes, it is aimed at their daily routines. Children are attacked going to and from school – even at school; women are attacked coming onto their estates and leaving them. Men are in danger at the bus-stops they use to go to work. It is violence directed at driving Bengalis out and keeping them out, block by block and estate by estate across the East End. To this end, a great deal of it has been focused on women and children when they are on their own.

Terror can be sustained by the persistence of attacks, just as well as by their ferocity. The range of weapons is enormous, as was reported to the Housing Committee in February 1987:

> Verbal abuse, spitting, physical assault by stabbing, kicking, punching, shooting with airguns, throwing stones, eggs, sticks, using iron bars; criminal damage to property e.g. windows being broken, doors damaged, burning material being put through letter boxes, cars damaged; excreta, stink bombs and rubbish being pushed through letter boxes, rubbish dumped on doorsteps, washing vandalized or stolen, graffiti daubed on doors or walls, banging on doors, thumping on ceilings; dogs, cars, motorcycles, knives, petrol bombs, shot guns and threatening letters have also been used to frighten the victims.

As the government and councils tried to close down people's options of better housing, more people used racism as a weapon in holding onto what they had got. There was an alternative. If the violence experienced by the Bengalis had instead been organized and channelled to fight for more housing on empty land, to stop the takeover of Docklands by the rich, to force more government money into the borough, to confront the councils' own divisive policies, it might have been a different story. As the next chapter shows, effective anti-racist organization often meant it *was* a different story. It is just as dangerous to stereotype white people as it is to stereotype ethnic minorities. There are indeed as many currents running against racism as with it.

10 | Fair shares?

Knowing there was racism in the allocation process was one thing; changing that process was quite another. After all, the GLC admitted such racism existed as early as 1975, following the Runnymede Trust report *Race and Council Housing in London*. From the 1971 Census it had found that white tenants had a much higher chance of being allocated to new GLC estates. The GLC's own research confirmed this but no action was taken. Spitalfields soon saw the results.

The GLC's published housing priorities had eight bands of housing need. Slum clearance cases were top, statutorily overcrowded tenants next, and homeless families third. Locally, Bengalis were certainly a large proportion of the clearance cases, made up at least half of homeless families, and in Spitalfields constituted 90 per cent of the GLC's statutorily overcrowded tenants. Yet the 320 new houses being finished at Granby Street and Virginia Road in 1978 didn't go to people from those top priorities, least of all the Bengali clearance cases from Spitalfields. Granby Street was mainly filled by existing GLC tenants in the fifth and seventh priority categories, while rents on much of Virginia Road were double the normal levels. Race and money rather than need seemed to be the criteria for allocating new housing.

The allocation system

Despite the requirements of the 1980 Housing Act, the GLC never published its allocations system in full. So to understand just how the estates were allocated was not easy for .

outsiders. The description that follows was pieced together over several years and was certainly not clear when people started campaigning to get the system changed. It is basically the system used for the London Area Mobility Scheme still in operation. A computer has the details of everyone needing housing. For every empty home, it picks people who are suitable. It is told the details of the empty place – for example it might be a three-bedroom, second-floor maisonette with central heating in Limehouse. It finds all the people who've asked for a maisonette that size in Limehouse who don't mind being above the ground floor but who do need central heating. It then lists, in priority order, the top 99 cases who fit the description. In theory the person at the top of the list gets the flat. But there's enormous discretion. Across London as a whole in 1985, the top person was successful in only 5 per cent of cases, while in half the cases none of the top 20 people was considered. There are some generally accepted reasons for not making the offer to the top name – for example, rent arrears or bedrooms being too small. Yet can there really be good reasons for ignoring the top 20 people half the time? The conclusion must be that lettings officers were making decisions outside the computer system, and no-one was even challenging them.

That wasn't the only level of discrimination. The council's housing visitors had the job of talking to people who wanted council homes. The visitors filled in forms giving people's details which were then fed into the computer. People who didn't understand the system wouldn't know how important it was to ask for exactly what you wanted. If, for example, you would have liked that flat in Limehouse, but hadn't specified you wanted central heating, the computer would not have picked your name out. English-speaking housing officers often just didn't give this information to Bengali families – whose records were then incomplete and who suffered as a result.

More insidious was the grading of people. Housing visitors made their own subjective assessment of whether people were worthy of 'good' (Grade A), 'average' (Grade

211

B) or 'bad' (Grade C) housing. People applying just didn't know this was going on. Whatever someone's priority, if they were graded C, the computer would never match them up with a Grade A flat. Bengalis in the slums were never considered to be 'worth' (to use Waterlow's expression) new housing. This secret system preserved the housing ladder.

Much of the GLC's housing list was made up of homeless families and waiting list cases referred to it by Tower Hamlets Council. These referrals built in further layers of discrimination, much of which was also reproduced in the housing allocated by the borough itself. For example, homeless families, when referred to the GLC, were always graded C, so they only got offered bad housing. In the borough's own stock, there was no such grading, but homeless families were similarly discriminated against. The Department of the Environment sponsored the Priority Estates Project, which provided specialist teams to help develop new management ideas on 'difficult' estates. The Project looked at 582 lettings made by Tower Hamlets between February and July 1985, by which time Bengalis made up over two thirds of homeless families. It found the borough was pushing homeless families towards some estates and excluding them from others – with 13 estates on which not a single offer was made to the homeless. The implication that the borough's allocations were also discriminatory was confirmed by the Commission for Racial Equality who found in the same year that Bengalis made up a very high proportion of the tenants in isolated old blocks like John Scurr House in Wapping and Electric House in Bow, while there were none on the modern Patriot Square Estate in Bethnal Green. This formed one of the grounds for a non-discrimination notice under the Race Relations Act, served by the Commission on Tower Hamlets, and against which the council didn't appeal.

Many Bengalis never got considered for housing at all, because of two rules which have consistently disqualified them from Tower Hamlets' waiting list. The first ensured that Bengali men with families still abroad couldn't spend more than three months away seeing them. Otherwise their places on the list were lost, and their cases not looked at until a year after they returned. For Somalis, who are still seafarers, this meant a lifetime of homelessness, as they are never in the borough for a year at a time. The Liberals have softened the rule slightly – allowing one month away for every year spent in the borough. The second rule concerns separated families. If a family is split up, with half in York and half in Tower Hamlets, it gets high priority for rehousing because it is effectively homeless. But if the second half of the family is abroad – in Bangladesh, for instance – the council doesn't recognize its existence. It gets no priority and no housing even if the first half of the family has lived in Tower Hamlets for 30 years. The Commission for Racial Equality deemed this to be unequal treatment in its Non-Discrimination Notice, and the council claimed the rule was under 'urgent review', with a report expected in early 1989.

The first challenge

The first new GLC estate developed after the campaign to rebuild Spitalfields got underway was at Hopetown Street. White and Bengali tenants were united that this should go to local people in greatest need. This was to stop the GLC from using the estate for tenants from across London when Spitalfields' conditions were the worst in the capital. Petitions were signed and meetings held. When the houses were ready in early 1981, the GLC knew all eyes were on the allocation. Yet the principles of Granby Street were repeated. The new tenants weren't all white – over a dozen Bengali families were included. But even they weren't coming from the GLC's top priority bands, while all but two of the terraced houses went to existing GLC tenants. It was flats emptied by these tenants on the Chicksand Estate which were given to Bengalis in Wentworth Dwellings. However, much had been achieved: the estate had gone mainly to local people, was multi-racial, and had an open

213

and friendly atmosphere. It was just that the ladder principle was still excluding those in greatest need.

Renewed attempts were made to break the ladder. With the Housing Rights Service, 22 Bengali groups targeted 15 new and good-quality estates in that arc surrounding Spitalfields where nearly 1,000 new lettings would be made over two years. This discounted the six borough council estates to the east and south which generated another 200 lettings a year, and where Tower Hamlets was starting to make offers to Bengalis. In 1982 the list of targeted estates was published in a report, *Bengalis and GLC Allocation in E1*. Rough estimates based on the electoral roll suggested just 4 per cent of the tenancies on these estates had gone to Asians – on eight estates it was less than 1 per cent. Most of the Bengalis who *were* on these estates were confined to four old blocks. The 'ghetto' policy was shining through. Bengalis held just 1.5 per cent of the tenancies in the rest of these estates. With this, they were being told that E1 was 'full up' and they'd have to move on elsewhere.

The report did not call for a shake-up in the allocations system. If the system had been used properly, there was no way so few Bengalis would have been housed, although because the GLC didn't keep ethnic records, it was impossible to say what proportion of the housing *should* have gone to Bengalis. GLC officers denied the evidence of racism, producing their own counter-evidence. Closely examined, this actually supported the accusations against them. On the targeted estates, only 50 flats had been accepted by Asian families over the previous two years – just 7 per cent of what was on offer. At that rate, Bengalis were never going to establish themselves.

GLC councillors neither supported their officers nor accepted the evidence of racism. They blamed the system, and looked for technical reasons to explain why Bengalis had been frozen out. (Indeed, Ken Livingstone in his book on the GLC years, *If Voting Changed Anything, They'd Abolish It*, published in 1987, was still maintaining that computers cut out discrimination.) Admittedly, this approach did lead to the GLC coming clean about the grading system, although they didn't do anything immediately to change it. Instead, in September 1982, the GLC tinkered with the allocations system in ways which the community organizations had not asked for. The biggest move was to abolish the quota of 33 per cent of new housing which was reserved for existing tenants. In fact, not just 33 per cent but virtually all new housing went to existing tenants, and abolishing the quota wasn't going to stop that. But it was going to make white tenants think that their chances of rehousing were being undermined. Community groups wanted to avoid this. They had argued instead that additional quotas should be set for homeless families and waiting list cases. That way, these groups, traditionally excluded from new housing, would be guaranteed some of it, without excluding existing tenants.

An organized response

The campaign to change housing allocation, started by those in bad housing, grew in momentum throughout the years of the 1981 GLC Labour administration, not least because that GLC funded organizations critical of its performance. The campaign tied many threads together. Bengali youth organizations, covering much of the borough, were united through their Federation. CAPA was drawn in because taking up complaints about police inactivity on harassment wasn't enough. The Tower Hamlets Association for Racial Equality drew in Chinese, Somali and Afro-Caribbean groups who were badly affected in their own way by the allocations policies. The Homeless Families Campaign was confronting the way the homeless were being used and abused. The Housing Rights Service was working with families being forced out and without council housing at all. The Tenants' Federation was anxious to challenge the racism inside the tenants' movement.

The centrepoint of the campaign was to get Bengali people in bad housing a real choice about where to live, and once that choice was made, to confront any racist opposition that might emerge. While supporting Bengalis under attack on other estates, it supported their right to move if they wanted to live somewhere else. East London Workers Against Racism (ELWAR), a front for the Revolutionary Communist Party, stood apart from this alignment. ELWAR didn't question the allocation process that dumped Bengali families on hostile estates. Once there, the family must be defended at all costs. Nayor Ali's survival on Glamis Estate, was due in great part to ELWAR's work. After his 'reception', ELWAR members visited everyone on the estate with a petition of support for Nayor Ali. They got a surprising number of signatures – over 300 of the 550 tenants – and from this a group emerged to oppose the prevailing ethos and provide support from *inside* the estate. They tried the same tactics on other estates, providing round-the-clock protection for families being attacked, and they continued to draw successfully on the anti-racist current amongst white tenants.

But for ELWAR any transfer of families under attack would be a victory for racism, thereby encouraging more violence against others. This led to the defence of families in flats they were desperate to leave. Moving a family off a hostile estate may appear to be a victory for racism, but tackling such estates must wait till people positively *want* to live on them. ELWAR argued black people couldn't make this choice freely until the estate had been cleared of the threat of attack. This is sometimes true. But for many Bengalis, Bow and Poplar were never going to be places they wanted to live.

Meanwhile the campaigning groups sustained their pressure on the GLC to end the racism in allocations. The GLC dithered. Not until the summer of 1983 did they support the idea that a Race and Housing Action Team be set up to monitor – and intervene in, if necessary – the allocations process. Even then, there was little movement in actually getting anything set up. Bengalis continued to be squeezed out. Not a single Bengali moved onto the new housing either side of the Ocean Estate in E1. Terraces of new houses at Rectory Square and a Docklands-style development at Globe Wharf by the Regent's Park Canal were set up by the GLC and became new no-go areas.

This left only three major new GLC developments – Davenant Street and Wentworth in Spitalfields and Royal Mint Square to the south. This last scheme of 153 homes was the first to be finished. It was attractively designed and in a valuable area for many Bengali families. Ashley Bramall, the GLC councillor who headed their local housing sub-committee, was pressed to monitor offers *before* they were sent out. He checked people's ethnic origin but not their relative priority for housing. As a result, 20 per cent of the estate went to Bengalis, including half the three-bedroom places. Again, a relatively harmonious new estate was created. There has certainly been none of the violence associated with Bengalis trying to move onto established all-white estates. White tenants who didn't want to share Royal Mint with Bengalis weren't going to accept an offer there. However, tenants on the nearby Peabody Estate were angry – they'd wanted transfers to new homes. The anger was defused when a posse from Spitalfields went down to meet Peabody tenants.

Success here underlined failures elsewhere. The 'London Against Racism' GLC administration was halfway through its term and hadn't mounted any serious challenge to its own racist allocations. A public meeting was organized to expose this contradiction and to get the GLC leadership to commit itself to taking action. Ken Livingstone, Tony McBrearty, Chair of Housing, Paul Boateng, Vice-Chair of the Ethnic Minorities Committee, and Ashley Bramall were asked to come. The wide spread of community organizations in the allocations campaign meant they could mobilize very effectively for this, and also draw in more people – for example, Bengali women's groups from both Spitalfields and Shadwell Gardens became involved. The meeting was set for 15th September 1983. That evening, as it got dark, a fleet of mini-buses weaved their way round the old estates picking people up. Coaches of homeless families came down from the Finsbury Park hotels. By the time the meeting was due to start, over 500 people were trying to pack into the Spitalfields Brady Centre. There just wasn't room for them all in the hall or the overflow room. The street was blocked with those who'd been disappointed. There had been nothing like it since the meeting to defeat the ghetto plan. Ken Livingstone had to give an impromptu speech on the steps before he could even get inside. He'd done his homework too. At the meeting he was able to announce that the Race and Housing Action Team jobs would be advertised the following week.

The Race and Housing Action Team

The Race and Housing Action Team was on the road, with eight workers and a brief to monitor lettings; to deal with racial harassment; to organize anti-racist training for staff; to co-ordinate interpretation, translation and information giving; and to service a joint advisory group of officers and community groups. The advisory group and Team Head had the right to take items to the Housing Committee. It would no longer be possible for senior housing officers to sit on things they didn't want discussed. This did threaten the power of senior officers and, by implication, criticized their past performance. Their reluctance to agree the idea had been a major factor in the delay in setting it up. That's why the community groups did not call that public meeeting until they knew they could get all the relevant senior GLC politicians and force them to make their commitment public. Without the meeting, the Team wouldn't have got started.

The two women – Nazia Khanum and Mithu Uddin – who were the Team's Head and Deputy, couldn't waste any time in getting things set up. There were only 18 months left before the GLC had to hand over its housing to the boroughs. They were quick to build a supportive advisory group of community organizations. They also established procedures for confronting racist attacks which became standard guidelines used elsewhere. People who had been attacked were believed until proved otherwise; transfers on the grounds of harassment were made possible; attackers would be evicted if there was enough evidence; Bengali tenants could talk to council staff in their own language; women could talk to women; the performance of estate staff dealing with harassment was monitored with the Team able to intervene where necessary. Above all, Nazia Khanum could order transfers when things were desperate.

It has always been difficult to measure the level of racist violence. When neither council nor police take action, reporting is low. If nothing else, the number of cases reported to the Action Team shows the level of confidence people placed in it Between the end of 1983, when it started, and January 1985, 24 new cases came in each month – 360 in all – of which 70 per cent were Bangladeshi.

It wasn't possible to meet the ensuing demand for transfers. Especially for larger families, there weren't enough places on 'safer' estates. The Team put more energy into making people stay. Community workers were introduced on the most violent estates. Mother and toddler groups, English language classes, and day outings were organized with the women on the Lincoln Estate. Although members of the Team in their reports described people under attack as 'victims', in their work they recognized the potential that such women's groups had, and the danger of stereotyping the women as isolated and defenceless. The Team felt, like ELWAR, that people weren't going to have a real choice about staying or going unless the support work was done. It wanted to see community groups organizing with them to defeat the attackers. Yet while the Team was carrying out this work with one hand, so to speak, it was being asked to sign its agreement to moving besieged tenants off with the other. It is therefore a bit unfair to characterize the Team as Chetan Bhatt did in the magazine *Foundations* in July 1987:

The Race and Housing Action Team was crucial to the wholesale bureaucratisation of responses (and resistance) to racist violence. The team, after investigating numerous cases of racist attacks in East London, rather than encouraging militant community defence, focused on the drawing up of extensive bureaucratic procedures for investigating and dealing with attacks on GLC estates.

It did encourage community defence, but neither the tenants nor the community organizations agreed that the Lincoln Estate was ground worth defending at that time. For them, the argument and the struggle should be about the estates that Bengali tenants *wanted* to live on. Both on the Lincoln and on the borough council's Teviot Estate, tenants organized to get away from intolerable violence. Ironically, they generated the mutual support network the councils had hoped for by moving them in 'clusters' – but they used this strength, not to stay but to get out of their hell.

The dispersal policies of both councils were being challenged. Through publicity, community group support, picketing of meetings and other pressure on councillors, both authorities conceded during the summer of 1984. Transfers were agreed to 'safer' estates, although it took many months before all the families got out.

Community support worked very differently where Bengali families were fighting to keep housing they wanted. The Ocean Estate, with over 60 blocks of housing from the 1930s to the 1950s, was one of Len Bennett's original 'designated' estates. However it was on the edge of E1, and many Bengali families had made a home there. There was plenty of trouble, but the tenants' association had strong anti-racist involvement. Soon after the Team was set up, Bengalis were offered new houses on the estate for the first time, at Beaumont Square. Violence erupted. But these families were determined to stay. Although attackers were known, the police took no action. Groups like the Bangladesh Youth Approach and CAPA gave support. Volunteers stayed with the families till the trouble died down, and the families are still there.

Confronting the allocations process

The overriding priority for the Team had always been tackling the allocations process itself. Not surprisingly, many senior staff wouldn't co-operate. Lettings staff, due to be moved into the same building as the Team, threatened to go on strike. The Team instituted 'racism awareness' training courses, but they weren't well designed, fuelling the latent racism until it burst out in all the familiar attitudes which trainers were unable to quell. People were leaving the courses feeling more self-righteous than when they started. Later courses, concentrating on people's work patterns rather than their attitudes, were more successful. Many staff did have a sense of how their jobs could change to combat racism in their work. What emerged was deep unhappiness about senior management – staff believed they acted high-handedly, and undervalued the positive approaches which the workforce had to offer.

The Housing Rights Service produced a follow-up analysis of lettings on the 'white cordon' estates. It looked at all the estates in the first report but also included a few more – 19 in all. In 1982-83, another 150 new homes had been finished and 850 places relet on these estates. Using the electoral roll, it appeared that Asian households got just 8 per cent of this housing. The GLC produced full information which established the true figure at around 12 per cent. But even this was hardly progress. In the same period the number of Asian tenants on Tower Hamlets-owned estates in the area had nearly doubled from around 140 to 270. Given it was a much smaller stock, this suggested Asians were getting nearer 30 per cent of the empty places on borough estates.

GLC officers hotly contested this second report; feelings between them and the community organizations became very bitter. This is when the GLC members asked Dr Deborah Phillips, the independent researcher mentioned in the last chapter, to look at the evidence. She studied all offers made between January 1983 and May 1984. Her final report *What Price Equality?*, published in 1986, supported much of what the Housing Rights Service had been saying. Although it still didn't establish what proportion of the housing should have gone to Asians, it did show that most Asian applicants had to have high priority to get offers, while 80 per cent of non-Asians who got offers were in the bottom five priority groups. It found that Asians and non-Asians were being directed to different estates even when they had the same priority and the same requirements and hadn't said what area they wanted to live in. It showed there *were* Asians graded for good-quality housing and that, despite this, non-Asians were more likely to get it. It confirmed that discrimination was most marked with homeless families. It showed the way housing visitors and estate officers discriminated by withholding information tenants needed in order to make choices.

The report completely exposed the GLC allocation system. A radical set of recommendations was agreed:

- The abolition of the grading of properties;
- All high priority cases to be reported on every eight weeks if they haven't had offers;
- Allocations to be monitored one day a week on a random basis *before* being sent out;
- Twenty per cent of new large houses to be reserved for the homeless;
- Targets to be set for the proportion of offers going to ethnic minorities in the top priority groups;
- Day release training for staff.

Monitoring offers before they went out meant there was the power to intervene to prevent racist allocations happening. Dr Phillips concluded that humans couldn't be cut out of the allocations process. By itself the computer didn't allocate housing effectively. For a three-month period offers were made purely on the basis of computer selection, which ensured offers to Bengalis on estates like the Exmouth. But overall many more people refused their offers and the number of empty flats grew and grew. Clearly some human judgements *had* to be made to supplement the computer's work. These judgements were going to be subjective. The only safeguard against that subjectivity was the monitoring which was agreed. The targeting which was agreed in the same package would ensure the council would know just how many people from ethnic minorities they would *expect* to house, when their need was compared with everyone else's.

Thus these recommendations, after three years of struggle, met the demands being made by the Housing Rights Service in their first report of March 1982. It didn't involve changing the GLC priorities for housing. But it did demand intervention at every level in the department, from changes in broad policy to the training of front-line staff. Because of the integral role given to the community organizations involved, it also implied that change wasn't possible from the inside alone. There had to be a partnership between councillors, the Race and Housing Action Team, and the community organizations to achieve anything.

Foundations undermined

But time ran out. The recommendations were agreed just four months before the GLC had to hand over its housing to Tower Hamlets. The person given the job of monitoring the lettings never even got a computer terminal. The advisory group lost its powers and then was disbanded altogether. With the amalgamation of GLC and Tower Hamlets stock, the officers who had run the GLC system were back sharing control. Tower Hamlets allocations were still not fully computerized by the beginning of 1988 – even though this was essential if lettings were to be decentralized as the Liberals wanted. Pre-allocation monitoring is virtually impossible on a manual system. Even if it had been technically feasible, neither the senior staff nor their new political masters wanted it. Tower Hamlets didn't even agree to the principle of keeping records of ethnic origin until October 1987, and by then many new obstacles had been thrown up.

The new Liberal administration planned to decentralize both the Race and Housing Action Team and its lettings. The decentralization of the Team spelt its disintegration. At its peak the Team had nearly 30 workers covering the entire range of activities in its brief. With the Team being split seven ways, these functions couldn't all be carried out at neighbourhood level. There was no obligation on the neighbourhoods to go on employing the workers at all – they could use the money for something else. Bethnal Green neighbourhood, which includes Spitalfields, abolished its Team altogether, and the job was devolved to estate officers, whose role Deborah Philips had criticized. In early 1988, no neighbourhood had a full Team, although during the year some Teams, especially in Labour neighbourhoods, did start to re-organize.

A few individuals were struggling on, but the Team had no central authority. The post of Head had its powers stripped away – and in any case no-one had been appointed to replace Dr Khanum who had left in despair. Neighbourhood lettings are controlled by the councillors from the neighbourhood. Monitoring of lettings may eventually be possible. But there will no power of intervention to prevent discrimination. Neighbourhood committees can decide about estates where homeless families are barred. There are no sanctions. The division of estates could become more institutionalized than it has ever been in the past.

This disintegration was also reflected in the Team's work on racist attacks. The number of cases referred to them was halved to 12 a month by the autumn of 1986, and had sunk to just eight a month by the summer of 1987. Between July 1985 and October 1986, the Team recommended 49 households for transfer, of which only 21 were agreed and just six actually housed. This drop probably reflects a recognition that the Team was no longer able to deliver the goods, rather than any drop in the level of violence. Certainly CAPA reported a 28 per cent increase in cases of harassment in 1985, although that too may just be a reflection of its own effectiveness. The Team hasn't managed to evict racist attackers. Those who believe in the willingness of the High Courts of England to do this have yet to have their faith confirmed. The first case was of the man who had clubbed a Bengali unconscious with a piece of the front door he'd just smashed in. The man said he'd acted in good faith on false information from his ex-wife who told him their son had been hit by the Bengali. This was good enough for the court, which apparently accepted that slugging people unconscious with smashed-up fragments of their own front door is reasonable behaviour. Other attackers have been identified, but this has not yet led to successful prosecutions.

Tower Hamlets allocations

The allocations campaign had concentrated on the GLC rather than Tower Hamlets, both because the GLC had much more of the housing in E1, and because the GLC's record was so much worse. Apart from Sidney Street in the heart of St Mary's ward, where in 1988 Asians still made up just 4 per cent of the 866 tenancies, Bengalis were able to move onto other Tower Hamlets estates in E1. Except with homeless families, lettings officers weren't working under the same sort of overall political direction from senior officers as was the case in the GLC. Leaving aside individual cases, councillors do not seem to have intervened either.

So when Tower Hamlets came to take over the entire housing stock, it didn't necessarily spell disaster. The principles which were fought for so hard between 1982 and 1985 did not sink without trace. In 1984 Tower Hamlets adopted a list of priority bands defining housing need similar to the GLC's and, to start with, some of the GLC's new ideas were acted on. Homeless families did get their 20 per cent of the large new houses at Scarborough Street and Davenant Street. Since then the proportion of offers to people in the top three priority bands has stayed above 60 per cent, while with the GLC in 1984 it was below 30 per cent. More people in serious need are getting offers. Figures reported to the Housing Committee in early 1988 showed the homeless were getting between 25 per cent and 30 per cent of all offers – up from 10 per cent in 1984. This was inevitable, given the exponential rise in homelessness. Those who were seriously overcrowded were getting 3 per cent of all offers – the GLC gave them virtually none. All this should have meant that Bengalis were getting more offers than before – but it can't be proved, as there isn't any published ethnic monitoring. However, the figures are distorted by the Liberals' decision to sell off estates. Tenants being forced unwillingly off these estates have to be given top priority for rehousing, even if they don't want to move.

A check on those estates in the arc round Spitalfields shows a mixed picture. There have been big increases in the numbers of Bengalis on some estates like Collingwood and Bigland. Other estates have been opened up for the first time – particularly Stifford, Cleveland, Barnardo Gardens and the Glamis. But there's still a hard core where Bengalis have been kept out – including Granby Street, Exmouth and the new estates at Rectory Square and Globe Wharf. On Glamis, from the half a dozen families in 1984, there were at least 16 by early 1988. Yet almost all this increase has been concentrated in the two large blocks – the tower block flats at Gordon House, and Roslin House which has maisonettes stacked on top of each other. The houses with gardens are virtually unaffected. On Exmouth there has been movement on and off the estate, but the net result is that Asians still hold just 2 per cent of the tenancies – scarcely any change from the position in 1982. The tenants of Exmouth may have given an undertaking to the court not to pressurize the council to discriminate, but the discrimination continues.

Yet the allocations campaign has had other important spin-offs. The big housing associations in the area – Toynbee, Samuel Lewis, Guinness Trust, Bethnal Green and East London, and Newlon – have all opened up to Bengali tenants. Particularly with the first three, the people they have housed have changed significantly. Toynbee at Toynbee Hall, Samuel Lewis at Bernhard Baron House were housing only professionals. The Guinness Trust had no Bengali tenants on their Bethnal Green estates. Now many Bengalis are living in the 500 units of housing at Flower and Dean village, in the revamped Fieldgate Mansions and at Guinness Court in Aldgate. On top of this are the 400 new homes in Bengali-controlled housing co-ops. Because all this housing has been publicly subsidized, the council is entitled to use over half of it for its own nominees, although it's been desperately slow to take up the opportunity.

The Liberals didn't seem wholly at ease with 60 per cent instead of 30 per cent of housing going to those with high priority. Many low-priority cases who expected rehousing under the GLC system are not getting it. These include a lot of the Liberals' new-found supporters, so the Liberals have invented their own ways of overriding the priorities based on need. The first change was that most people whose parents live in Tower Hamlets can now move automatically into the priority system half way up because they're 'sons and daughters' of the borough. Secondly, anyone can now phone up and ask for a named empty council flat: if it's been turned down twice or if it's just been ready and empty a month, the person with the highest priority who phones up gets it. It harks back to the 'Bingo' draws under Labour ten years before. Most Bengali applicants still haven't got parents in the borough – which counts them out of the first scheme. The second scheme has more sinister undertones. It hardly discourages the 'reception committees' which have 'persuaded' Bengalis to turn down good flats. Even assuming there is no violence, Bengalis are less likely to know about empty places on good estates, and won't be phoning up about them.

The Liberals built on this in 1986 by sending ballot papers to every tenant in English (translations were only available at district housing offices). Seven thousand tenants voted on telephone lettings, with nearly ten to one in favour. Only half that number voted on sons and daughters but they were

227

20 to one in favour. Such majorities cannot be ignored, even when less than 15 per cent of tenants are voting. The proposals drew on very real concerns. You didn't have to be a racist to vote for them: the telephone lettings idea taps into that frustration many people feel at the sight of empty council housing when they are desperate. But the ballots also reasserted the old values – housing for the people who have 'been here longest', housing for those who know how to use the system. The ballots both offered real power and re-established the bond between the housing authority and its English-speaking tenants. Those still waiting for council housing were excluded from the ballot altogether, while those who can't speak English were marginalized. As a means of holding onto political support, it was impressive.

Although the sons and daughters scheme successfully cut out virtually all Bengalis, it didn't provide much housing. Just 78 places were allocated through the scheme in its first year – with only one going to a Bengali. In October 1988, the borough-wide housing priority system was abolished. Each neighbourhood could establish its own priorities. By March 1989 Bethnal Green neighbourhood had introduced a new 'experimental' system which makes housing need a secondary consideration. People needing housing are divided into six groups, each getting a target number of lettings each year. As a result, the target for sons and daughters will be 20 per cent of all voids, instead of the 2 per cent they got in 1988. That takes away 18 per cent from the overcrowded and those seeking urgent moves because of Closing Orders, harassment or major repair. The Chief Executive and independent solicitors advised that this breached the Race Relations Act. Their advice was ignored. As the minutes of the meeting at which the decision was made put it:

Councillor Goodchild felt that families from Bangladesh were prepared to accept a degree of overcrowding but in *the existing community* couples would not have families until they had accommodation. [My emphasis]

Racists must feel once again that the council is validating their views. As has been shown, that is potentially very dangerous.

At the same time the Liberals are accelerating the process of forcing Bengalis onto estates where they don't want to live. With decentralized lettings, every neighbourhood has to house a quota of homeless families. Eleven a month are arriving in the Isle of Dogs. One hundred and four racist attacks were reported to the decentralized Race Team there between December 1987 and June 1988, including eight physical attacks. There are only 260 Bengali households on the Island, and most of these attacks are directed at them. Flats are getting wrecked between the Bengali tenants going to look at them and the day they move their furniture in. Three or four homeless families have been transferred out again. No-one has been prosecuted.

Bearing all this in mind, the Liberal administration's response to the Commission for Racial Equality's investigation is significant. When the CRE published the report in September 1988, proving discrimination in the allocation of John Scurr House under Labour, council leader Brenda Collins was quoted in *The Guardian* as saying the council accepted this and 'clearly wishes to comply with the non-discrimination notice and will have to discuss with the CRE further ways in which to do this'.

Less than two months later, the Liberals had produced a special four-page edition of the council newspaper, *Tower Hamlets News*, exclusively dedicated to refuting the CRE report with a banner headline screaming 'OUT OF DATE, OUT OF TOUCH, OUT OF ORDER'. It is true that the CRE did take three years to produce something, and they made mistakes to boot. But *Tower Hamlets News* didn't accept the evidence of discrimination at John Scurr House. If the Liberals didn't accept that about another administration, they are clearly in no mood to accept it about themselves. They claim to have started ethnic monitoring – but by May 1989 no figures had been publicly reported to the neighbourhood committee which covers Spitalfields.

Fair shares?

Here to stay

The allocations campaign had many component parts but, above all, it had the active involvement of hundreds of individuals who were waiting for council housing – both the homeless and those on the waiting list. They turned up time and again at meetings, understood the issues, and expected to see change. It has played an important part in ensuring there is now a strong Bengali presence not just along the City border, but spreading out north into Bethnal Green, and east through Stepney to Mile End. Spitalfields still remains the centre of this – especially for work and shopping. Over the next generation, this is going to be a presence which will be very hard to shift.

11 | Taking on the homeless

This Tory government has increased homelessness by attacking council housing. No council could stop this, least of all Tower Hamlets, where the number of homeless families in temporary housing went up from 230 in 1981 to 1,345 at the end of 1986. Yet Tower Hamlets is lucky – its homelessness problem has always been small compared with other inner London boroughs. Between 1980 and 1987 their position in the 'league table' remained unchanged – in both years there were 13 London boroughs accepting more homeless families while only Southwark has more housing at its disposal. So Tower Hamlets – with a relatively low number of homeless and a large housing stock – should be in a better position than any other inner London borough to tackle homelessness.

This isn't the way the present council presents things. If the Liberal administration were to be believed, Tower Hamlets is in a uniquely impossible position which demands action at a national level. Behind this rhetoric lies the most invidious assault so far on the Bengali community's right to live in the area. Bengalis have been hit hardest by this increase in homelessness: while half the homeless families in 1981 were Bengali, this figure was nearer 90 per cent in 1987. All the policies documented in this book which have attacked the Bengali presence in Spitalfields should make this no surprise. But the Liberals have found that the old policy of distributing the homeless round the unpopular estates of the borough hasn't been enough to meet this new crisis in numbers. They have taken two drastic steps: working to take away the right of Bengali men to live with their families in Tower Hamlets, while at the same time effectively trying to drive families who are already living here back to Bangladesh. It amounts to repatriation by the back door. It is certainly the most fundamental challenge so far to the Bengali presence in Tower Hamlets.

Deterrence and punishment

In the 1960s Tower Hamlets Council accepted tiny numbers as homeless – just 40 between June 1965 and February 1966, for instance. It would have been a simple matter, with such a large council housing stock, to move these people straight onto the council estates. Instead, they were put into half-way houses like Beechcroft Buildings, built in 1892 as the first council block in London, and awaiting its turn for demolition. Conditions were atrocious, but people who'd been evicted for rent arrears were held there until they paid up – creating 20th century versions of the debtors' prisons. Half-way housing punished people for their improvidence and, through word of mouth, deterred anyone else from applying to the Homeless Persons Section.

Things improved in the 1970s, when short-life houses were more often used for the homeless. But from 1980 onwards, the use of bed and breakfast hotels came in with a vengeance. While the overall numbers of homeless families didn't increase much between 1980 and 1983, the numbers in hotels went up fast from just 26 in June 1980 to 166 in July 1983. Then, by the end of 1986, when overall numbers had gone up enormously, 928 out of a total of 1,345 homeless families were in hotels. To begin with, families were concentrated in places around Finsbury Park, where property spivs were buying up houses as fast as they could get their hands on them and turning them into hotels for the council's convenience. But this couldn't meet the demand, and families were sent out to Bayswater and then as far afield as Heathrow and Southend.

It's very hard to convey just how desperate hotel conditions are if you haven't experienced them (and I haven't). But take the family of Shofor Ali (later to be active in organising homeless families) in a Finsbury Park hotel throughout 1982. Their top-floor room was long and narrow, with a dormer window at one end. The door wouldn't open fully – the entire length of the room was taken up with a collection of beds, wedged together, on which two adults and seven children were expected to sleep. There was no room for other furniture, no table round which the family could eat together, nowhere to play. The hotel only provided breakfast – all other food had to be carried upstairs from cookers shared with the other families staying there. There was no fridge: keeping milk cold meant using the window sill in winter and doing without in summer. Access to hot water was erratic – use of the bathroom had to be negotiated with half a dozen families. And this was no one-night stand. It had gone on from month to month, without a single offer of rehousing.

There was worse. At another hotel, 80 people shared two cookers, taps in bathrooms had to be used to fill kettles, wash clothes, wash up dirty saucepans, and fill babies' powdered milk bottles. Beds were pushed against windows with bad window catches or bottom-opening sashes. Children played on staircases with missing banisters: there were serious injuries as a result. Infections slopped round the hotels like flash floods. Gastro-enteritis was rife. Where possible men struggled back to the East End to work. Usually they lost their jobs altogether but would still travel back regularly to buy food and see friends. It was the women who had to try and make a life for their children inside these hotel bedrooms. For some, the hotels were their first experience of Britain and city life. Hard enough in itself, they also had to cope with their children going through the same initiation.

Support was minimal. Local health visitors struggled to provide a service – but they were an obvious threat to the hoteliers, who tried to keep them out. The local social

233

services department saw it as Tower Hamlets' duty to cover the hotels – and Tower Hamlets could not provide enough cover. Education welfare officers had their own problems. It was hard enough to trace who was moving in and out of the hotels. Even if they did get the children to a local school, the school roll would change week by week. Both local kids and those from the hotels had their schooling disrupted. Staff from Tower Hamlets Homeless Persons Unit itself virtually never visited families. It was chronically understaffed. Indeed, understaffing became yet another weapon. Stresses were so intense even sympathetic officers couldn't respond to demands being placed on them. This made it more likely that the homeless would experience abrupt, uncaring, aggressive and even dismissive attitudes. From the staff's point of view, they might be forgiven for feeling that the only way they were going to get through the day was by telling people to go away.

This use of hotels was never necessary. Rarely during the 1980s were there less than 2,500 council homes standing empty. The end of 1986, the high point of the use of hotels, was also when the number of empty flats peaked at 3,543. Admittedly, the government was to blame in many cases for refusing the money for major repair. But many flats just needed inspections, minor repairs, cleaning and decorating. Tower Hamlets' record had always been worse than the GLC's on this – with 8 per cent of its stock void against 3 per cent of the GLC's. In 1982 the Shelter-funded Housing Emergency Office (HEO) listed dozens of simple administrative changes which would have ended this scandal, apart from the straightforward expedient of employing a larger workforce which would have paid for itself by bringing more flats into use. But the council did nothing decisive. The Empty Property Unit (HEO's successor) was goaded into presenting a report in 1984 which explained succinctly what was wrong with Tower Hamlets management practice. But things only got worse. Even the Liberals, who had constantly expressed outrage at the level of voids and who have got numbers down, were still responsible for 2,600 voids nearly two years after they took office. These voids were not just in unpopular areas, they were spread evenly across the borough with a minimum of 5 per cent being empty in Globe Town and a maximum of 8 per cent in Wapping. Progress on reducing numbers has however been maintained.

An obvious by-product of this failure is that many homeless families, rather than face the trauma of the hotels, simply squatted the empty council flats. At Arthur Deakin House in Spitalfields, over half the 40 flats were squatted in 1980. The squatters organized, and after two years living under the threat of eviction, the council conceded tenancies. At a meeting in the weights gym at the Brady Centre, the top brass of the housing department sat behind a table while the squatters filed up one at a time to sign for their rent books. More often the council succeeded in carrying out evictions, with the squatters moving on to fill other empty flats, while new homeless families would come and squat the places they'd just been chucked out of.

Other council policies have deliberately kept the level of homelessness much higher than it need be – and this is especially true since the Liberals took power. They've sold council estates; sold housing land; brought in the new management practices we looked at in the last chapter which allow people with low priority to take housing which could be used for the homeless; they've even turned down money from the Housing Corporation to build rented housing when it's been on offer, while the 1988/89 budget showed no intention of increasing the proportion of empty housing going to the homeless from its 25–30 per cent level. Despite this being an increase on the 10 per cent going to the homeless in GLC days, it remained the smallest percentage in any of the London boroughs with a serious homelessness problem in 1987.

Just before the Liberals took over, it was still true that even if most homeless families chose to live in and around E1, this would take up less than 20 per cent of the small empty flats, and half the three-bedroom places. It was the large families needing four or more bedrooms who were in difficulties. In 1984, nearly 100 large families became homeless – and there were only about 100 empty large flats in the whole borough. So things were already critical. Yet by February 1988 there were 495 such families waiting for offers. Every opportunity the councils have passed up to get large houses built is a deliberate decision to keep these people in desperate temporary housing.

The council took the most expensive option – using bed and breakfast hotels. In the autumn of 1986 only Camden, of the London boroughs, had more families in hotels, while Greenwich with 20 per cent more homeless families didn't use hotels at all. The cost for Tower Hamlets rose astronomically. Only £100,000 was budgeted for hotels in 1980 (although this overran somewhat). By 1987 the bill had reached £18 million a year – around 15 per cent of the council's entire budget. Why spend all this money when it's quite unnecessary?

The bed and breakfast procedure wasn't just for punishment and deterrence. It had other effects. Hotel conditions were so terrible, they 'softened up' the families so that when they were given an offer of somewhere they didn't want to move to, they'd be prepared to go. But as the homelessness crisis escalated through 1986, the bed and breakfast bill served yet another purpose. By that point, with perhaps a fifth of the entire Bangladeshi population of Tower Hamlets suspended in the limbo of temporary housing, the council was aiming for the ultimate solution of getting the law changed to prevent any more families from joining their men.

With the 1988 homelessness budget being quoted at £24 million, there began to be suggestions that Bangladeshi immigration was causing the homelessness crisis, a crisis which threatened the council with bankruptcy. This was linked to new government restrictions on people from the Indian sub-continent who wanted to visit Britain. From the summer of 1986, these people would need visas to come as tourists. With visas or without, almost all this group of people was made up of holidaymakers. With visas or without, they weren't coming here to stay.

But this led to a gutter-press campaign about a 'new wave of immigrants' coming here to 'beat the visa restrictions'. The *Daily Mail* put on its best prose. On 20th October 1986, under the headline 'ASIANS START NEW HOUSING CRISIS', it recorded:

> The sudden influx of Asians into Britain is taking its toll. Tower Hamlets Housing Chairman Jeremy Shaw said: 'We are now feeling the effect of the rush to beat visa regulations and it is exacerbating the desperate situation we already have. The housing problem is totally out of control.'

The same week, the *Evening Standard* joined in:

> As Britain began yesterday to send back some of the thousands of immigrants who tried to beat new tougher visa regulations, the frightening costs of absorbing the new wave began to emerge . . . One of the most hard-pressed areas is the East End borough of Tower Hamlets . . . Mr Eric Flounders, leader of the Liberal-controlled council said: 'We are simply not able to deal with a problem of this size. No local authority could. The law is an ass because it makes this a local problem when it needs to be tackled at national level.'

The truth was rather different. Twenty-one families, fed up with delays in Bangladesh, came over before the restrictions started in October to claim their right to settle here. A previous case had established their right to make this claim from British soil. While their claim was being assessed, the council was asked to house them. If any of the families' claims were successful, they would become the permanent responsibility of the council anyway. Yet these 21 families were sending the homelessness situation 'out of control', thus demanding action 'at a national level'. With less than two dozen families, the Liberals had managed to rekindle national hysteria about being swamped by a new wave of immigration.

Shaw wrote to Douglas Hurd, the Home Secretary, demanding that the government foot the bill. Hurd offered no money, but a year later changed the immigration rules so that families can't stay in Britain while trying to establish that they have settled status. On 2nd February 1988 Tim Renton, Under-Secretary of State at the Home Office, admitted to Parliament in written answer 223 that the change had been brought in as a result of Tower Hamlets Council's lobbying of Douglas Hurd in December 1986. As we shall see, the open doors to the Home Office were also being successfully used to press for far more Draconian changes in the 1988 Immigration Bill.

By the time the homelessness budget for 1988/89 was set, it had plunged to £8 million, while providing temporary housing for *only a hundred fewer* families than in 1986. Even this budget was excessive. In the event, the homelessness bill for the first half of 1988/89 was less than £2 million. In 1987 the council switched its short-life housing from the hotels to houses which the council had rented on the private market – as early as 1983 the homeless themselves had suggested using privately rented housing, but only inside Tower Hamlets. Results were astonishing. From 928 families in hotels at the end of 1986, only 233 remained two years later. Every family taken out of the hotels saved the council £20,000 a year, because the homeless pay the full cost of privately rented places – averaging £450 a week. Housing benefit covers this. But if people are in work, every pound earned is taken from the housing benefit. So, though such short-term rented housing has more space, more control over cooking and washing facilities and is often self-contained, the drawbacks are that this housing is spread all over London, and it condemns wage-earners to unemployment or jobs where they effectively earn nothing at all.

This switch away from the hotels failed to avert the danger of ratecapping. Tower Hamlets 1988/89 budget was capped at £126 million, when they were planning to spend £156 million. This was an added incentive in bringing down the homelessness bill. But if the Liberals had been seriously worried by the amount homelessness was costing, they would not have allowed their Homeless Persons Unit to degenerate to the point where the Fraud Squad had to be called in, as reported in *The Times* in January 1988. The Unit was chronically understaffed – 20 per cent below par, and par was only 31: half the size of the workforce in other boroughs with similar numbers homeless. Hotels were overcharging; the council was paying for rooms long since empty; homeless families' housing benefit hadn't been collected. These are not the signs of a borough worried by a homelessness budget they claimed was approaching £24 million.

Intentionally homeless

The newspaper hysteria of 1986 presented the women and children walking through the gateways at Heathrow much as the Jewish paupers of the last century had been depicted walking down the gangplanks of ships in the London docks. Then and now, migration to the East End has been a springboard for racists campaigning for immigration controls. The Aliens Act of 1906 came in the wake of hysterical anti-semitism, spearheaded by Bethnal Green's Tory MP Major Evans Gordon. The British League of Brothers, forerunners of the Blackshirts and National Front, held mass meetings in the East End, drawing in trade unionists and winning the TUC's support. Whitechapel's Tory candidate for the 1906 General Election, D.H. Kyd tried to inflame a predominantly Jewish constituency where many Jews didn't have the vote:

> It is intolerable that we should have dumped down amongst us the very scum of the unhealthiest of the continental nations.

The local Liberal MP, Stuart Samuel, and the Liberal opposition in Parliament spoke against the Bill. Just weeks after it became law, the Liberals won a landslide victory in that 1906 General Election. But the new Act was not repealed.

The present-day Liberals in Tower Hamlets have centred their campaign on the homeless. In particular, they have drawn on the long tradition of presenting the homeless as feckless and inadequate people who've only become homeless through their own fault. If the homeless are responsible for homelessness, then obviously no-one should help them find somewhere to live. These were the attitudes of the 1960s when welfare departments dealt with the homeless. Social workers were sent in to sort out people's personal inadequacies. If they were successful, the family presumably found somewhere to live. *People without Roots*, a report published in 1967 by Tower Hamlets Council for Social Services, recorded the consequences, if not:

> The Welfare Department stated that a social worker is attached to a [homeless] family where mental illness or other *defects* exist; but if there is no response on the part of the family to help given then eviction from the establishment might follow. [My emphasis]

Such treatment was outlawed by the Homeless Persons Act, passed in 1977. It puts a duty on local authorities to house all the homeless people who have what's called a 'priority need' – the largest group being families with children. In theory this provides a safety net, ensuring that no family ends up sleeping rough on the streets. This directly contradicted previous practice, but councils still have a get-out. If the family made itself homeless 'on purpose', had become 'intentionally homeless', no-one has to rehouse it, although the Act expected that very few families would be refused housing on such grounds.

Something of the terror of being declared intentionally homeless is conveyed by this example. In 1980 a family approached the Spitalfields Housing and Planning Rights Service after their hotel booking had been cut. A whole day was spent trying for a reprieve while the six children kicked their heels on the office sofa, the younger ones not understanding what was facing them. Towards evening, when the final attempt failed and the parents were told, the father's eyes clouded as if someone in the family had died. The office was closing, they had nowhere to go. A friend kept them one night on his living-room floor. They squatted two attic rooms the next day, with no furniture, to begin, with, sleeping on the bare boards with nowhere to cook or wash. They lived like this for months before being turned out again. If experiences like this don't force people back to Bangladesh, they certainly 'persuade' them to accept unsuitable offers of rehousing, when they would be declared intentionally homeless if they refused.

Four years went by after the Act came into force before councillors even discussed how their officers were carrying out their new duties. Thus the officers were free agents, and in that time they thought they had found a way of refusing housing to many Bengali homeless families on the grounds that they'd made themselves homeless intentionally. This was built on by the Liberals when they came to power nearly ten years later. Their argument is technical, but because it has such far-reaching consequences, it is important to understand.

Until the 1988 Immigration Act, any Bangladeshi settled here before 1973 had an absolute right to bring his family. Applications to do this are now tailing off. From a national figure of over 15,200 in 1977, there were 5,500 in 1986. But the actual numbers arriving have been far more constant – because of the artificial controls imposed by the entry clearance system. Delays of several years are built into the system on purpose. People have been routinely told they don't belong to their own families – the insults and degradation of 'proving' marriage and parenthood follow. But Britain's new 'lie detector' has backfired badly. It is now possible by testing DNA to prove genetic relationships. Ninety per cent of cases which in the past have been refused on all other grounds now have to be conceded. The only way of stopping these people now is to change the rules.

In any case, DNA tests haven't speeded up the interview procedure, nor can they always confirm marriages. The

British High Commission still likes interviewing the man in London and his wife in Dhaka asking the same set of questions, and then discrediting the marriage because the two people, who may not have even seen each other for several years, can't give identikit answers to questions like 'Which side of the bed does your partner sleep on?' To avoid this, men often go back to Bangladesh, where they can get stuck for several years awaiting interview. No-one knows when entry clearance will come through. But when it does, it's only valid for six months. Because entry clearance is unpredictable, housing in London can't be planned ahead. Because it runs out quickly, the family's got to move, whether there's somewhere for them in London or not. If they miss that six month deadline, they go down the snake and have to start the whole procedure again. Often they do miss it – through illness, pregnancy, death or just through savings running out. Intense family loyalty and respect for the elderly mean that if other family members are seriously ill, those about to leave for London will stay, often for long periods.

This last group of families was easy prey to Tower Hamlets homelessness officers. The families had all been away together for several years so they must have had homes in Bangladesh, which meant they had made themselves homeless on purpose by leaving them for London. One officer made the council position clear at a meeting of the Tower Hamlets Association for Racial Equality in August 1980. She said no family should have the right to enter Britain unless it already had somewhere suitable to live; the council should decide whether a given address was suitable; and that therefore the council should become an agent of immigration control. As a result of this approach, families were asked if they had homes in Bangladesh. If they said yes, their troubles were just beginning. They'd be put into a hotel, but soon afterwards their booking would be cut. Because of their 'home' in Bangladesh they were declared intentionally homeless.

The difference between a home here and in Bangladesh is so great that it makes any translation of the word meaning-

—less. In Bangladesh 'home' doesn't relate to one building. An extended family, of up to four generations, living in a collection of small houses of perhaps one room each, will focus their lives around a central courtyard or short street through the complex of buildings. Cooking, water, washing and toilet facilities will be shared. People have such a place which they will want to call 'home' until the day they die. Whether they would be able to live there is quite another matter. It won't belong to the men individually, and almost certainly wives and children will have no private space. These dependants rely on the breadwinner being in London. The people drafting the 1977 Homeless Persons Act cannot have imagined it was going to be used to decide whether it was reasonable for someone to move back to a village in Bangladesh 25 years after he'd set up home in Britain.

Yet dozens of families had been told they had homes in Bangladesh during 1980, under the Labour administration. Court action had prevented them being thrown onto the street while a test case was heard. Tower Hamlets had lost that case because the judge ruled that the council had failed to make any real inquiries about this particular family's housing in Bangladesh, and he considered that the family had been treated abusively. From then till the end of the Labour administration, such cases had been treated more cautiously. Although the council had still found that some families had homes in Bangladesh, they had usually given them concessionary offers of housing rather than face another legal challenge. It was these people with concessionary offers, in the weakest position of all, who had been used to 'open up' estates like the Teviot. However in its last year, the Labour council had put pressure on the Home Office to stop Bangladeshi men bringing their families over here.

The Liberals sustained this pressure – writing to the Department of the Environment about the 'problems' created by Bangladeshi families arriving. At the same time they tried once again to throw families onto the streets for having homes in Bangladesh. Again they picked on those who'd suffered immigration delays, serious illness, or bereavement. Under Labour, just 1 per cent of homeless families were declared intentionally homeless for having homes in Bangladesh. With the Liberals, it's nine times as high, while only one family in six gets a concessionary offer. In July 1987, more test cases went to the High Court, which this time supported the council and went further. Not only was there no duty to house these families under the Homeless Persons Act, social workers would have no duty towards the children under law. This is terrifying. Until now, all judicial decisions about childcare have been based on establishing what is in the best interests of the child. This ruling suggests that it is reasonable for the State to act negligently towards a child because of the behaviour of its parents. The families appealed.

The setting of the subsequent court proceedings spoke volumes. Several rows of Bengali men sat on benches dwarfed by Victorian Gothic arches just like those of the courtrooms and East India Company offices of Calcutta. In Court Number 8 the men's faces were taut with concentration, trying to follow the arcane exchanges between barristers. In front of them, several feet above their heads sat the three elderly, white, male, bewigged judges, their plummy accents almost incomprehensible. These three wise men, who had never wanted for anything, were going to use their sagacity to allow hundreds of children to be thrown onto the street. Although they did quash the High Court decision, it was on a technicality. The letters to the families had not explained exactly *why* the council thought it reasonable that they should continue living in Bangladesh. New letters were sent, and the council was covered. Tower Hamlets had spent enough money on court fees to build a new home for each of the families fighting the test case. It realized that an important principle was being set which they wanted to use to drive out many hundreds of people.

In June 1988 the first ten families were turned onto the streets, after living for 18 months with this sentence hanging over their heads. The Bishop of Stepney opened up a church hall for them to stay in. Another 26 families soon followed, and there's been a trickle more every month since. Councils and voluntary groups all over London were alerted to find some temporary sanctuary. Not since before the days of the workhouse has the British State washed its hands so thoroughly of its own homeless.

The persecution of these families usefully coincided with the drawing-up of the 1988 Immigration Bill. The point wasn't lost on the Home Office. The Bill was Draconian. No British citizen will be allowed to live with a foreign spouse in this country without the government's permission. The promises made in the 1971 Immigration Act to people who were settled here by 1973 have been torn up. All the taxes paid and national insurance contributions made by those people count for nothing. Their families won't be allowed in if they 'have recourse to public funds' – and housing under the Homeless Persons Act will count as using public funds. More than once, the government has justified this by quoting the 'problems' of Tower Hamlets Council.

The changes were not supposed to make any difference in the immediate future, as the 9,000 outstanding applicants were told their cases would be processed as before. But reports of interviews in Dhaka suggest that the new rules are already being applied to everyone, even when there is no legal basis for doing so. This is the real victory for the Liberals in Tower Hamlets. Many families now seem to have been separated forever – and that separation ensures they will not be making demands on the precious land in Tower Hamlets.

The Homeless Families Campaign

Traditionally, each homeless family is isolated, facing its own problems alone. By definition, it's difficult for the homeless to contact each other and organize. Hence, councils can afford to treat the homeless badly, without fearing repercussions. Despite this, organizations have emerged. The Faceless Homeless confronted Paul Beasley in the 1970s. In 1981 a group of advice agencies – Tower Hamlets Law Centre, the Citizens' Advice Bureau, and the Housing Rights Service – brought out a report, *The Law, the Homeless and the Council*, which demanded an end both to the use of bed and breakfast hotels and to the use of 'intentionality'. Its 15 demands had little impact, the only concession being an increase in the number of offers allowed to the homeless – from one to two.

However, in the bitter winter of 1981/82, a Homeless Families Committee was born out of the terrible conditions in the hotels. Shofor Ali and a small band of friends trudged the snow of Finsbury Park, seeking out as many families as they could. Contact with one family in any hotel led on to others. In those days you could get past the reception desk if you said you were a friend of someone staying there, though this later became impossible. At that time there were reckoned to be around 100 families and they contacted at least half of them. A meeting was called in a Finsbury Park community hall. Anger erupted. Days later, there was an occupation of the Homeless Persons Unit which was defused by its Head, Francis Menezes, after he arranged a meeting with relevant councillors.

To begin with, the Committee had two main aims: getting everyone out of the hotels, and getting more control and choice in the permanent rehousing of homeless families. In the spring of 1982, in talks with Bob Ashkettle from Tower Hamlets and Deirdre Wood of the GLC, agreement was reached on giving the homeless three offers and a reserve percentage of new houses. But these two councillors couldn't get the agreement through their Joint Housing Committee. Nothing happened.

The Homeless Families Committee had a tough job on. Conditions were getting worse – new hotels were being used that didn't even have cooking facilities. Meanwhile hotel managements realized they'd be out of business if the Committee was successful. They turned violent. Abdul Mannan, the Committee's Chair, was beaten up, and a film crew covering the issue was attacked in the street. In February 1984, a semi-paralysed man was dragged down the hotel steps and thrown to the ground when the council cut his booking after sentencing him as intentionally homeless. There was an outcry. But the hotelier knew the council would back off when he threatened to evict the 104 families he was then housing.

The Committee also had to tackle the allocations system, which as we've seen discriminated viciously against the homeless. Between 1981 and 1983, half of all homeless families housed by the GLC had ended up on just seven estates – Wapping, Boundary, Ocean, Lincoln, Coventry Cross, Burdett and Will Crooks. The Committee renewed its presssure on the councils when, in 1983, under the influence of new left-wing councillors, Tower Hamlets set up a Housing Committee.

The campaign organized regular meetings, first in Finsbury Park, then in Bayswater and even at Heathrow. It picketed council meetings, used the media well, got funding to employ a researcher (Richard Backes) and as result was able to produce reports. *Hotels and the Homeless – Our Way Out*, in 1983, and *The Next Steps*, a year later, exposed hotel conditions and showed in precise detail how families could be housed without using bed and breakfast. 1983 to 1985 were years of success. Jeremy Shaw, later to become the Liberals' Housing Chair and to behave rather differently, got a motion through the Housing Committee agreeing to 'end the use of hotel accommodation for homeless families as soon as humanly possible'. The rate of rehousing speeded up slightly. More Bengali families got offers in E1. They stopped the automatic grading of the homeless for the worst estates. They stopped the use of the worst hotels. For a fleeting moment, homeless families were even given a 20 per cent quota of new housing – and moved into Ashfield Street, Davenant Street and Scarborough Street. The homeless were moved off the Lincoln and Teviot. An attempt to take away their two offers was fought off. Some families even agreed to move beyond E1 if they could *choose* estates which suited them. To help in this, the council offered to provide a 'profile' of all its estates (although it is yet to materialize). These successes partly explain why the Campaign didn't follow Camden's example, where the homeless occupied the Town Hall after a Bengali family had been burnt to death in a hotel fire at the end of 1984.

The experience gained in these struggles has not been lost. Several of those active in the committee kept up the fight after they were housed. Shofor Ali became a tenants' representative on the GLC Housing Committee, and more recently was involved in the fight against Housing Action Trusts. Two others went on to chair tenants' associations. One of them, Gulam Mustafa, continued to work with homeless families long after he had been rehoused. Abdus Subhan was a prime mover in getting families off the Lincoln Estate. Mujib Osmani became a housing rights worker.

But the Campaign's task has become much harder. The growth in homelessness and especially the use of private rented housing which has dispersed the homeless across London has made activities more difficult to organize. The Liberals' attack has put them on the defensive. The only compensation has been that as the plight of the families has worsened, the Campaign has been given much greater financial support by organizations like Save the Children. A war of attrition has set in, with the Campaign trying to isolate Tower Hamlets Liberals from their national party, while the council has worked hard to divide the homeless off from other badly housed people in the borough.

The Liberal Party prides itself on its 'record in local government'. Homeless families picketed Liberal conferences in 1986 and 1987, and ran successful fringe meetings. As the Party debated the International Year of the Homeless, MPs like Simon Hughes and Michael Meadowcroft were feeling distinctly uneasy. As Patrick Curry, a constituency delegate put it after the 1986 Assembly:

> Liberals at their Assembly in September had an unsettling experience. It was possible to turn a blind eye to cries of

'Liberal racism!' (a whole new concept, for many), but reassurance that these accusations were indeed all lies – whether sought privately or in meetings – was simply not forthcoming.

The Liberal Party leadership spent a year privately trying to get its Tower Hamlets councillors to change their minds, without success. When the families were put onto the streets, Simon Hughes publicly dissociated himself. Even though the Campaign hasn't been able to stop evictions, it has kept in touch with all the families as they're forced out. Thus it has not only been able to help find temporary places for them, it has made sure that each eviction continues to damage the credibility of Liberal local government through effective use of the media.

Dividing off the homeless

The Liberals have responded by insisting that their 'obligation' to the homeless is harming everyone else. Estate improvements can't happen because of the hotel bills. Tenants can't get transfers because the homeless are taking the flats. The council's own newspaper announced in its Christmas 1986 edition:

> Expenditure on homeless families has crippled the Council's economy . . . The Council is powerless to prevent this bill from rocketing because they have a legal obligation to house homeless families.

This way the homeless are stigmatized as they were in the summer of 1986 when the Liberals announced they were going to pack homeless families into a ship moored on the Thames. They actually started talks with shipping merchants which, if successful, would have crammed people unwillingly onto boats to create latter-day versions of the 18th century prison hulks where overcrowding triggered enforced deportations to Australia. In the climate the Liberals were creating, the idea of enforced deportation can't have been far away in the minds of some homeless families, whose men had first arrived on ships in the Thames three decades before. The idea came to nothing. Maybe it was never serious. But it was a propaganda coup. At the least it was an appealing fantasy for racists, while intensifying the sense that homelessness was becoming an unmanageable crisis. Was this the way Jeremy Shaw had foreseen getting families out of hotels as soon as humanly possible? As he said to the *Hackney Gazette* in June 1986:

> Homeless families are just going to have to be less choosy about accommodation.

While 'launching' the ship idea Tower Hamlets invited its *tenants* to decide on how the homeless should be treated. The suggestions were that two offers would be cut to one; that families would have no choice of area, could be put on any floor of a tower block no matter how young the children, and would be forced to live at just below the level of criminal overcrowding. This meant families of eight in three-bedroom flats. But this 'new deal' would only apply to families needing more than two bedrooms. This was a neat division making sure most Bengalis were penalized, while the bulk of other families would still get two offers. The council got a Counsel's opinion to say the deal was not racially discriminatory. It was not an opinion shared by the Commission for Racial Equality which in their non-discrimination notice of September 1987 demanded changes. The old principle was being resurrected. The council wanted to involve its tenants actively in pushing the homeless to the bottom of the ladder, which they did by 4,585 votes to 962. According to the Labour Party pamphlet *The Right to Evict*, the leader of the council, then Eric Flounders, wrote to the Director of Housing in November 1986 asking:

> Why can't large established families move to better areas and their places be taken by homeless families in less good areas?

The new restrictions had nothing to do with speeding up rehousing. An officers' report showed that giving two offers instead of one didn't slow down rehousing, so long as the two offers were made at the same time. This had been done experimentally and had worked. It gave homeless families a real choice – they could weigh up the relative merits of two places at once. Despite this, the Liberals took their choice away. Meanwhile, the new Labour opposition along with the Homeless Families Campaign were pushing for half the council's empty flats to be given to the homeless and for the dropping of the 'charges' of intentional homelessness. The Liberals voted these proposals out, after homeless families, who'd come to watch, had been cleared from the public gallery and refused the opportunity to speak.

As a result of the new restrictions, Bengali families are being moved all round the borough. Their only safeguard is the requirement that allocations officers 'exercise discretion as to safety and suitability of each offer', and an appeals procedure to the very councillors who set the system up. We've seen that violent receptions have been prepared for families being moved to the Isle of Dogs in this way. With neighbourhood lettings, every area of the borough will have a 'quota' of homeless families to house. This will guarantee that homeless families are arbitrarily spread thinly across the borough, regardless of choice, while councillors within neighbourhoods will have the discretion to continue the practice of targeting the homeless on the estates other people don't want.

Far from home

Despite these massive attacks on the homeless, the Liberals are far from reaching their objectives. Until they cut the numbers of homeless families, there won't be enough empty flats to decant tenants from the estates they want to sell off. Their estimates for 1988/89 assumed they would taking on another 1,345 homeless families. Perhaps next year's estimates will reflect their hope that the new Immigration Act will cut numbers, because the court decision only allows them to discriminate against those families who, through immigration delays, bereavement or other misfortune, had to spend time together in Bangladesh before arriving here. The Immigration Act holds the real power to divide families. It's a great incentive to sell off land and council housing. That way the homeless will have no hope of showing immigration officers they have somewhere suitable for their families over here. The Liberals may relax in the knowledge that these families will be separated for life. Yet the men are here through economic necessity. They did not come under the regulations governing the Turkish gastarbeiter of West Germany or the black hostel dwellers of Johannesburg. When they decided to settle here they had the right to live with their families. They are unlikely to come to terms with the principles of apartheid now.

We've all paid the price. No British national will now have the absolute right to live with a foreign spouse in this country. Because of EC law, EC nationals have more rights in Britain than the British! When they work here, they can not only live with their spouses and children, they can bring their parents and grandparents too. The Liberals' campaign has also paved the way for the repeal of the Homeless Persons Act. There has already been talk about redefining homelessness as 'rooflessness' to reduce the numbers which councils have to house. It now seems only a matter of time before the government finds ways of releasing councils from many of their obligations to the homeless – and assisting them to sell even more of their land.

12 | Back to the future

There's plenty of space and plenty of public money to move people into the East End. So long as they are the right people. But the Bangladeshis weren't the right people. Poor and unskilled, they came from a rural economy that Britain had asset-stripped for 200 years. They were given neither space nor money to help them settle. The rich of Wapping would still be making money no matter where their home was. They don't depend on the East End for their living. They can afford to live elsewhere. The Bengalis of the catering and clothing trades can't. They don't have a choice. They must live in the area to survive. If the Bengalis do move on, it won't be because they are trying to better themselves as the Jews did. It will be because the East End will have 'bettered itself' to the point where working-class people can no longer afford it.

From necessity, the Bengalis have sunk very deep foundations in Tower Hamlets. This book has documented some of the ways they managed to do it – resisting dispersal from slum clearance areas, getting well over 1,000 new rented homes built, stopping the sale of housing land, developing their own industries, breaking open racist council allocations policies, challenging office developers and organizing the homeless. In many of these struggles they have not been alone. What has been won has not just been for the Bangladeshi community, it has been vital in protecting the interests of all working-class people in the area.

Working-class communities have had successes in other parts of London too. There are nearly 1,000 council and housing association tenants in Covent Garden. Four

253

hundred new rented homes are going to be co-operatively controlled at Coin Street on the South Bank. The Courage Brewery site next to Southwark Bridge now has rented housing and industrial units. But nothing really compares with the scale of public sector building in Spitalfields and the other wards on the City fringe. Almost all of it has happened during the 1980s, while the Tories have been trying to wind up public sector housing altogether.

The results are dramatic. The population of Spitalfields, from its all-time low of 1981, clocked up a 23 per cent increase by 1987 to take the numbers over 8,000 for the first time for over a decade. This rate of growth can only be matched by that of neighbouring St Katharine's, where the increase is explained by the private development of Docklands. In Spitalfields most of the population increase came from extra rented housing. Both because of the campaigns against racism in allocation and the growing co-operative movement, Bengalis were able to move onto new estates at Royal Mint Square, Burslem Street, Guinness Court, Davenant Street, Wentworth Street, Scarborough Street, Ashfield Street, Thrawl Street. There's still more to come at Peace Street, Newark Street, Selby Street, Folgate Street, Brick Lane and Backchurch Lane. Meanwhile most of the housing squatted in the 1970s has never been knocked down. Instead it's been modernized, with the squatters themselves as tenants, in Parfett Street, Myrdle Street, Fieldgate Mansions, Adelina Grove, Varden Street, Nelson Street, Whitehorse Lane, Bromley Street, Belgrave Street, Aston Street, Commercial Road and elsewhere. Old terraces have also been bought up and improved in virtually every street in Whitechapel.

In less than 15 years this has transformed the area. In the early 1970s, the Bangladeshi community was still composed almost exclusively of single men sharing tenements where they could find them. The few families in council housing were restricted to the oldest estates of E1. They owned virtually nothing, had the right to occupy virtually nowhere and were facing racist violence so intense that they couldn't be sure they would ever be able to establish themselves. Now they have much of the new housing, and although the violence has moved out across the borough it is no longer a big factor in Spitalfields. As a result there is new youth and vigour in the community. Families have settled. Thirty per cent of the population is under 20. A new generation is growing up committed to living and working in the area. Primary schools are opening again, Brick Lane is burgeoning, corner shops have become supermarkets, women's centres are opening, the support structures are in place. A generation of child-bearing age left the East End in the 1960s and caused Tower Hamlets so much angst. How were the wage-earners going to be attracted back? What could be done to prevent Tower Hamlets becoming a haven of the elderly and unemployed? Yet when the old heart did get a new pacemaker, when new families who wanted to live *and* work in the area moved in, the council didn't want it. The wrong people had arrived.

At different times Labour, Liberal and Conservative administrations at Tower Hamlets and at the GLC have been involved in schemes that took the land away from Spitalfields people. They didn't pre-plan anything, they haven't always acted in unison. But the pressure experienced by people suffering from bad housing in Spitalfields has been a constant combination of these different policies working against them. The councils have tried to disperse Bengali people they've been responsible for housing, sold land they could have housed them on, promoted office development and undercut the clothing industry. They tried to use divisive allocations policies to split up local working-class people, and to force Bengalis into designated areas. These policies have been so formidable because they have locked together. Even when barriers to the building of new housing were overcome, the barriers of housing management were still in place. And trying to stop the sale of council housing has thrown up the problems of land values generated by office development. There has been no easy way.

The Conservative government has shared the aspirations of these councils, and has encouraged them. We've seen the joint work on changes to the immigration rules, and the softening up of opinion to change the Homeless Persons Act. Occasionally the councils have excused themselves, suggesting the government has given them no alternative to the actions they have taken. But there have, as we have seen, always been alternatives presented to them which they've ignored.

Although the alternatives have often won through, Spitalfields is now under greater threat than ever before. The machinery to dig out the foundations of the Bengali community is being bolted together. This isn't surprising as the very success of the Bengali community has created the biggest differential in land values anywhere in Britain. The difference in value between their council houses and clothing workshops against the studio flats and offices which surround them is almost unquantifiable. As the planner Alison Ravetz has defined property development, the 'greatest profits are made when low-value functions are converted into high-value ones'. In the East End now, the land with the lowest present value becomes the most desirable.

A central purpose of the British planning system, developed during the Second World War, was to prevent these forces dictating the use of land. Ending planning restrictions releases 'hope value', delivering vast unearned profits to developers who are simply making money out of other people's need to use the land. By investing a billion pounds and taking away all democratic controls, the Tories engineered this lift in land values in Docklands, allowing unheard-of profits to be made out of land which had been the life blood of the East End for centuries. In a tiny way the Spitalfields Trust had the same effect in the Fournier Street Conservation Area where their activities caused house prices to rise until only people rich enough to afford Georgian restoration could buy them. City fringe land for office development is being freed up too. Planning powers to stop offices have been destroyed – so more land gets office hope value. And although Public Enquiries are still sometimes held into controversial schemes, they have no meaning since ministers at the DoE will overturn the findings of Inspectors who are not prepared to give land away to profiteers.

What has not been so easy is to introduce the same process into the council estates. The 'right to buy' certainly helps. People now buying council flats on Spitalfields estates are getting enormous discounts. If they sell up, other local people won't be able to afford the market value of the flat. But with the government getting rid of controls on minimum wages which will increase the rate of exploitation in industries like catering and clothing, there are few people on the estates who can even afford the discounted prices. The government's answer to this was a Housing Action Trust. But this was defeated by a combination of united tenants' action and the sheer depth of the East End housing crisis. The government could not find the space to move the council tenants to, nor was it prepared to pay the price of making the estates fit to privatize. The defeat of the Tower Hamlets HAT amounts to one of the biggest victories yet chalked up against Thatcher's government. Out of this comes the vital point – black and white tenants were acting in unity against the Trusts. They had the same interests. On a local level, the same has often been true. Some of the great successes in Spitalfields – on slum clearance, on new house building and holding up office developments – have come from broad-based campaigns, involving organizations representing all groups that were going to be affected. Recognizing this unity of interest has been important in stopping the councils helping turn Spitalfields over to the rich.

This raises the question of just what political forces have been at work to confront council policies. They haven't been the traditional organizations of the left. Trade unions have had little impact on Spitalfields. Neither clothing nor catering is well organized – although great gains could be made if they were. Support from public sector unions has been patchy. At times, local people have recognized the impossible position in which council workers are placed – often wanting to help, but being prevented from doing so by council policy and staff shortages. Occasionally there have been more formal links. The Trades Council attempted its own enquiry into homelessness, although this never bore fruit. Shop stewards from the Union of Construction, Allied Trades and Technicians explained what changes they wanted to speed up the turn-round of empty flats. On the other hand, we've seen that the GLC Staff Association published racially inflammatory material and did not criticize officers with such views. Although often significant, union contributions were never central to the campaigns to save Spitalfields.

As for the political parties of the left, they have been successfully involved in combating racist violence. Both the Socialist Workers Party and what was then the International Marxist Group (IMG) took part in the street battles of the late 1970s. As part of the Socialist Unity electoral front in 1978, the IMG got a very respectable vote in the Spitalfields local elections. The Revolutionary Communist Party, the presence behind East London Workers Against Racism, gave political activity much more direction, fighting off racist attacks on council estates. But none of these parties wanted to be involved in any challenge to the power of the local state when it was being used against Spitalfields.

The Labour Party has stepped into this area. It has had problems, first in disassociating itself from the administration that bore its name, then in building up a base within the Bengali community. Neither of these things has been easy: the process has been documented by John Eade in his book *The Politics of Community*. While Labour held office in the Town Hall, ward councillors who opposed the regime were marginalized. At the same time, though, these councillors were in touch with the work of community groups and other members of the party were involved in local campaigns. But the ward party as a whole was not central to the direction of any of them. With the election of a Liberal administration this has changed somewhat. There are no longer the contradictions of opposition to the regime. But more significantly, the Labour Party has filled one of the big gaps left by the demise of the Spitalfields Local Committee. The campaign to Save Spitalfields from the Developers, fighting the development of the Market, was established by Labour Party activists, who still provide its backbone.

In the end though, the Labour Party is a machine directed at winning electoral power. Two Labour administrations were elected at the GLC which had manifesto commitments to support policies which Spitalfields people wanted. The first set up the Spitalfields Project, which achieved little before being taken over by a Tory administration. The second was Ken Livingstone's 1981 administration, which supported controls on offices, the building of rented housing and the rooting out of racist housing management practices. It took nearly two years of local campaigning to get the GLC to agree to actually build rented housing and three years to get them to *start* tackling the racism of their housing management system. It took four years to shape a new office policy for the revised Greater London Development Plan, then prevented by direct government intervention. It could not deliver its manifesto on its own – it was the strength of local organization which forced it into action.

But there is a complex dynamic between the radical Labour administrations and community activity. The manifesto and even the election of such an administration is dependent to some extent on the strength of such community organizations. The subsequent financial support for such community groups establishes contradictory tendencies. On the one hand, it makes them dependent on the political regime; on the other, it can vastly enhance their ability to organize and fight for their political demands. Those demands are often for change inside the political administration. The likelihood of their success is increased by sympathetic councillors and officers on the inside.

During the last GLC administration all these elements did sometimes work together, as in the campaign against office development. To be successful, the most extraordinary alliance of forces was needed. In Spitalfields there were 40 active community groups, directly connected with people's everyday concerns. They had their own umbrella organization. They had links with similar organizations in Docklands and with other working-class communities also under threat in other parts of central London. They had succeeded in getting their policies adopted in the GLC Labour manifesto. But they also had sympathetic councillors in key positions and officers who were committed to the policies. This same alliance was needed before there were any real changes to the GLC's housing allocations policies. In that case it involved the setting-up of the Race and Housing Team. In demolishing such power structures, work has to be done inside the building as well as out. This dynamic was threatening to the Tories; it was part of the reason why they had to abolish the GLC.

The contradictions of such a dynamic have been amply exposed by the GLC's abolition. Community organizations round Spitalfields made political gains by confronting the GLC which had funded them, while at the same time becoming dependent on that funding. Some of these organizations established themselves without money, expanded with grant aid and then collapsed when they lost the money. When the Liberals cut the funding of groups that opposed it, many became ineffective or disappeared. It is true that in some cases money allowed the organization to operate without keeping in touch with its own grass-roots, but in others recent defeats and the general political climate have made it difficult to find the extra energy to sustain organizations without money.

This book has given some idea of the workings of umbrella organizations like the Spitalfields Local Committee. But it has not gone into the internal dynamics of community organisations, nor has it attempted to assess individual Bengali organizations – like the youth groups or the

Welfare Association. Most of them are headed by sophisticated politicians. But what should have come through though is that the central force behind the fight for Spitalfields has been those in the front line – the tenants' groups in slum clearance areas, the Homeless Families Campaign, the squatters, the co-operatives, the people on the council waiting list. Time and again, individuals in appalling housing conditions have been able to come together to forge formidable alliances. These people have been at the heart of every success.

In the 1990s Spitalfields will no longer stand out as such a 'special' case. The Bengali community is now firmly rooted in all the western wards of Tower Hamlets. But the war for this land is coming from almost all sides. One front is trying to push up from Docklands, another is spreading out from the City, and a third is trying to force a corridor down the Liverpool Street railway line by way of the Bishopsgate Goodsyard. Against enormous odds, Spitalfields will end the 1980s with a larger and stronger working-class community living in much better housing than it had ten years before. But the enemy has renewed strength, and the odds against Spitalfields in the 1990s are greater than ever.

Notes

To avoid footnotes, I have tried to make it clear in the text where I have drawn my information from. Figures which are not credited are the result of my own calculations. When exact surveys weren't done, I make estimates of population for small areas by the following method. I look at the preceding Census. I establish what proportion of the Census population for the vicinity appeared on the electoral roll in the Census year. For the sake of argument, let us assume that 71 per cent of the Census population are on the electoral roll. I then take the year and area I'm concerned with, count the numbers on the roll that year and assume they are 71 per cent of the population at that time. It is not going to be exact, especially in an area where the Census itself is often questioned as underestimating numbers. But it is the best method I've been able to come up with.

There are some sources I have found particularly valuable, and I list them below. Throughout, I have made heavy use of council committee reports, of the 1971 and 1981 Census data, and of the Spitalfields Survey carried out in 1980 by the Catholic Housing Aid Society and Spitalfields Housing and Planning Rights Service. Election figures, where not credited, are from records in the Tower Hamlets Local History Library.

Chapter 2: Point of departure; point of arrival

Abercrombie, Sir Patrick, and Forshaw, J.H. *County of London Plan*. (1943) London County Council.

Ambrose, Peter. *Whatever Happened to Planning?* (1986) Methuen.

Sharp, Thomas. *Town Planning* (1940) Pelican.

Young, Michael, and Willmott, Peter. *Family and Kinship in East London* (1957) Routledge and Kegan Paul.

Moye, Andy. *Post-war Redevelopment of Stepney and Poplar*. Unpublished thesis, Tower Hamlets Local History Library.

House of Commons Home Affairs Select Committee Report *Bangladeshis in Britain* (1987) HMSO.

Adams, Caroline. *Across Seven Seas and Thirteen Rivers* (1987) THAP Books.

Casey, Sean, and Shukur, Abdus. 'Profile of the Bangladeshi Community in East London' (1985) *New Community* Vol X11 No 3.

Burney, Elizabeth. *Housing on Trial* (1967) Oxford University Press.

Chapter 3: The battlelines

Leach, Kenneth. *Brick Lane 1978: the events and their significance* (1980).

Bethnal Green and Stepney Trades Council. *Blood on the Streets* (1978). Report on racial attacks in East London.

Spitalfields Health Survey (1983) Jointly sponsored by Tower Hamlets Community Health Council, Tower Hamlets Health Education Unit and Spitalfields Local Committee.

Chapter 4: Down with the slums

Tower Hamlets, GLC and Spitalfields Project Officers Working Party. *Development in Spitalfields* (1979).

Tower Hamlets and GLC Allocation: Policies and Practice (1977). Report by the GLC Director-General's Department (largely written by Rhoda Brawne).

Wates, Nick, and Wolmar, Christian, eds. *Squatting: the Real Story*. (1980) Bay Leaf Books. Firsthand account of the Parfett Street squats.

White, Gerry. *Rothschild Buildings* (1980) Routledge and

Kegan Paul. *Race Today*, especially July/August 1978 edition.

Statistics on Closing Orders etc from committee records and by correspondence with the Environmental Health Office.
The 'ghetto meeting' was extensively covered in the national press at the time. See also *East London Advertiser* (9th June 1978) and *Evening Standard* (5th June 1978).

Chapter 5: Building on Brick Lane

Figures for new housebuilding are very difficult to collate. They change from week to week as schemes are dropped and others are worked up. The figures in this chapter for new housebuilding were first compiled in early 1987 and updated during the summer of 1988. The figures were compiled by phoning every single public sector organization known to be developing housing in the area, and by using reports submitted to the Bethnal Green Neighbourhood Committee. They will, of necessity, be out of date by the time you read them.

Tower Hamlets Association for Racial Equality. *Housing – a Plan for Action* (1987). Paper for the Bangladeshis in Britain Conference, November 1987.
Docklands Forum. *Housing in Docklands* (1987).
Joint Docklands Action Group. *Housing in Docklands* (1987).
Tower Hamlets Information Research Resource Centre. *Taking Stock* (June 1985).
Spitalfields Housing Co-op. *Give Peace Street a Chance* (June 1984).
Spitalfields Housing and Planning Rights Service. *Save our Sites and The Big Sleep* (1979).

Chapter 6: Spitalfields for sale

The information on the Spitalfields Historic Building Trust comes largely from their own newsletters, available in the Tower Hamlets Local History Library.

Chapter 7: Space invaders

Tables on office space have been compiled directly from planning applications submitted.

Joint Docklands Action Group and Spitalfields Housing and Planning Rights Service. *Empty Premises: Office Policy in Tower Hamlets* (June 1983).

Spitalfields Housing and Planning Rights Service. *What's Happening to West Spitalfields?* (May 1980).

Evidence on office policy submitted by a panel of community organizations to Public Enquiry on Tower Hamlets Borough Plan (May 1984).

Secretary of State for the Environment's decision on the appeal against refusal of planning permission for two sites in Puma Court and No 3,5 and 7 and 14 and 16 Wilkes Street (17th October 1980).

Chapter 8: Unpicking the seams

London Strategic Policy Unit, Economic Policy Group. *Sewing up the Pieces: Local Authority Strategies for the Clothing Industry* (December 1987).

Buxton, Toby. *Off Our Backs: the State of Industry and Employment in Tower Hamlets* (March 1986) Tower Hamlets Information Research Resource Centre.

Perry, Nigel. *The Leather Garment Industry in Tower Hamlets* (1983). Report for Tower Hamlets Council.

Association of Clerical, Technical and Supervisory Staff. *The Battle for the Brewery* (1983/4).

Chapter 9: Breaking the bounds

GLC Police Committee. *Racial Harassment in London*. Report of a Panel of Enquiry and adopted by GLC in October 1983.

Jacobs, Joe. *Out of the Ghetto* (1978) Janet Simon.

Tompson, Keith. *Under Siege* (1988) Penguin Special.

Chapter 10: Fair shares?

Owen, Lesley. *Allocation in Tower Hamlets* (April 1986). Report for Priority Estates Project.

Spitalfields Housing and Planning Rights Service. *Bengalis and GLC Housing Allocation in E1* (March 1982). Follow-up report in Spring 1984.

Phillips, Deborah. *What Price Equality?* GLC Housing Research and Policy Report No 9, on allocation of GLC housing in Tower Hamlets (December 1985).

Eade, John. *The Politics of Community* (1989) Gower.

Chapter 11: Taking on the homeless

Federation of Advice-giving Agencies in Tower Hamlets. *The Law, the Homeless and the Council* (June 1981).

Tower Hamlets Homeless Families Campaign. *Hotels and the Homeless: Our Way Out* (1983).

Tower Hamlets Homeless Families Campaign. *Rehousing Homeless Families: The Next Steps* (1984).

Tower Hamlets Homeless Families Campaign. *Out in the Cold: The Use of Intentionality to Evict the Homeless in Tower Hamlets* (1987).

Commission for Racial Equality. *Homelessness and Discrimination* (September 1988). Report of a formal investigation into the London Borough of Tower Hamlets.

Latest estimates of allocations to estates in E1 have been compiled using the electoral roll which came into force February 1988.

Index

References to maps are in italics

Index

Index

Index